BLOOD ON THE SADDLE:

The Life of Doc Scurlock

by

David Garrett & Mica Pharris

FIRST EDITION

BLOOD ON THE SADDLE: THE LIFE OF DOC SCURLOCK

By David Garrett and Mica Pharris

INTRODUCTION	1
PROLOGUE: THE SCURLOCK FAMILY PRIOR TO DOC	3
PART I – BLOOD ON THE SADDLE: THE LIFE OF DOC SCURLOCK	9
FROM ALABAMA TO TEXAS	11
INTERLUDE 1: FIRST ESCAPE	17
CHISUM	21
INTERLUDE 2: FIRST HANGING	27
EARLY DAYS IN LINCOLN	31
INTERLUDE 3: FIRST KILLING	39
NOT ALWAYS A CALM BEFORE THE STORM	43
INTERLUDE 4: THE MOST DANGEROUS STREET IN AMERICA	51
LINCOLN COUNTY WAR	53
INTERLUDE 5: THE WORST IN THE BUNCH	63
THE BATTLES OF LINCOLN	67
INTERLUDE 6: LAST ESCAPE	79

FROM NEW MEXICO TO TEXAS 83

PART II – YOUNG GUNS AND DOC 99

PART III – DOCUMENTS PERTAINING TO DOC'S GENEALOGY 107

PART IV – DOCUMENTATION OF DOC DURING HIS LIFE 137

PART V – DOCUMENTS IN DOC'S OWN HAND 211

PART VI – AFTER DOC'S PASSING 247

PART VII – DOC'S LEGACY AND THE BUCKBEE LETTERS 259

PART VIII – AUTHENTICATED PHOTOS OF DOC 287

PART IX – CENSUS RECORDS FOR JOSIAH GORDON SCURLOCK 315

INTRODUCTION

It's a rather daunting task to attempt to follow in the footsteps of the likes of Philip Rasch, Maurice Fulton, Robert Utley, Robert Mullin, William Keleher, Leon Metz, Frederick Nolan, and Nora True Henn. Among numerous others, these are the people who have exhaustively researched and written about Billy the Kid, Pat Garrett, and the Lincoln County War.

In writing about the life of Josiah Gordon Scurlock, it's absolutely necessary to re-travel the roads that all of the wonderful historians have paved for the simple fact that Doc was so heavily involved in so much of that history.

There are, however, numerous instances where the historical record has blank spaces that no one but the people who were there could fill. Unfortunately, as we approach one hundred and fifty years since the Lincoln County War, there are fewer and fewer stones to overturn to answer the plethora of questions still lingering out there.

Of course, what people tend to do is speculate. Doing so should always be done with caution, though. While it's fun to wonder if Billy the Kid found a gun in the privy behind the Old Lincoln County Courthouse to effect his escape from Sheriffs Brady and Bell, unfortunately, there are other theories that are at odds with this being provably true.

In the following biography, each chapter of Doc's life is sourced and represents what should be considered the closest we have to the historical record with ample citations. In between chapters, though, are presented interludes that are flights of fancy based on the history, but take great liberty with those perplexing gaps in the historical record. Please keep in mind that these interludes are presented purely for the fun of it and aren't necessarily the way things actually happened. Each interlude includes a disclaimer that explains the history on which it is based.

Finally, and most importantly, we would like to thank our extended Scurlock family for allowing Mica to scan their photos through the years. An enormous amount of our knowledge of Doc comes from the descendants who have preserved and so graciously shared their heirlooms. Without the collective family blessing from numerous elders we consulted, this wouldn't be possible.

Special thanks to Peg Johnson for her valuable set of eyes. We would also like to thank Drew Gomber, the resident historian of Lincoln. Drew has been gracious with his time while we've visited Lincoln and gracious for encouraging us to dig even deeper into Doc's life.

I (Mica) wouldn't have the largest collection of Doc items and Scurlock pics if it weren't for the Scurlock elders and their allowing me to do so. A special thanks to Brenda Buckbee and Stephanie Holland. And a special dedication to the late Audrey Parker who helped as early as 2002 with the first seeds of this project.

And I (David) would like to give a special thanks to Col. Reagan Scurlock who has been our coach and encouragement to keep diligently working on this project. Maj. Garrett and your favorite cousin finally finished it, Colonel.

PROLOGUE – THE SCURLOCK FAMILY PRIOR TO DOC

This is the story of the life of Josiah Gordon "Doc" Scurlock, one of the last American frontier gun fighters of the Wild West. For some reason, Doc has eluded his place of prominence in the telling of the history of the Lincoln County War and the life of Billy the Kid. For the serious historians of the war, Doc is a known player, but he has yet to be treated in a book-length biography. Why is that? After all, he was likely one of Billy the Kid's closest friends. The only other one of the Regulators who can say that they spent more time with Billy is likely Charlie Bowdre, who was with the Kid till Charlie was gunned down by Pat Garrett's posse at Stinking Springs near the end of Billy's life.

Other Regulators who spent considerable time with Billy the Kid are Fred Waite, John Middleton, and Doc Scurlock. And it's almost certain that Doc and Charlie knew Billy longer than either Fred Waite or John Middleton did. Tom O'Folliard became a very close companion of the Kid, but he entered the tale later than the other Regulators.

Furthermore, Doc and Billy spent a very lengthy prison sentence together. It was almost three full months. Even though this jail sentence was in the home of Juan Patron, there is no doubt that Billy and Doc were the main leaders of the Regulators at the time in 1879 and had spent much time together.

Hopefully, this treatment of the life of Josiah Gordon Scurlock will help those interested in the Lincoln County War and the life of Billy the Kid to see the important part he played in the history of, not only Lincoln, but Ft. Sumner, the Pecos, and the Texas Panhandle as well.

Lincoln County, New Mexico at the time of the events precipitating the Lincoln County War, through the war itself, and on into the fallout from the war, would certainly qualify Lincoln as a frontier town. New Mexico did not become a state until 1912. During the 1870's and 80's, the best guess estimate of the entire territory's population was around 100,000 people. At the time that Doc Scurlock was living in Lincoln, New Mexico there were certainly many frontiersmen who lived seemingly contradictory lives as both contributing citizens and hunted outlaws depending on the current status of the powers that be and the attitudes of the citizenry.

New Mexico Territory, during the Postbellum era, was a vast area where law and order was rather hit or miss, depending on the location. Miles of sparsely populated mountain country provided easy escapes and perfect hiding places for outlaws and rustlers to evade justice. Many times, vigilante citizens took the role of judge, jury, and executioner upon themselves. To many citizens, these groups of self-appointed justice dealers seemed to be ill-conceived and over the line. Many blood feuds and revenge killings were justified on the grounds that the lack of presence of full-time lawmen or local judges were simply unacceptable obstacles where a swift pursuit could mean the difference between capture and evasion.

There was also rampant corruption within the territory among the government, business, and community leaders. Lincoln County, at the time, was New Mexico's largest county and was a fifth of the entire territory. The infamous Santa Fe Ring, which controlled much of the politics and business of the territory was a classic "good old boys" network who sought to maintain a tight control on the lucrative economy driven largely by cattle and mining. And where the money goes, criminals soon follow.

Unlike the movies where two gunmen face off on a deserted street to duel, the typical gun fight was usually an ambush by a posse or a group of united men taking advantage of surprise on a lone or inferior number of men to exact revenge for an earlier transgression.

How did this culture evolve? For Doc, the foundations have their roots in the Anglo-Scots-Irish culture that took root in the early days of migrants streaming to the New World into the British colonies of North America. They spanned all levels of society, from indentured servants all the way to wealthy planters and landowners. They were predominantly Protestant, but Catholicism wasn't unheard of. They participated in early rebellions such as the War of Regulation and Bacon's Rebellion. The Revolutionary War was the first major upheaval that helped to solidify their cause and pave the way for other conflicts across the ever growing frontier. These conflicts against native tribes, The War of 1812, The War for Texas Independence, and The American Civil War, helped form their uniquely American culture.

In particular, the Scurlocks claim ancestry in Scotland, Wales, and Ireland. Most likely, the Scurlocks were initially Welsh Gaels that adopted the Norman language and way of life and were present at the conquests of Richard de Clare, also known as Strongbow, the Anglo-Norman who led invasions into Ireland in the 1100's. The Scurlocks were awarded estates on both sides of the Irish Sea in Pembrokeshire, Wales and Rosslare Harbor, Ireland, as well as other estates in Ireland.

They seem to have been able to play both sides of a royal vacillation between Catholic and Protestant monarchies, so it's tough to say at what point they adopted Protestantism. One of the earliest records of a Scurlock was Rowland Scurlock. The healing arts seemed to be a family

Scurlock Genealogy Sources

Martin, E. (1985), *The Scurlocks: Seekers of Freedom,* (Self-Published at author's own expense (much thanks to Mica for finding, securing, and sharing this rare but wonderful book!)

Neal, R. (1998), *Tidewater to Texas: The Scurlocks and Their Wives*, BookCrafters

Scurlock, H., (Extensive documents contained in pdf chapters. This amazing series of files comprises twenty one family members' and family genealogists' research!)

PART I – BLOOD ON THE SADDLE: THE LIFE OF DOC SCURLOCK

FROM ALABAMA TO TEXAS

You'd be hard pressed to find a place more befitting the stereotypical lawlessness of the Wild West than Lincoln County, New Mexico Territory in the 1870's and 1880's. Of all the colorful characters who inhabited that territory and took part in the numerous conflicts, one of the most enigmatic and contradictory people of them all was Josiah Gordon Scurlock. Better known to the residents of the area as Doc Scurlock. While Billy the Kid and Pat Garrett have become a part of Pop Americana, Doc Scurlock stands as a figure who is worthy of a much closer look.

Doc was daring, hot tempered, and just as rough and rowdy as Billy the Kid, but he was also intelligent, well-read, and sly as a fox. He was just as likely to be reading one of the classics as he was to be participating in the lynching of a horse thief. He wrote poetry, taught school, practiced medicine, as well as engaged in gunfights. He was a renaissance man living in a rough and tumble world of revenge and bravado.

In order to understand the upbringing of Doc Scurlock, it is important to understand the time period in which he was born and reared. Doc's grandfather, William Scurlock, fought in the Revolutionary War, at the Battle of King's Mountain, under "Old Roundabout" Colonel Benjamin Cleveland[5], when he was just a teenager. He would go on to marry Rhoda Ann Simmons, who was a neighbor of the Scurlocks in North Carolina. Rhoda's father and several of her brothers also

[5] Part III, Kitty Scurlock Collins letter and William Scurlock's pension letter.

fought in the Revolutionary War at the Battle of Cowpens, so that Doc had a proud heritage of the revolutionary fire from both of his paternal grandparents' families.[6] William and Rhoda had numerous children who dispersed throughout the South as westward expansion began to occur. Of these children, three moved to Alabama in the area of what is today Montgomery, Alabama. One sister named Caroline Matilda settled in Texas.[7]

The three children who settled in Alabama were Daniel Norman Scurlock, Priestly Norman Scurlock, and Katherine "Kitty" Scurlock. They all settled near each other in the 1830's. Daniel Norman Scurlock settled near Tuskegee, Alabama along the Federal Road and had a large cotton plantation in the town of La Place. La Place was later renamed and is known today as Shorter, Alabama. Kitty settled in Wetumpka, Alabama and married Joseph Collins. Priestly Norman Scurlock settled just a few miles southwest of present day Dadeville, Alabama, where he taught school to the local children.[8]

After the Indian Removal Act of 1830, resulting in the mass relocation of Native Americans of the Creek tribes, commonly known as the Trail of Tears, the county of Macon was formed. Macon County was founded December 12th, 1832. The Scurlocks were among the first Anglo settlers in the area when this land became available for homesteading.

Daniel is listed as a signatory testifying to the integrity of one of the first county elections. Priestly apparently lived either with, or close to, Daniel as he is listed on the muster rolls of the Tallassee Guard in the Second Creek War of 1836. Priestly purchased his own land north of Daniel in Tallapoosa County in 1837.[9]

Daniel Scurlock died January 31st, 1838 and the running of the plantation was left to his surviving wife Lucena Turk Scurlock, their children, and numerous slaves. Lucena was a spirited woman who managed the cotton plantation quite well up until the economic turmoil the South would face preceding the outbreak of the Civil War. Surviving letters preserved by her son Theodocius Scurlock attest to her strong-willed character and the influence she exerted over her family.[10]

A couple of years after Daniel died, their father William Scurlock died on September 1st, 1840 while living in Georgia. William's wife Rhoda moved in with her daughter Kitty in Wetumpka, Alabama.[11]

Priestly then served as one of the Macon Guards in the Mexican American War of 1846 under Lt. Col. Philip Raiford. His unit was deployed to Mobile, but they saw no combat during their guard duty there.[12]

Josiah Gordon Scurlock was born to Priestly Norman Scurlock and Esther Ann Brown on January 11th, 1850. Very little is known about his mother's family other than that her parents were Nathan Brown and Ann Holsomback.

---

[6] Babits; (My grandmother Rosa Lee Chesser Garrett, daughter of Nancy Gordon Scurlock, used to tell me that her great great grandfather got his kneecap shot off in the war).

[7] Neal; see also Part III, Kitty Scurlock Collins letter.

[8] Part III, letter dated March 1910 from William Lafayette Scurlock and Part IX, 1850 Tallapoosa, Alabama census.

[9] Alabama Historical Quarterly.

[10] Neal.

[11] Part III, Kitty Scurlock Collins letter.

[12] Alabama Historical Quarterly.

By the time Josiah was born, he already had three older brothers and one older sister. The fact that Priestly was a school teacher – and also because he reiterates to his nephew William (his brother Daniel's son) in a letter dated May 16th, 1869 – suggests Priestly placed a great deal of importance in getting a good education. Surely, Josiah was pushed quite hard to learn to read and write from a very early age. Something that he would carry throughout his entire life.[13]

Doc's grandmother Rhoda died on March 13th, 1851 when he was just a small boy.

Around 1855 Doc's cousin Theodocius Scurlock, a son of Uncle Daniel and Aunt Lucena, decided to move to Texas. Theodocius, who went by the nickname of "Dosh", was 10 years older than Doc and would prove to share many traits with Doc. For one, he studied medicine. He also lived in both Texas and Mexico and even dabbled in writing poetry. Cousin Dosh arrived in Texas and lived with his Aunt Caroline, who was already living in Texas. This would precipitate an exodus of Scurlocks moving to Texas to escape the economic trials that would hit Alabama immediately before, and especially after, the Civil War. Lucena was none too happy that her oldest son left her and the responsibility of managing a large plantation to go to Texas. Further fuel was added to the fire when a large family rift was opened between Lucena and her sister-in-law Caroline. This was due to the fact that Caroline believed that room and board was owed her for hosting Theodocius while he established himself in Texas. This feud would grow to grand proportions as the years went on. Theodocius would go on to graduate from medical school. During the Civil War, Dr. Theodocius Scurlock served in Texas as a physician. After the Civil War ended, Dr. Scurlock was so bitter that the South had lost the War that he moved to Mexico and never returned to the United States. He was murdered in Tuxpan, Mexico in 1886.

After Theodocius moved to Texas his brother Daniel followed and later his other siblings would too. Lucena finally decided to sell the plantation – except for the plot of land where the family cemetery was – and move to Texas herself. She arrived in Texas about a year before the Civil War broke out. Her home in Texas is now preserved as a historical landmark in Polk County, Texas.[14]

The Scurlock Cemetery located in Shorter, Alabama has been reclaimed by the pine forest after neglected maintenance for nearly fifty years. It's impossible to identify the locations of most of the graves and would require a herculean effort to restore it. The location of Uncle Daniel's grave is lost amongst the thick foliage and ground cover.

The Scurlock numbers were dwindling in Alabama when the Civil War began. Doc was too young to fight, but all three of his older brothers would serve. His two oldest brothers, William and Sampson, went to fight at Dauphin Island at the mouth of the Mobile Bay. They were both in the 1st Battalion, Alabama Artillery. William was in Company D and Sampson was in Company B.[15]

Dauphin Island was a strategic location guarding the entrance to the Mobile Bay. In 1821 construction of Fort Gaines was begun and the construction wasn't complete until 1861. The Confederate Army took possession almost immediately after its completion. Fort Gaines would become famous for the Civil War naval battle known as the Battle of Mobile Bay on August 5th, 1864.

---

[13] Reagan Scurlock, Doc's grandson, attests to Doc teaching him his letters and numbers as a boy.

[14] Neal; also see Part III, letter dated March 1910 from William Lafayette Scurlock.

[15] Part III, Civil War records.

But it appears that neither William or Sampson fought in this battle. William died at Fort Gaines, Alabama of illness on July 31st, 1861 shortly after the soldiers manned their post.[16]

Sampson was pulled away from Fort Gaines and sent to Georgia to defend against Sherman's advance. He fought at the Battle of Kennesaw Mountain on June 27th, 1864; the Battle of Jonesborough on August 31st – September 1st, 1864; and the Battle of Franklin on November 30th, 1864.[17]

Doc's brother Daniel, who was only a couple of years his elder, wouldn't enter the war until October of 1863, but he wasn't present at the Battle of Mobile Bay, either. Daniel was, however, at the Battle of Fort Blakely at the northern part of the Mobile Bay. This battle took place April 2nd – 9th, 1865 and is famous as being the last major battle of the Civil War. Daniel was captured and taken to Ship Island as a prisoner.[18]

Both Sampson and Daniel survived the Civil War, but hard times hit the family, as it did so many other families in the South.

It was likely during the days of the Civil War that Doc began to assist a local family doctor.[19] He had aspirations of following in his cousin Dosh's footsteps. During the 1860's, Dadeville, Alabama's population was about 500-700, but, Dadeville had acquired a reputation as a place for doctors to learn. In 1852 the Graefenberg Medical Institute was founded. It was the first functioning medical school that was chartered by the Alabama Legislature.

The driving force behind the school was Philip M. Shepard, a doctor who had served in the Seminole Wars. Dr. Shepard was granted a ten year charter for his school and under his guidance, about 50 individuals graduated from it. When Shepard died in 1861, the school closed. Doc must have felt the school's influence even though it closed prematurely.

In about 1868 Doc went to school in New Orleans at Charity Hospital.[20] Charity Hospital changed locations six times over the course of its history and unfortunately, very little records have been preserved from the time period Doc would've attended.

He never graduated, however. The family story goes that Doc fell madly in love with a nurse while he was an intern. It's not known whether or not he actually proposed, but he certainly had intentions. Unfortunately, the nurse fell for another intern and Doc was left devastated. As a result, in 1869 Doc dropped out of medical school and joined a party of travelers bound for Tampico, Mexico who were going to treat an outbreak of Yellow Fever. He stayed with this group for two years. In 1871 he grew ill and was convinced he had contracted Tuberculosis. Because of this he decided that he needed to remove to a climate that was more beneficial to his lung condition. Although he never really did have Tuberculosis, this was the reason he decided to head towards Texas, possibly with the intention of reaching New Mexico or Arizona.[21]

Considering there is no documentary evidence for the early movements of Doc's life, there is a brief allusion to an alternate storyline worth covering, just for the sake of being thorough. In December of 1880, after the Lincoln County War, Agent Azariah F. Wild of the

---

[16] See Part III, Civil War records.
[17] Ibid.
[18] Ibid.
[19] In correspondence with Reagan Scurlock dated 24 May 2016, Reagan sates this as well.
[20] Rasch doesn't cite this in "Man of Many Parts". Rasch and Buckbee contacted Tulane and Auburn Universities inquiring about whether or not Doc attended. Payne, D. Scurlock, and J.D. Scurlock cite Charity.
[21] Rasch, "Man of Many Parts"; D. Scurlock; J.D. Scurlock; Payne.

Treasury Department was in Lincoln investigating forged currency in circulation there. He compiled a list of suspects with many questionable tidbits of information on each suspect. One wonders if people were purposely feeding him wrong information. For example, he had that Charlie Bowdre hailed from Virginia, which is false. In his entry for "Dr. Joseph G. Scurlock" he had that he came from Georgia and had killed men in both Louisiana and Texas.[22]

Could Doc have actually killed a man in Louisiana and fled to Mexico before returning to the U.S via Texas? Was his romantic story of spurned love just a cover for something more nefarious? While it doesn't seem likely, there may just be a kernel of truth that can never be confirmed in the rumors which Agent Wild somehow acquired.

In 1871 Doc, with his newly acquired command of the Spanish language, crossed back into United States territory at Eagle Pass, Texas.[23] He was heading west and his journey would lead him right into the service of one of the richest ranchers in the region – John Simpson Chisum. This would change the course of his life dramatically.

---

[22] Nolan, *The West of Billy the Kid*.

[23] D. Scurlock; J.D. Scurlock.

INTERLUDE 1: FIRST ESCAPE

Silver City, New Mexico, September 1875

Henry listened as Sheriff Whitehill unlocked the heavy wooden door to the jail house and entered closing the door behind him. He heard him pause long enough to stoke the dying fire back to life and then he proceeded to walk to the back corner cell where a young Henry Antrim sat trying to look as sullen as an old ugly spinster sitting the bench at the local Saturday night baile. Only Henry was sitting on a cot in a cold cell stewing about the news that he wouldn't be able to go before the court until the middle of December. Sitting in jail for three months for a crime that Sombrero Jack committed was something that Henry surely didn't cotton to at all.

Whitehill leaned on the bars and said, "You hungry, Henry?"

Henry put on the act heavy and launched into the speech he had been rehearsing in his head all day yesterday.

"Yes, sir, Sheriff. And tired. I can't sleep because it gets so cold at night. Look, Mr., I mean, Sheriff Whitehill, I know that Mrs. Brown is disappointed in me and wants me to learn a lesson, but you got to believe me, sir. I'm innocent!"

"Henry, listen, son, I don't think you grasp the severity of the situation. Now, after your poor mother passed on, Mrs. Brown was kind enough to take you and your brother in. And you go and repay her by stealing two guns and who knows how much in clothes? You know, the value of the theft makes it more severe in the eyes of the law?"

"But it wasn't me! It was Sombrero Jack who did the stealing. He set me up!"

"Oh, stop calling George Shaefer by that stupid name. He ain't no outlaw, he's a bricklayer; hell, he's barely older than you."

Henry wrung his hands and stood up. "Well, maybe I was wrong for holding Charlie Sun's stolen property for George, but he's the one that needs to be charged for the theft! That S.O.B. set me up, I tell you!"

"Henry, you can sort that out with the court, but right now I'm steppin' over to get some victuals. Anything I can request for you?" Sheriff Whitehill turned to go.

"Sir, I get it. Talking you out of it's like talking a tired ole mule into running a race. If you won't let me go, can you at least show more mercy than the deputy? He don't let me get no exercise at all, and he never stokes the fire so it's always freezing in here at night. I can't sleep!"

"I'll talk to him."

"You did, though! He hates me." He grabbed the bars and pressed his face as far as he could between the bars. "Can I at least have the run of the hall. I can keep the fire fed and walk around. There ain't no way a kid like me can break that great big ol' door down. You said it yourself! And I'm so cold."

Whether it was the charm or his luck, the sheriff stopped at the door and rubbed his chin.

After a moment, he finally relented. "Fine. I don't want to be accused of mistreating no kid."

Sheriff Whitehill walked over and unlocked the cell door. As Henry stepped out of the cell the sheriff placed a hand on his shoulder and said, "Listen, Henry, why don't you just send a letter to your step-dad? I'm sure he would come help you out."

"No way. Don't get me started on him. That bastard ran off to Arizona and left Momma and me and Joe when she was sick."

"Well, I thought he was kind of good to ya'll. At least he might help you out." Sheriff Whitehill turned to leave again.

"He never cared for us; just tolerated us for Mom's sake," Henry said as he went towards the fire to warm his chilly hands.

Just before the sheriff got out the door Henry said, "Sheriff Whitehill, will you please tell Mrs. Brown and Miss Richards what I told you and that I'm sorry?"

"I think you should tell them yourself, son."

No sooner had Henry heard the sheriff locking the jail door than he began to put the fire out. Not bothering to care about all the soot and ashes getting all over the floor and himself, he cleared the fireplace out.

Thirty minutes later, Sheriff Whitehill returned with a platter of food balanced on one hand. He set it down outside and unlocked the door. He cracked the door and peaked in as he started to get the tray. But there was no Henry.

After a frantic search of the cells, he ran outside looking in every direction. There happened to be a New Mexican walking the trail at the top of the ridge.

"Did you see a boy get out of here?"

The man smiled and pointing said, "Si, he came out the chimney."

Henry Antrim made his way to Clifton, Arizona. When he left Silver City he hadn't intended on seeking out his step-father, but the more he thought about it, Sheriff Whitehill was right. Billy Antrim had failed him and Joe even if he wasn't their biological father. He had a responsibility.

Henry walked up to the closest miner in the mining camp and said, "Do you know Billy Antrim? I'm Henry Antrim. His son. I've come a long way to tell him something important."

The miner regarded Henry and replied, "Yep, he works here. He's working right now. Down there," he said pointing to the mine entrance.

Henry gave him the sympathetic eyes and said nothing. The miner looked the kid up and down, sighed and said, "Wait here."

When Billy Antrim emerged from the mine, he made no effort to hide his annoyance at finding the reason for his work interruption was his step-son Henry.

"You're in trouble," he said so matter-of-factly that Henry thought the news had somehow preceded him.

"What do you know about it?"

"Nothing at all; I just figured that'd be the only reason you'd show up here."

"You good for nothin' old sot. You abandoned us!"

"I'm just trying to earn an honest living. Unlike you. You're nothing but a trouble maker and that's all you'll ever be."

Henry let the stinging words bore into him while he tried to withhold his anger.

Billy Antrim continued as he pulled his wallet out. "Here," he said as he pulled out a few dollars. "Take this and go and don't ever let me see you again."

And with that, Billy turned and headed back to work.

Henry looked at the money in disbelief.

He walked over to the miner who had sought out Billy Antrim for him and said, "Mr., my Pa said I could spend the night with him before I leave tomorrow. Can you point me to his room?"

The miner explained where Henry could find his step-father's room.

As Henry rode towards Fort Grant with Billy Antrim's guns and pocket watch, he decided a change was in order. As a boy, William Henry McCarty had gone by Billy. When his mother married William Henry Antrim, who also went by Billy, she had insisted that young Billy take his step-father's last name, too. But, then, there was the confusion of having two Billy Antrims in the household, and he was suddenly required to go by his middle name of Henry.

Now, Henry decided he didn't want to be told what name to go by anymore. He was taking back Billy. Come to think of it, he didn't want the damn name of Antrim anymore, either.

From now on, he was going by "the Kid". He liked the sound of it. It had a certain ring to it.

[DISCLAIMER: While liberty has been taken with the dialogue, this follows closely the first escape of Billy the Kid.]

CHISUM

In 1871 John Chisum was doing quite well. He had weathered the turmoil of the Civil War and had actually come out of it for the better. Even as early as 1860 he was running 5,000 head of cattle, valued at $35,000. He was well known for being one of the major businessmen in the cattle industry in Texas.[24]

John Simpson Chisum was born August 16th, 1824 in Hardeman County, Tennessee. In the summer of 1837, John, with his parents and his siblings, along with other relatives and families, relocated to Red River County, Texas. It was either enroute or shortly after their arrival in Texas that John's mother Lucinda died. John applied himself to business and community service and soon entered the cattle business a partner in the Half Circle-P brand.[25]

Shortly before the Civil War, John's father Claiborne Chisum died in 1857. John would become the defacto head of the family for the remainder of his life with his younger brothers James, Jeff, and Pitzer playing very critical roles in John's cattle empire.

---

[24] The Handbook of Texas Online

[25] Ibid.

During the Civil War, John Chisum was successful enough as a businessman in the cattle and horse business to be appointed a quartermaster supplying beef under contract to the Confederate States. He was appointed an honorary position in the cavalry.[26]

His first delivery to the Confederates was at Vicksburg in the fall of 1861. This was well before the fall of Vicksburg to the Union in 1863. At the time, Vicksburg was a Confederate stronghold and Chisum was paid $30,000 for this first delivery. He would go on to make four more deliveries before war's end, three to Little Rock and one to Shreveport.

One of the smartest decisions John made during the war years was to put his proceeds into usage rather than banks. By doing this, when the war ended and Confederate money became essentially worthless, Chisum had expanded his empire through more land, cattle, and facilities to show for his efforts.[27]

While Chisum was building his fortunes in Texas, in the fall of 1862, Brigadier General James Carleton established Bosque Redondo, New Mexico as a location for the Mescalero Apaches. By 1864, over 6,000 Navajos were relocated there as well. The Indian Agency served as a headquarters and focal point for relations with the Apaches and Navajos and was closely tied to lucrative contracts supplying the reservation with beef and supplies. In August of 1867, Chisum established his Bosque Grande ranch. Also during 1867, Dr. Joseph Blazer would purchase an old mill built around 1846. Dr. Blazer had studied dentistry and served in the Civil War in the Iowa cavalry before relocating to New Mexico. Under its new name, Blazer's Mill would achieve a legendary status in the coming years.[28]

In 1868, the Indian Agency at the Bosque Redondo reservation was relocated to Fort Stanton. Lucien B. Maxwell purchased the Bosque Redondo. Lucien also purchased the abandoned Fort Sumner in 1870 and turned it into his home and a popular little town. After Lucien died, his son Pete took over ownership.

The little New Mexican village of La Placita, that was just 15 miles from Ft. Stanton, became Lincoln, just as the county was known, in 1869. John Copeland, who sometimes worked as a butcher for the Indian Agency, established his ranch in 1870 nearby. Also, that year, Dick Brewer arrived on the Rio Ruidoso.

Dick Brewer was a mid-western boy who, like Henry Newton Brown and the attorney McSween, went to work for The House early on before breaking with them. Brewer was a neighbor to the men who would become the Regulators. They lived sufficiently far enough away from Lincoln to have created their own community of ranches. The closest "town" was actually San Patricio just over ten miles from Lincoln, a place where the Regulators would frequently take refuge.

By 1872 Chisum had pretty much abandoned his base in Paris, Texas and was operating out of his Bosque Grande location in New Mexico.

As for Copeland, he and later Dolan-man John H. Riley got embroiled in a small race war with the local New Mexican citizens in 1873. Copeland would eventually wind up giving his allegiance to the Regulators' side. George Coe also mentions that at this early time, Riley was

---

[26] John Chisum's cavalry sabre is currently on display at The Billy the Kid Museum at Ft. Sumner.

[27] O'Neal.

[28] Mehren.

simpatico with their faction, before going into business on the side of The House.[29] Jimmy Dolan had even tried to shoot Riley but the two men let bygones be bygones and Riley eventually became Dolan's partner after Lawrence G. Murphy bowed out of the partnership due to health issues.

So, even this early in Lincoln's history, connections across the factions merged and changed.

After the Civil War, Chisum set his sights on the future of his business, and that was westward expansion. He could foresee that the ranges to the west and the need to supply the native tribes through the Union occupation of that land was a burgeoning business opportunity. Then in 1874, Chisum won the contract to supply beef to the reservations in New Mexico.[30]

By 1875, operations of the Indian Agency in the Post Trader's Store ran by L. G. Murphy had reached breaking point. Due to a bad relationship with the military, poor accommodations, and allegations of selling whiskey to the Indians, the agency was relocated first to John Copeland's ranch, and then in March close to Blazer's Mill.[31]

Doc worked for Chisum as one of his line riders. In this capacity, Doc learned the cattle trade. In 1873 Doc moved up to Chisum's Bosque Grande ranch north of Roswell, New Mexico. Other notorious cowboys who were reportedly riding for Chisum at this time include Jessie Evans, Frank Baker, Tom Hill, Jim McDaniels, Nicholas Provencio, Jesus Largo, and Jim Jones. All of these men would play both ally, but more frequently foe, to Doc and the Regulators over the coming years.

In the days of open ranges, before barbed wire fences demarcated property boundaries and contained herds of cattle, the job of the line rider was a most important job. Not only did these cowboys help to keep cattle and horses from wandering too far afield, but they also served as sentries and deterrents to would-be thieves.

It was in this frontier environment, far from regular law enforcement, that Doc likely learned about the brand of justice common to Chisum and his men. Lily Casey Klasner relates a time when Chisum confided in her the story of several cowboys implementing summary justice by hanging a fellow cowboy for the killing of a well-liked range foreman.[32]

Another story related by S. R. Coggin, a neighbor rancher of Chisum's who was visiting his Bosque Grande ranch, tells how Chisum's cowboys were executing summary justice and Coggin asked Chisum why he didn't turn the case over to Las Vegas, New Mexico. Chisum's response was that it wasn't his business to interfere in the cowboys' form of justice, and that it would be too time consuming to go the Las Vegas route. While the offenses spanned all manner of law breaking, the main offense Chisum endured was cattle theft.[33]

John Chisum's troubles began primarily with the Comanches, Apaches, and Navajos as early as 1868, but things progressively worsened over the ensuing years. Ultimately, he would lose close to 1,700 cattle, horses, and mules worth more than $90,000. While some of these losses were due to theft from Anglo rustlers, the embittered Native Americans, who had been

---

[29] Coe.
[30] The Handbook of Texas Online; Mehren.
[31] Mehren.
[32] Klasner; O'Neal.
[33] O'Neal.

progressively robbed of their land, would account for many thefts of Chisum's cattle and killings of Chisum's cowboys.[34]

Doc narrowly avoided losing his life on two occasions where conflicts with the natives were involved. Sources don't agree on whether the killing of his line partner Jack Holt occurred before September 1873 or after, but Doc's grandson Joe Buckbee recounts the story as it was related to him by Doc himself:

> Grandad and Jack Holt were working together as line riders for John Chisum. The two of them were out riding line when suddenly as they approached a canyon they were surprised by approximately five Indians (Grandad said there were from five to seven altogether). Almost immediately Holt was killed, as were both horses. Grandad hid among the rocks and exchanged shots with them most of the evening. As the evening wore on, it became evident that he was getting lower and lower on ammunition. He decided to let up on the shooting . . . not knowing how long he would be able to hold out against them. When he did quit shooting and the atmosphere grew quiet, the Indian chief came forward (thinking he was out of ammunition) and Grandad stood up quickly and shot him. At this the rest of the Indians began to yelp like a pack of coyotes and took cover.
>
> He waited for night and safety before he walked twenty miles for help. When he returned with help they found the dead chief gone. Holt's body was still there however and they were amazed that he had not been scalped but Grandad and his companions were shocked to find that his right arm had been removed at the elbow. They wondered at this and could not imagine why the Indians had done this.

The second of the two tales was recorded in the Santa Fe newspaper as occurring on September 13th, 1873. Doc returned to their camp and found his partner, Alexander "Newt" Huggins, had been scalped and his nose cut off.[35]

It was likely in late 1873 or in 1874 that Chisum reached his limit with the depredations of the Indians. He put together a force of around 100 of his men, including Doc, and headed for Ft. Stanton. The story goes that Chisum plied the officers there with liquor before his men arrived. A fierce gun battle broke out and the Chisum men, their bloodlust fueled, began to kill Indian men, women, and children indiscriminately. Supposedly Doc witnessed the braining of an Apache infant and was so revolted by this action that he claimed it to be one of the most horrible things he ever witnessed in his life.[36]

In Bill O'Neal's biography of John Chisum this incident is cited as occurring in the fall of 1877 which would be over two years after Doc had left Chisum's operation. There is also the possibility that this incident didn't actually occur exactly as it has been reported. Regardless, it is certain that Chisum was not averse to his cowboys dispensing frontier justice in retaliation to thefts and rustling and that Doc witnessed the overzealous slaughter of natives by Chisum cowboys while on one of these retaliatory raids.[37]

---

[34] Ibid.

[35] See part III, 7 October 1873 article; part VII, Joe Buckbee's letter to *True West* and Ketring's letter to Joe mentioning Maurice G. Fulton's note on Huggins; Douglas; D. Scurlock; Fulton; Klasner.

[36] Douglas; D. Scurlock.

[37] O'Neal.

Several versions of Doc's life story cite the killing of either Huggins or Holt as being the catalyst for his severing ties with Chisum, at least for this period of his life, as the two men's destinies were to be entwined yet again.[38] Unfortunately, the dates don't seem to match up for this to be the case. Even after the raid by Chisum on the Mescalero reservation, Doc continued to work for Chisum about another year.

Whatever the final straw might have been for Doc, having set his mind, he headed to the big ranch and asked John Chisum to pay him his due earnings, that he was quitting his outfit. Not wanting to lose one of his best men, John would have none of it. So Doc took it upon himself to square up with John. He took several horses, saddles, and a rifle in exchange for the money owed him and took off towards Fort Sumner, or even further west. Chisum sent two of his best ruffians to catch Doc and retrieve his stolen items. When the two men caught up to Doc, he explained the situation and the two men actually sided with Doc and let him go.

The *Santa Fe Daily New Mexican* carried the following item on Saturday, May 15, 1875 – the first of many times Doc would appear in the newspapers.[39]

> We received information too late for last week's issue, that a young man by the name of J. G. Scurlock, usually known as Doc Scurlock, a little previous to the 11th instant, stole three horses, two saddles and a gun from parties living in New Mexico, and made his way to Arizona. He is described as being 22 years of age, between five feet eight or ten inches high, light hair, light complexion, front teeth out, writes a very good hand, quick spoken, and usually makes a good impression on first acquaintance.

He wasn't 22; he would have been 25 by this time. It's also obvious that by this date Doc had already lost his front teeth. The exact date on when Doc lost his teeth isn't known, but it supposedly happened while he was gambling. He was in a card game when things took a sinister turn. There was likely liquor and allegations of cheating involved, but regardless, Doc and one of his card opponents drew on each other and both men fired simultaneously. And both men's aims were true. Doc took a bullet right in the mouth that knocked out his front teeth and exited through the back of his neck. His opponent fell dead. Doc certainly thought himself dead as well, one would imagine, but he was one tough fellow and, amazingly, he survived. After that Doc affected a mustache that helped to conceal the scar.[40]

Again, we are reminded of Agent Wild's notes on "Dr. Joseph G. Scurlock" having killed a man in Louisiana and Texas. Could the killing of a man in Texas be a reference to the incident in which Doc lost his front teeth?

There is no source that can shed any light on this story, such as the other man's name or what the circumstances were that precipitated the whole incident. It's just one of those mysteries about the individuals involved in the Lincoln County War of which we will probably never know the truth.

---

[38] Gomber; D. Scurlock; J.D. Scurlock.

[39] Part IV, article dated 15 May 1875.

[40] Rasch, "Man of Many Parts"; Gomber; D. Scurlock; J.D. Scurlock.

After Doc left Chisum's service, family tradition takes over again without certain proof. Supposedly he did arrive in Arizona where he befriended Charlie Bowdre, a friendship that would last until Bowdre's death.[41]

Charlie Bowdre was born Charles Meriwether Bowdre sometime in either late 1848 or early 1849 in Wilkes County, Georgia. When he was about three years old, the Bowdre family moved to DeSoto County, Mississippi. Little is known about the details of his early life or why he decided to head west. It is believed that he went to Silver City, New Mexico in 1874.[42]

It was during this time that Billy the Kid was known to be living in Silver City, as well. His mother, Catherine Antrim, died in Silver City on September 19th, 1874, which would lead directly to his peripatetic lifestyle.

Billy the Kid's early life is notoriously vague. His birthdate is usually ascribed as November 23rd, 1859, but opinions vary. November 23rd also happens to be Ash Upson's birthday, and he was the man who assisted Pat Garrett in writing his book. Either Ash used that date because he loaned it to Billy, or he remembered it because he happened to share it with Billy.

It's also impossible to say which state, or even country, Billy was born in. What we do know, is that Billy's mother married William Henry Antrim and they resided in Silver City, New Mexico at the time that Billy set off on his extraordinarily eventful, yet short life.[43]

Initially after his chimney escape, it is believed that he did go and see his step-father, who showed him nothing that would indicate Antrim wanted anything to do with his step-son. Billy wandered through Arizona at the same time that Doc and Charlie are reputed to have been in Arizona. Doc and Charlie decided to try their hand at mining. In order to raise quick capital, the two men opened a cheese factory on the Gila River and supposedly hired on Billy the Kid for a short time. Whether or not Billy did work for Doc and Charlie, he for certain shows up in Fort Grant by 1876. He was involved in rustling, as he usually was, and was caught, whereupon he escaped, shackles and all from jail.

While it's hard to determine the truth of whether or not Billy's movements line up with Doc and Charlie's, it is certain that Doc and Charlie were close friends by the time the two men showed up in Lincoln in late 1875 or early 1876.[44]

---

[41] Rasch, "Man of Many Parts"; Payne, "The Ture Doc Scurlock Story" and "Doc Scurlock, Frontier Legend".

[42] Nolan, *LCW: A Documentary History.*

[43] Bell.

[44] Rasch, "Man of Many Parts"; Payne, "The Ture Doc Scurlock Story" and "Doc Scurlock, Frontier Legend"; D. Scurlock, "Physician, Gunfighter, and Family Man".

INTERLUDE 2: FIRST HANGING

Lincoln, New Mexico, December 1875

Doc Scurlock, Charlie Bowdre, and Fernando Herrera rode in Fernando's buckboard wagon down the road leading into Lincoln. They were on their way to watch the first public hanging in Lincoln County. Communication between the three men was a bit difficult because Fernando spoke Spanish and Charlie spoke English. Doc would talk to one and then translate the information for the other.

"So you knew this guy William Wilson?" Doc said to Charlie, referring to the man sentenced to be hanged.

"Not really. Supposedly he quit working for Mr. Casey because he was taking off to California, but I guess he never left. They say he was from back east and had once done time at Sing Sing, but I don't know. But him quitting just made a job for me."

"He had already quit Casey's place before you got there then?"

"Yeah."

Doc and Charlie had known each other prior to their coming to Lincoln. The two had decided to try and work locally in order to make enough money to go into ranching together. Charlie had found a job working for Robert Casey while Doc had gone to work for Fernando Herrera.

Doc translated the information into Spanish and Fernando replied.

"He wants to know if you know why Wilson killed Mr. Casey," Doc said.

"I heard it was over back wages that Wilson was owed, but I don't know. Now that my boss is dead, I'm worried I won't get paid, either."

Doc spoke to Fernando again then asked Charlie, "Is it true Wilson shot him in the face?"

"Yep, shot him twice. Ed Welch told us about it. Ed's the clerk in the Casey store and he went with Mr. Casey to Lincoln for a political convention being held there. Ed said that he and Mr. Casey bumped into Wilson and everything was perfectly cordial. The three even ate dinner together at the Wortley and Mr. Casey paid the bill. Then, inexplicably, after the three parted company Wilson came back to find Mr. Casey and shot him in the hip. Mr. Casey tried to take cover and Wilson shot him a second time in the face. Ed hightailed it back to the Casey place and told poor Mrs. Casey the news."

Doc translated again for Fernando and then the three fell into silence as they came into view of Lincoln. The town was crowded from one end to the other. It seemed that the entire community for miles up and down the Rio Bonito had come out to witness the spectacle.

Even with the grim specter of a hanging looming over the town, there was a lot of animated talking, chatting, and gossiping as the citizens, who didn't get together on this scale very often, mingled with each other. Fernando, who had been living in the area for many years introduced Doc and Charlie to numerous people, both American and New Mexican.

The crowd coalesced around the newly constructed gallows that had been completed just that morning for the gruesome purpose of this inaugural hanging. Just before 11 o'clock a hush fell over the crowd as the military escort entered the west end of town from Fort Stanton.

Doc recognized the Federal soldier's rank of captain that drove the ambulance. The ambulance was accompanied by another officer – a lieutenant – leading an entire cavalry company on horseback.

Fernando began to explain to Doc who these men were. The captain was Captain Stewart who was the current post commander at Fort Stanton. With him were Dr. Carballo and Padre Antonio Lamy. He didn't know the name of the other officer, though. Fernando explained that Padre Lamy was from Manzano but was the only Catholic priest to serve the entire parish.

While Doc explained this to Charlie, the majority of the soldiers broke off and encircled the gallows and began to push the crowd back. The captain and the ambulance stopped in front of one of the houses. Wilson was brought from the wagon and ushered into the house.

Fernando explained that the house belonged to Sheriff Saturnino Baca. Baca had once served under Kit Carson. He also provided the additional detail that Baca had been largely responsible for naming both the town and the entire county of Lincoln. While serving in the territorial legislature a motion was made to name the county after Baca, but he demurred and proposed naming both the county and the town for the United States President who had been assassinated several years prior.

Several minutes later, the contingent emerged from the house, this time with Sheriff Baca. As they approached the gallows, Doc observed Wilson, now clothed in black, shaking hands with several people in the crowd.

As the priest, doctor, sheriff, and Wilson climbed the steps of the scaffold, Captain Stewart remained below, but another man with red hair and wearing fine civilian clothes did ascend the stairs. The crowd began to boo and shout various insults towards the condemned man. Charlie pointed out the Widow Casey who was one of the more vocal residents.

Doc recognized the red-haired man as Lawrence Murphy. He was formerly a Federal officer and had served as a quartermaster. After exiting the military, Murphy became a prominent figure in Lincoln affairs. He served as the District Probate Judge as well as being the most prominent businessman in the area. Murphy had been removed from his office as Probate Judge recently when $20,000 in tax money had gone unaccounted for. Doc had been introduced to him on an earlier visit into town with Fernando.

Sheriff Baca stepped forward. Wilson, flanked by two soldiers appeared calm as Baca addressed the crowd, trying to calm down those that were the most vocal. He produced a piece of paper and read the death warrant, first in English and then in Spanish. Next, he produced another piece of paper and read Wilson's final statement, again in both English and Spanish. Doc noticed Murphy's agitation and wondered what role he served on the platform.

Padre Lamy then approached Wilson and performed the rite of the Extreme Unction. As this was going on, Murphy and Baca exchanged words, but it was impossible to make out what they were saying.

Once Padre Lamy was finished, Baca stepped forward. Doc took note of the fact that Murphy and Wilson exchanged words as one of the soldiers placed the hood and noose over Wilson's head. Doc quickly ascertained that Murphy was playing at something, but it was impossible to hear the details.

Baca made the announcement that there would be a half hour reprieve for the condemned man. The soldier placing the hood hesitated. With this announcement, the crowd became so vocal that several dismounted soldiers were forced to push and shove several citizens back.

On the platform, Baca and Murphy began to exchange words again and Captain Stewart marched up the stairs to join in the conversation. Stewart ordered his soldier to complete his duty. Finally, Baca, announced that the hanging would proceed as originally planned. Wilson began to plead with Murphy through the hood and Murphy responded by kicking the lever that sprung the door. Wilson fell and the crowd cheered.

As Wilson flailed at the end of the rope, the crowd grew silent. All eyes were glued to the gruesome scene. After a minute the struggle lessened and finally, Wilson's body was still. He hung that way for nearly ten minutes and then Baca made the order to cut him down.

The body was placed in a coffin in front of the gallows so that everyone might view the body. Fernando, Doc, and Charlie turned to make their way back to Fernando's wagon when suddenly, one of the New Mexican women began to scream.

"What's she saying?" Charlie asked Doc.

"She says that the man is still breathing."

Murphy, who seemed to insert himself into the affair at every opportunity, was making the argument that a man couldn't be punished twice for the same crime, but the crowd was having none of that. A general chaos ensued as the citizens grew more and more agitated. Sheriff Baca and Captain Stewart tried to restore order. It was to no avail, though. Before Doc's disbelieving eyes, the people of Lincoln had produced a rope and taken it upon themselves to haul Wilson back into the air to dangle once again at the end of the rope. This time, he was left for twenty minutes.

As Fernando, Doc, and Charlie rode out of town Charlie said, "Who knew we'd get two for the price of one?"

Doc translated for Fernando and Fernando also chuckled at the morbid joke. Then Fernando said something back to Doc.

"Don Herrera says that if things don't shake out at the Casey place, he recons he could use an extra set of hands at his place."

This time, Charlie said straight to Fernando, "Gracias, Don Herrera. Muchas gracias."

[DISCLAIMER: It's not proven that Doc, Charlie, and Fernando attended the "double hanging", but it is possible. As far as the details of the hanging of Wilson, this follows closely with how it was reported as well as Lily Casey Klasner's account of it.]

EARLY DAYS IN LINCOLN

Upon arriving in Lincoln, Doc and Charlie made the good graces of Fernando Herrera and were given temporary lodging in exchange for work around the Herrera ranch. Fernando would eventually become father-in-law to both men.

Fernando was born Jose Fernando de Herrera on July 2nd, 1836 in Santa Cruz de la Canada. He married Maria Juliana Martin, who was four years his elder, October 13th, 1856. Sometime in 1866 or 1867, Fernando decided to head south and determine whether or not the news was true about the availability of fertile land in the area of El Bonito. Fernando became a squatter on the Rio Ruidoso and later made claims for this property under squatter's rights laws. He applied for water rights in 1867.

At first, Fernando remained on his land, which he dubbed *San Juanito,* in honor of his home in San Juan County, New Mexico, and began farming while ensuring no one else laid claim to his land. Once he had established relationships with his neighbors, he made occasional trips back to Santa Cruz to visit his family, even bringing his eldest son Jose Andres to help him build an adobe house. In about 1870, everything was prepared; Fernando and Jose returned to Santa Cruz to relocate the family.

At the time that Doc and Charlie arrived in Lincoln, late 1875 or early 1876, and made the acquaintance of Don Herrera, Maria Juliana had died from complications while giving birth to their youngest son Teodoro. Further tragedy befell the household when two of the youngest children were killed by lightning striking the roof and grounding through the stove where the children were playing. Fernando was left as a single father with eight children: three sons and five lovely daughters (one daughter's twin had also died at only a few days of age).

Fernando did remarry to Marta Rodriguez, but it's not known whether this was before the arrival of Doc and Charlie or afterwards. But, it seems very probable that the single Fernando needed help around his place while the two men got settled. And Doc's fluency with Spanish likely made the arrangements easier. Plus, the bachelors would both succumb to the charms of two Herrera girls.[45]

Doc and Charlie lived with Fernando for about two years. Even though they didn't occupy them right away, they borrowed money from L. G. Murphy in order to purchase their ranches on the Rio Ruidoso. This business transaction would turn out to add more fuel to a fire that would become the Lincoln County War. During the time leading up to the War, Doc served on posses trying to retrieve stolen cattle as well as serving as a sometimes physician and even following in his father's footsteps by serving as a school teacher. But Doc, ever the contradiction, would also be accused of theft, assault, threatening other citizens, and even disguising himself to obstruct the law.[46]

Jimmy Dolan, in a letter to the *New Mexican* dated May 16th, 1878 and published May 25th, confirms Doc and Charlie borrowing money from the House. In 1876 Dolan was the junior partner to Murphy, but by 1878, Dolan was the senior partner and John Riley was the junior partner.

Interestingly, this same letter mentions an accusation that is worth taking a look at, even though it is the obvious bias of the enemies of Doc and Charlie. Dolan stated that about a year and half prior, that is, at around the time that Doc and Charlie had just arrived in Lincoln, that they approached Riley with an offer to sell him cattle at a low price with the understanding that the cattle would be stolen cattle from Chisum's range. Riley then declined and went on to notify Chisum of the incident in a letter. Chisum, upon receiving the news, then forwarded the letter to Doc and Charlie. Doc and Charlie then vehemently denied the accusations and swore vengeance on Riley.[47]

Lest it seem that Riley was above such practices as dealing in stolen cattle, he was known to facilitate Jessie Evans and his gang's rustling. The House had the questionable business sense to buy rustled cattle at a cheaper price and sell them in order to increase their profits. So, it seems a bit suspect that Riley would deal with Jessie and the Boys and not Doc and Charlie, unless Riley considered it a breach of etiquette to operate outside of the Jessie Evans Gang.

Could Doc and Charlie have been involved in cattle rustling between the time that Doc left Chisum's employment until they arrived in Lincoln? Many stories about Billy the Kid's involvement with rustling cattle with the likes of Jessie Evans and his gang would place them all in a likely scenario where they were moving stolen cattle between Chisum's ranges on the Pecos and through southern New Mexico into Arizona. Besides, Doc had already been caught red handed with Chisum's property he had taken claiming it was owed to him. Also, on August 12th,

---

[45] Sanchez.

[46] D. Scurlock; Part IV, Cases 220, 226, & 230 dated October 9th, 1876; Part IV, J. J. Dolan letter dated May 25th, 1878.

[47] Fulton.

1877, Sheriff Brady arrested Doc for possession of stolen horses. Was a "cheese factory" just a euphemism for an entirely different business practice?

Jessie Evans, the eponymous leader of the Jessie Evans Gang, was born about 1852. He arrived in New Mexico from Texas in 1872 and went to work for John Chisum. A bold and effective fighter and leader, Chisum sent him on numerous excursions with other cowboys under his employee in retaliatory raids against the Mescalero Apaches for the retrieval of stolen horses and cattle. It's possible Doc accompanied Jessie on one or more of these raids.

Apparently, these expeditions only served to make Jessie a more effective cattle rustler when he decided to defect from Chisum's outfit and prey upon his former employer and other residents in the area. Colonel Albert Jennings Fountain, the attorney and editor of the *Mesilla Valley Independent* waged an editorial war against Jessie and his gang, sometimes called "The Boys". In these scorching recounts of their dastardly deeds, he dubbed the group "Banditti" and Jessie as "Captain Evans".

Around the same time that Doc left Chisum's employment, Jessie did too. Jessie initially found work on John Kinney's ranch on the Rio Grande in the Mesilla Valley. Kinney was five years older than Jessie and only served as a mentor in the ways of rustling.

John Kinney was born in 1847. He served in the U. S. Cavalry. He discharged from the military at Fort Selden near Las Cruces as First Sergeant in 1873 and began work in the cattle business. Kinney was another victim of Col. Fountain's editorial wrath. Fountain summed up the situation when he wrote that Kinney's ranch served as the headquarters and rendezvous for all of the rustlers in that region.

While Jessie Evans and the Boys roamed the vast stretches between the Pecos and the Rio Grande, Kinney remained ensconced around the Rio Grande. He would go on to lead the John Kinney Gang, also known as the Rio Grande Posse, during the Lincoln County War.[48]

On New Year's Eve that ushered in the year 1876, John Kinney and Jessie Evens, along with several other notable gang members were celebrating in a Las Cruces saloon. Soldiers from the 8th Cavalry were on hand and a brawl broke out with the outcome that John Kinney was severely beaten and thrown out.

In retaliation, Jessie Evans, Jim McDaniels, Frank Baker, Tom Hill, George Davis, Nicholas Provencio, Manuel "The Indian" Segovia, and others all fired at will into the saloon through doors and windows. A soldier and a civilian were killed and two people were wounded.

The fact that they got away with the crime against Federal soldiers goes to show just how untouchable the gang must have felt themselves.[49]

Jessie and his gang continued their spree of mayhem across the region through 1876 and well into 1877. Billy the Kid made his first confirmed appearance with the Boys in October, 1877. They held up a stagecoach seven miles east of Fort Cummings. The Kid was identified by name as being a part of the posse.

Billy the Kid is notorious for all of the names he went by over the years. He seemed to go by Billy as a child, Henry Antrim as a boy and teenager, Billy Antrim and Kid Antrim during his years in Arizona. By the time he joined the Jessie Evans gang he was styling himself Billy Bonney and William H. Bonney. It's not certain whether or not this surname was his birth father's name,

---

[48] Utley.

[49] Bell; Utley.

or a name he concocted himself. While it wouldn't be until the newspapers branded him "Billy the Kid" at the tail end of his life, we'll continue to refer to him as Billy the Kid because it is the name that history has most identified him with.

On August 17th, 1877, Billy the Kid was at Fort Grant, Arizona where he killed what most believe to be his first man. Gus Gildea confirmed that Billy came to town dressed like a "country jake" with his pistol in his waistband. Billy got involved in a poker game that turned violent. Frank "Windy" Cahill, the local blacksmith, was known to pick on Billy. This evening, however, Billy decided to end the bullying. Windy tackled Billy and sat atop him slapping him. Billy managed to free his pistol and shot Cahill in the stomach. Cahill died the next day and Billy fled the territory into New Mexico Territory.

After the stagecoach holdup in October, 1877, the Jessie Evans gang, now with Billy Bonney riding with them, next went to Mule Spring. The gang now numbered eleven and they held off a posse that pursued them. The posse lost their nerve and quit the chase.

On October 9th, the gang entered Tularosa and shot up the town. They visited John Ryan's store near the Mescalero Apache Indian Agency. That night, they adjourned to the summit of a nearby mountain and set up camp.

A rendezvous with John Riley and an employee of The House, James Longwell, was obviously planned. The Jessie Evans gang turned out along the road in mock-military fashion to meet the buggy carrying Riley and Longwell.

Returning to the mountain top, a bonfire was built and the revelry began. Jessie addressed the group and congratulated them on their successes. He then went on to promote himself to the rank of colonel and bestow upon Nicholas Provencio and Frank Baker the ranks of captain.

In a letter to the *Independent* making light of the night, Riley, signing himself "Fence Rail", told of how the gang drafted resolutions outlining the rules of engagement of their crime outfit. Nicolas Provencio consigned an issue of the *Independent* to the pyre in a symbolic funeral while Frank Baker played the "Rogue's March" on a comb.

The gang then split up and made their way to the Pecos area where Jessie Evans and the gang were sheltered at the Hugh Beckwith ranch. The Beckwiths were enemies of Chisum and had had run-ins with John Chisum and his men on numerous occasions. Chisum knew that Hugh was one of the people who sponsored the fleecing of Chisum's herds.

Another family in cahoots with the Beckwiths were the Jones family. Heiskell Jones and his wife Barbara "Ma'am" Jones had nine sons and one daughter. Several of their sons would figure prominently in the coming Lincoln County War on the side of the Seven Rivers Warriors.

For some inexplicable reason, While Jessie Evans and the Boys were at the Beckwith ranch, Billy was staying with the Jones family. Billy and John Jones formed a friendship.[50]

Also, Lily Casey Klasner mentions in her memoirs that Charlie Bowdre worked for her family for a while on their Feliz ranch and she also recounts a meeting with Billy the Kid and her mother.[51]

It can be inferred from the various accounts of Evans, Billy the Kid, Charlie, and Doc that these men were on very familiar terms with each other.

---

[50] Nolan, *The West of Billy the Kid*; Utley.

[51] Klasner.

On June 22nd, 1876 Doc's father, Priestly Scurlock passed away in Chappell Hill, Texas. Priestly had moved the family to Texas around 1874. This news must have been a tough blow for Doc to receive, but there is nothing to record the relationship that Doc had with his parents, so it is tough to say how much communication existed between them.[52] During the summer of 1876 a smallpox epidemic swept through the region killing numerous people. Priestly's death might likely be the result of this epidemic.

Besides Dick Brewer and Fernando Herrera, neighbors of Doc and Charlie's in those early days along the Rio Ruidoso just outside of Lincoln, included some recent arrivals of Coe cousins. Frank Coe, and another cousin-in-law named James Albert "Ab" Saunders had arrived from Missouri in the Spring of 1876. They set up their ranch and then returned to Missouri to bring back more kin.

George Coe, Frank's cousin, accompanied their small family band who crossed the distance from Missouri to New Mexico with a considerable crop of potatoes and fairly robust farming equipment. They also drove a small group of cattle and horses the entire route. The group arrived in Lincoln in time for St. Patrick's Day at Fort Stanton arriving March 17th, 1877.[53]

During the time period between 1876 and 1877, the small Ruidoso community fell prey to horse and cattle thieves. The thieves came from every ethnic group present in the area, there was a gang led by three notorious New Mexicans (Meras, Gonzales, and Largo), a Mescalero Apache gang led by a chief named Kamisa, and various largely Anglo groups (The Boys, The Seven Rivers Warriors, and The Rio Grande Posse).

The name that Doc and his friends Dick Brewer, Charlie Bowdre, Billy Bonney, Frank Coe, George Coe, Ab Saunders, Henry Newton Brown, Fred Waite, Frank MacNab, Jim French, John Middleton and various others took for their group was the Regulators.

In colonial times, there had been various groups of self-styled justice dealers who had used the term "Regulators". There was even a civilian uprising over taxes in the Carolinas that was dubbed the "War of the Regulation" or the "Regulator Movement" with members of the rebel faction calling themselves Regulators.

Vigilantism had a long history from the colonial era America and on the borders as westward expansion steadily pushed the demarcation of the American Frontier from the Carolinas and across the lands to the west. There was also a history of groups forming for similar purposes of raiding and retaliatory raiding among the New Mexicans and Native tribes of the Southwest.

The first incident occurred in July of 1876. Several notorious horse thieves named Nicas Meras, Jesus Largo, and Juan Gonzales made the mistake of stealing some horses from Frank Coe. This was before Frank returned to Missouri to retrieve his cousin George Coe.

Frank pursued well enough to get the identities of the three thieves, but he couldn't take them alone. Coe put together a posse consisting of his cousin Ab Saunders, Doc, Bowdre, Joe Howard who farmed on the Hondo, a man they derisively called Chihuahua of Cherokee/Mexican mix who worked for Joe on his farm, and John Jones.

The posse was certainly determined. They chased their prey into Puerto de Luna, which is northwest of Fort Sumner and deep into San Miguel County.

---

[52] Neal.

[53] Coe.

Juan Gonzales had earned some local notoriety for leading a posse of angry New Mexicans jointly with local authorities including Sheriff Ham Mills against the Horrell Gang during the Horrell War. He operated as the informant to the others of where to strike. Nicas Meras was a man who lived a double life. In the days he posed as a respected citizen, but he seemed to live more for the nocturnal hours, when he liked to operate his thefts. The last man was Jesus Largo. Jesus had worked for Chisum at the time Doc did. Jesus was described as having a flat nose due to a "six-shooter blow". He was big and knew how to handle horses and cattle.

When the gang made it to Bosque Redondo, they stopped at Pete Maxwell's place. Pete said he could feed them and send them on their way with a letter of introduction to a prominent New Mexican rancher that resided further up the road named Pablo Anallo, but he couldn't spare any men.

This might have been the first time that Doc met Pete Maxwell, or he might've had the opportunity to meet him when he worked for John Chisum on his Bosque Grande ranch. Fort Sumner is about 40 miles north of Bosque Grande so there is the possibility of Doc and Pete meeting then.

Before Coe's posse made it to Anallo's place, they arrived at John Gerhardt's ranch. John had valuable intelligence and told them that two of the men they were after were holed up in a canyon with two women. The posse boldly stormed the place only to find two hysterical women; the two men, Largo and probably Meras had fled. The posse did, however, recover the stolen horses. As they gathered them and made to depart, Largo and his partner rained fire down from above the canyon. In the race to escape, the bold New Mexican bandits captured Chihuahua.

The men made it back to Gerhardt's ranch and decided to leave the stolen horses there while they pursued their prey further north. They made it to Anallo's ranch but he counseled them not to use any local help that he could provide because he felt his men would side with Largo and Meras and ultimately betray the Lincoln men. Frustrated, the posse returned to Gerhardt's to decide what to do. When they arrived back at Gerhardt's however, they found their horses had been re-stolen. They were also given a note of truce terms from Jesus Largo.

They agreed to the terms that provided for the returning of Chihuahua, which was done, but not all the horses. After leaving, this didn't sit well with everyone in the posse, so they decided to make one more attempt to retrieve the horses before returning to Lincoln. During this stealth mission, Chihuahua suspiciously got separated from the posse and caused some dogs to begin barking, thus alerting their prey yet again.

The men gave up their efforts and an argument over what to do with Chihuahua ensued. Doc and Jones wanted to suspense with justice on the spot, but Bowdre and Coe didn't want to cause such trouble. Joe Howard assured them that he would settle the matter once they were back home. So, the men returned to Lincoln and a few days later Joe Howard shot and killed Chihuahua while they were in Joe's garden.

Later, Ab Saunders would testify along with Joe that Howard killed Chihuahua in self-defense.

Coe and the boys, still with a mind for vengeance, got word that Sheriff Saturnino Baca had captured Jesus Largo. The capture had occurred in Las Tablas just north of the Capitans by New Mexicans, but Largo was supposed to be brought to Lincoln and held in the jail there.

Coe, Saunders, Doc, and Bowdre intercepted Baca as he was escorting his prisoner to Fort Stanton and relieved him of the accused. The men proceeded to take Largo out of town into a local canyon.

Largo, who had supposedly ridden with Doc during earlier Chisum days, tried to plead with Doc for mercy, but Doc pushed him away claiming he didn't know him. Largo was lynched and the next day Billy Mathews cut the body down. Not long after this Saunders and another unnamed man extracted further revenge when they laid in ambush for Meras riding alone. They called for his surrender, but he tried to escape and Saunders shot and killed him. Meras' blood trail went for a mile before his body was discovered against the canyon wall. The canyon was named Meras Canyon after him.

Juan Gonzales was shot and killed by a sheriff's posse at Bernalillo on November 18th 1876.[54]

Another crime that Doc was charged with was holding Martin Baca at rifle point in a threatening manner. Unfortunately, the details of why are lost. Saturnino Baca's son, Boni Baca, a protege of L.G. Murphy, married Martin Baca's daughter, Telesfora Baca. Doc Scurlock would have the dubious honor of saying that he had held both of the fathers at gunpoint on different occasions.[55]

In one tragic event that must have haunted Doc for the rest of his life, he accidentally shot his close friend Mike G. Harkins. This occurred on September 2nd, 1876. Mike was the manager of John Riley's store at Blazer's Mill. The two friends were examining a gun in the carpenter's shop behind the Murphy-Dolan store, most likely in a business transaction, when the self-cocking pistol accidentally fired killing Harkins.[56]

Or was it an accident? If the story of Doc and Charlie's run in with Riley occurred the way Dolan alleged, the killing might be something a bit more sinister. Colonel Fountain presided over the case that found Doc not guilty of the killing.[57]

Harkins was embalmed under the direction of Dr. Carballo and Dr. McLean. He was buried in Lincoln with Major Murphy conducting the ceremony as Lincoln had no protestant preacher at the time. Harkins was an Episcopalian. Murphy read the Church of England commitment prayer and said a few words over the grave.[58]

On a much happier note, Doc was wed to his young bride on October 19th, 1876. Maria Antonia Miguela Herrera was the daughter of Fernando Herrera. The Herrera's were of Basque descent and had lived in New Mexico for some time, originally in Santa Cruz.[59]

Antonia was born June 13th, 1860 in Santa Cruz, New Mexico, making her only 16 years old at the time of her marriage to the 26-year-old Scurlock. This union wasn't wholly supported

---

[54] Haley; Fulton; Nolan, *LCW: A Documentary History*; D. Scurlock; Rasch, "Man of Many Parts"; Gomber, who characterizing all of the hangings of horse thieves during the winter season of 1877 as Lincoln Christmas ornaments.

[55] Part IV, criminal case 230.

[56] Part IV, articles dated 11 Sep 1876 and 12 Sep 1876 as well as cases 220 and 226; Rasch, "Man of Many Parts"; D. Scurlock; Gomber.

[57] See Part IV, criminal case #226.

[58] Keleher.

[59] Part V, Doc's Bible; D. Scurlock; J.D. Scurlock; Sanchez.

by Fernando, but he ultimately relented and even went on to participate in many of the events during the Lincoln County War on the side of the Regulators.

Doc and Antonia were married in the Catholic tradition by Padre Sambrano Tafoya. Most people simply called him Padre Sambrano or Father Sambrano.

Padre Sambrano was born April 3rd, 1829. Before arriving in Lincoln as the Parish Priest, he lived in the area of Manzano. While in Manzano he had become a father figure to the orphan Martin Chavez who would play an important role in the Lincoln County War. Padre Sambrano removed from Manzano permanently to Lincoln just a couple of weeks before George Coe arrived.[60]

Initially, the newlywed couple stayed with the Herreras, but Doc quickly grew infuriated by the way his bride was bossed around the home. He decided that no one, not even her own family, would treat his wife so unkindly. They moved back to his ranch on the Rio Ruidoso.

Prior to the Herrera's moving from Sant Cruz, New Mexico their daughter Manuela grew extremely ill. When the family moved south, Manuela was left in the care of a family friend with the intention of the two catching up to the family once Manuela was well enough to travel. It's not certain what the delay was, but it wouldn't be until 1875 that Manuela was reunited with her family. Manuela was nine or ten by this time. Sadly, Juliana Herrera, Fernando's wife and Manuela's mother died in 1873, making Manuela's reintroduction to the Herrera family difficult. Even though there was a language barrier and Charlie Bowdre was eighteen years her senior, the two developed a friendship that would eventually culminate in marriage and make Doc and Charlie brothers-in-law.[61]

[60] Cummings.

[61] Part V, Doc's Bible; Payne; Sanchez; D. Scurlock.

INTERLUDE 3: FIRST KILLING

Open plains outside of Fort Griffin, Texas, November 1876

Pat Garrett sat watching the cook Grundy Burns attempt, yet again, to get a fire going in the damp, cold weather. Everything seemed to be soaked, including everyone's spirit. The buffalo hunting was still good, but the conditions made it miserable work.

It was Pat's second winter on the plains as a hunter and he was already beginning to grow tired of the monotony of this life. Calling it hunting was a bit misleading as there was very little in the way of tracking skills involved. The buffalo were so thick on the plains that the critical skill for the hunter was a true aim. And flawless aim was something that Pat had grown quite good at.

A couple of years back he had dabbled in farming and stock driving until he met Willis Skelton Glenn. Skelton, as he liked to go by, was a Civil War veteran who had also migrated from Louisiana to Texas and had dabbled in farming and driving cattle and horses. The two men became acquainted with each other. When the two men met Luther Duke, a Kentuckian, it seemed that they had finally gotten enough pieces in place to make a go at the lucrative trade of buffalo hunting. So, they pooled their money and purchased supplies.

Pat brought into the mix a young Irishman named Joe Briscoe who he thought could be useful around camp. Skelton found two other men to round out their hunting operation in a local saloon. Nick Buck claimed to be one of the finest skinners around. This was a valuable trade because the cleaning of the carcass took much longer than the shooting.

On a good day Pat could kill between 60 and 100 buffalos. The skinner, even on a good day, could only skin between 60 to 70 before the loss of daylight made the job impossible. It was dirty, thankless work, but Nick Buck was truly a master and he had been teaching Briscoe the trade.

The second man that Skelton had found in the saloon was the fellow who Pat now watched feebly trying to catch a fire so that maybe the group could have a hot breakfast in the miserable chill before setting off to work. Grundy Burns was their camp cook, but it didn't appear much cooking would get done if Grundy didn't get the damn fire lit.

Pat, who was six foot four inches tall, tried to wring the moisture from his pants. It was impossible to find clothes to fit a man of his height back at Fort Griffin, the nearest supply depot. His pants were too short so he had come up with the idea of attaching two strips of buffalo hide to his pants legs to make up the difference. Unfortunately, the fur soaked up moisture and made the pants weigh a ton.

Finally, Grundy managed to get some buffalo chips kindled and everyone except Briscoe crowded around the small fire.

Briscoe had gone in search of water. It seemed that the skinner's clothes were perpetually smelly, dirty, and bloody. Briscoe was continually attempting to clean his clothes. This particular day, he had only managed to find a place where the rain had collected. The water was dirty and ice cold, but it wasn't bloody.

Having scrubbed his clothes, he marched back into camp cursing his numb fingers, cursing the lack of clean water, and cursing the overall state of the weather.

Pat, already ill over the dampness of his pants said, "Only a stupid Irishman would go clean his clothes in a mud puddle."

This wasn't the first time Pat had made remarks to Briscoe, but for whatever reason, this was the straw that broke the camel's back for Joe.

"You long-legged son of a bitch. I've just about had it with your condescending remarks about the Irish when you're the one who looks like a damn fool walking around in those godawful pants!"

"You better watch your tongue, Joe, before I use one of these long legs to kick your ass back down to that mud hole."

And with that, it was on. Joe launched towards the squatting Pat but Pat anticipated it and rose to meet Briscoe. Just as Briscoe came within the long reach of Pat, Pat had grabbed his collar and swung him to the ground.

Briscoe rolled over and took one look at the dirt now staining his only clean shirt and the ire of the Irish kindled higher than Grundy's buffalo chip fire. Briscoe tried to tackle Pat but Pat danced away and swatted Briscoe an open-handed slap across the side of the head.

Things escalated quickly then. Briscoe, infuriated beyond reason, tried desperately to come at Pat. Pat's height and reach made the task impossible for Briscoe and after a couple more open-hand smacks to Briscoe's head, the boy was soon sprawled on the ground and huffing air.

"It's futile, Joe. Don't get up and embarrass yourself anymore. It's not even fair sport now."

Briscoe looked around at all the men laughing at his expense. He didn't say another word as he yanked the hatchet away from Grundy, who was trying to split wood and feed the fire into life.

Brandishing the hatchet he recovered and came at Pat again. This time, Pat decided that he needed to put the wagon between himself and Briscoe because he didn't care to catch a wild swing from the enraged man.

Briscoe meant business and Pat was sure that, given the chance, he would bury the hatchet in his skull. Pat, while circling the wagon away from Briscoe scooped up his Winchester and decided that things had gone far enough. He gave Joe Briscoe one final warning but the Irishman didn't heed it. He ran at Pat with the hatchet held high and then the air echoed with the shot.

Joe Briscoe took the bullet right in the gut and fell backwards right into the newly built fire of Grundy Burns. Everyone rushed to pull Briscoe out of the flames. He groaned, spit up a mouthful of bloody froth, and then died.

Skelton talked Pat into going back to Fort Griffin and turning himself in. Pat felt horrible about the killing and quickly agreed that Skelton was right and struck out immediately.

One year later, the buffalo were nearly hunted out.

Pat had gone to Fort Griffin and did turn himself in, but no one really seemed to care to press the matter. The deputy listened to his tale and agreed that it sounded like an unfortunate act of self-defense. He talked to the constable and they elected not to prosecute any charges. And with that, Pat was free to return to his outfit.

Over the next year Duke sold his rights to Skelton, they endured two devastating raids by the Comanches as the Indians attempted to stop the extermination of the buffalo herds, and the trio of Skelton, Pat, and Buck decided to take a vacation to St. Louis before deciding which direction to go next.

By November of 1877, Skelton had bought out Pat and then hired him as a hunter for one more hunting excursion. They chose to go further west in order to determine the situation on the Texas/New Mexico border, but the buffalo were so sparse that they abandoned most of their equipment and headed for Fort Sumner.

On their first morning at Fort Sumner in February of 1878, they sat eating breakfast along the Pecos. As they ate, a herd being driven by several men was passing by.

Pat said, "Nick, go on over there and see if those men need any employees."

Nick agreed and left, but soon returned to say that they didn't.

"I don't think you understand the gravity of our situation," Pat said. "Let me try."

Pat mounted his horse and rode over to one of the ranch hands.

"Which outfit do you fellows belong to?"

"Pedro Maxwell," the man replied.

"Can you point me to his whereabouts?"

The man pointed to a wagon a quarter of a mile to the rear of the herd. Pat road over and introduced himself.

"The New Mexicans call me Pedro and the Anglos call me Pete," he explained as he introduced himself to Pat.

"And what can you do, Lengthy?" Pete Maxwell asked after Pat entreated him for a job.

"Well, I can ride anything that has hair and I can damn sure rope better than your boys there."

Pat and his companions went to work for Pete Maxwell. His partners didn't last, though. Skelton Glenn and Nick Duke decided to move on.

Pat worked for Pete only a short time. While he did, though, he took the opportunity to learn Spanish. Pat then decided to work as a bartender in Beaver Smith's saloon. Before long, everyone in the area knew him as Juan Largo because of his height. He had the opportunity to encounter people from all walks of life as they passed through the saloon. And he became quite conversant in Spanish.

[DISCLAIMER: Liberty was taken with the dialogue, but this follows closely to the events of Pat's first killing and how he came to arrive at Ft. Sumner.]

NOT ALWAYS A CALM BEFORE THE STORM

It must be understood that the relationship between Scurlock, Bowdre, the Coes, Saunders, and others who would one day become members of the Regulators and those members of the Jessie Evans Gang was never as cut and dry as two opposing forces before the outbreak of the Lincoln County War. In many instances, allegiances and friendships spanned both groups. Jessie and fellow members Frank Baker, Tom Hill, and Nicholas Provencio likely knew Doc from their time working for Chisum together.

Just as allegiances and friendships of the rowdy citizens were never clearly aligned, so too were the relationships between the power set. And so things stood in August of 1877 when the small farmers were feeling not just a little animosity towards John Chisum as he tried, at least to their view, to appropriate the entire county for his personal range.

Another couple of recent settlers to the area were Frank Freeman and Billy Mathews. Freeman was also born in Alabama, but bore an overt racial prejudice that got the best of him in the end. He first went to Texas where he met up with Billy Mathews. The two purchased a ranch near Lincoln close to the Ruidoso and Hondo on the Rio Feliz.

Freeman's first act of racial hatred came in December of 1876. Freeman was on an errand between home and Ft. Stanton and decided to stop at the Wortley Hotel in Lincoln for a bite. He refused to share a seat with a black Union soldier from Fort Stanton and the incident escalated to Freeman shooting the soldier.

Even though the soldier would wind up surviving the wound to his leg, Freeman thought he had killed the soldier. A posse was assembled and captured Freeman and he was turned over to a contingent of federal soldiers from Fort Stanton to stand charges. This contingent just so happened to include more Post-Slavery, African-American soldiers. Understandably, Freeman began to believe that these men would seek their revenge enroute. Somehow, Freeman managed to escape. Scared for his life, he fled back to Texas.

Freeman stayed away from Lincoln for almost a year, when he did return, he was up to his old antics again.

On August 5th, 1877, Charlie Bowdre and Frank Freeman became drunk and disorderly and paraded through the streets of Lincoln firing their guns at will. Their spree began at the Montano store where they forced the proprietor to provide liberal amounts of whiskey.

They then ransacked the place and got into a standoff with another soldier from Fort Stanton. Freeman, making to shake hands in a friendly manner, grabbed the soldier's hand and placed his gun against the soldier's head. He pulled the trigger but, again, another resilient soldier would survive.

Leaving the soldier for dead, the two men then went up to the McSween house where John Chisum was visiting and demanded, "If John Chisum or his corpse was not turned over to them, they would burn the damned house down". They then proceeded to fire their guns into the house. A servant returned fire and the two men retreated.

Sheriff Brady was summoned and met up with the two at the Murphy building where they had left their horses. Bowdre shoved Brady, then Brady and Freeman nearly drew down on each other. Billy Mathews and Jimmy Dolan intervened and saved any further violence.

The two were taken to Fort Stanton. Freeman and Bowdre later raised bail.

On or about the 14th of August a posse aided by troops from Fort Stanton received the news that Freeman, a man named Armstrong, and Nicholas Provencio were boasting of returning to Lincoln and taking revenge on the town.

Brady and his deputy gathered posses and went after the group of threatening loudmouths. Deputy Sheriff Francisco Romero and some men killed Armstrong in a shootout.

Meanwhile, Sheriff Brady appealed to Capt. Purington at Ft Stanton for assistance and was given the assistance of Lieutenant Smith and fifteen soldiers. The posse picked up the trail and found Freeman, Scurlock, George Coe, and Bowdre at Bowdre's ranch. A fight ensued which resulted in the killing of Freeman and the capture of Doc and Coe. Bowdre escaped down the river. Doc was charged with having stolen horses in his possession. According to George Coe's retelling of the incident, Brady forced Doc and Coe to share a horse as he took them into custody. The two men were tied together with Doc in front and George in back. They were tied so tightly that George averred the discomfort was tantamount to torture. Whether it was meanness or outright torture, Doc and George had every reason to hold a grudge against Brady.[62]

Next month, Jessie Evans and The Boys, who the press (Col. Fountain) dubbed "The Banditti", were up to no good in the vicinity. It began with some thefts from the area of Blazer's Mill and the Apache Reservation's stock. Indian Agent Maj. Godfroy filed a complaint about the

---

[62] Rasch, "Man of Many Parts"; Coe; Payne; D. Scurlock.

incident and about the general lawlessness all around. He even hinted at being on the verge of quitting his job and leaving the area.[63]

In November of 1876, a young, entrepreneurial-minded Englishman with an eye on expanding his family's wealth by using his father's business funds and investing them in the cattle business, had arrived in Lincoln.

John Henry Tunstall was born March 6th, 1853 in London, England. His father was of the upper middle-class and had business ventures in Canada as well as England. John first came to Canada to assist in the family business, but by 1876, he found his way into the cattle and mercantile business in Lincoln. His interests were aligned with John Chisum and the town attorney, Alexander McSween.[64]

At the time that The Boys absconded with some of Tunstall's brand new horses, he had hired Dick Brewer to be his ranch boss. He had also taken a liking to Robert Widenmann. Robert's parents were German, but Robert was born in Michigan. He was sent to Germany for a formal education and returned to the United States before drifting into Sant Fe where he met John Tunstall. John and Robert were about the same age and seemed to enjoy each other's company. McSween, however, distrusted Widenmann and thought he was essentially living off of Tunstall.

Dick Brewer recruited Doc and Charlie to help pursue the gang deep into Dona Ana County to Las Cruces. Dick probably thought Doc and Charlie knew several of the members of The Boys well enough to retrieve their stolen horses.[65]

On September 22nd, 1877, the *Mesilla Independent* ran the following item:

> THE BANDITTI AGAIN
>
> Mr. Richard Brewer, a well-known citizen of Lincoln County arrived at Las Cruces on Thursday from his rancho on the Ruidoso. He reports that on the early part of the week the notorious Jessie Evans and a companion in crime whose name we did not learn, stole four fine horses from Mr. Brewer, and two were the property of Mr. Widenman. The animals were taken in daylight and in Mr. Brewer's presence. Mr. B., having obtained assistance followed the thieves who came in the direction of San Nicholas; upon arriving at that place Brewer left his posse with directions to continue following the trail and he came into Las Cruces and obtained a warrant for the arrest of Evans and his companion. On Thursday night one of the posse sent word in to Mr. Brewer that Evans and his companion had been captured at San Augustine that we have long intended to say may as well be said right here. That place has the reputation of being the headquarters, the haunt and the rendezvous of the worst gang of thieves and cut-throats that ever cursed any civilized community with its presence. The mountains and canyons in its vicinity afford hiding places for stolen stock, and lurking places for the banditti that have been plundering the citizens of Dona Ana and Lincoln counties. Our authorities have for some time had an eye on this den, and it is about time they took steps towards breaking it up.

---

[63] Fulton.

[64] Nolan, *LCW: A Documentary History*.

[65] Part IV, article dated September 22nd, 1877; Fulton; Nolan, *LCW: A Documentary History*; D. Scurlock.

> A thorough search of the canyons on the east side of the Organ mountains would not prove unprofitable to persons who have had stock stolen from them in Dona Ana and Lincoln counties during the past year.
>
> LATER – Messrs. Scurlock and Bowdre who accompanied Mr. Brewer, arrived in town this morning, they report that they went to San Augustine and found the four stolen horses at the house of W. F. Shedd in possession of Jessie Evans, Nicholas Provencio, Frank Baker, Tom Hill and three others of the band. They demanded the horses; the thieves refused to deliver them saying in effect that they had been at too much trouble to get them. Finding it impossible to take the animals, the two men came in town and reported; and thus the matter stands.
>
> These Banditti are well armed and mounted. They are here in our country openly defying the laws. It appears that they cannot be arrested, and they know it. There is no telling who may be their next victim.

It's very likely that this parley went so peaceably because Doc would likely have known, or at least been acquainted with Jessie Evans from working for Chisum at the same time[66]. Certainly Charlie and Doc knew Nicholas Provencio well enough considering the Frank Freeman incident.

Doc and Charlie's entreaties to return the horses were for naught, so they returned to Lincoln much as they had on the pursuit in the opposite direction for Jesus Largo.

When news arrived that The Boys were southeast of Lincoln in Seven Rivers, Dick Brewer and Sheriff Brady, who was more or less forced to assist the effort due to public sentiment, assembled a posse that conspicuously didn't include Doc and Charlie.[67]

The posse caught up to Jessie Evans and his partners at the Beckwith ranch. After a brief exchange of fire, Brewer and Brady succeeded in capturing them.[68]

Tunstall, returning to Lincoln from a visit to St. Louis for supplies for his store, ran into the sheriff's posse and prisoners on the road and at first couldn't decide if the situation was that Evans had captured Brewer or Brewer had captured Evans.

The men began to joke and Tom Hill asked Tunstall if he had a drink. Tunstall offered to get them a drink back in Lincoln. Because they'd be in jail, they told him to bring it by the jail. And he actually did go to the jail to visit the men.[69]

Tunstall's motive for doing this was largely geared towards trying to charm the men into revealing the whereabouts of his stolen horses. The Boys told him that they were now in Mexico. There is the possibility that they incriminated Billy the Kid with having in his possession Tunstall's favorite horses, Tunstall never mentions this is any letters, though.[70]

While the group was incarcerated, Tunstall was beset by another problem. This time his troubles stemmed from the widow Ellen Casey. After Robert Casey was murdered in Lincoln by

---

[66] Rasch, *Warriors of Lincoln County*, see pieces entitled "The Story of Jessie J. Evans" and "The Chronicles of Jim McDaniels".

[67] Fulton.

[68] Nolan, *The West of Billy the Kid*.

[69] Nolan, *LCW: A Documentary History*.

[70] Lily Casey Klasner claims Billy was one of the men arrested with Jessie.

William Wilson, Widow Casey mismanaged her family affairs to the point that she was in financial straits.

In May of 1877, Alexander McSween served a writ on her for her debts. The court ordered Sheriff Brady to impound 400 head of cattle as a security against her settlement. If she could not settle, the cattle were to be auctioned publicly. Instead, McSween and Tunstall came up with a rather ingenious solution. They gave her a loan worth half the price of the cattle. Should she pay the loan back she would get the cattle back. But if she failed to pay back the loan, the cattle became Tunstall's. Believing that she wouldn't raise enough money to pay back the loan, Tunstall effectively got the cattle for a great price.

Ellen Casey was obviously rankled by this deal. She was also furious over Tunstall acquiring land on the Feliz that she felt still belonged to the Casey family. Unfortunately, Robert Casey never filed the proper paperwork to claim this land. Around the middle of October, Ellen decided that it was best to cut the family losses and head back to Texas. She packed up her five children, and with the help of family friend Abner "Ab" McCabe, gathered her remaining cattle and headed for the Pecos region. In addition, she also took the cattle that Tunstall had just acquired back into her possession.

Tunstall once again enlisted Dick Brewer to journey to the Seven Rivers region of the Pecos and catch the Caseys before they crossed into Texas. It was while the Caseys were visiting the Jones or Beckwith families on their trip that Lily and Ad Casey recounts Billy the Kid's presence there.

Billy attempted to sell Ellen Casey the horses he had in his possession, but Ellen Casey recognized the horses as Tunstall's. When she informed Billy that she didn't want to buy a stolen horse, even though she was in possession of considerably more of what was technically Tunstall's property, he informed her that she was already in possession of Las Cruces Sheriff Mariano Barela's daughter's horse, which was stolen. Indignantly she objected and Billy replied that he knew this because he was the one who stole it. She, however, had a bill of sale from Frank McCullum, the man who Billy admitted to trading the horse for another with.

Billy, nevertheless, attempted to join the Caseys as they moved on, but the Widow Casey refused his company. For the time being at least, Billy avoided Dick Brewer, who did catch the Casey family and manage to retrieve Tunstall's cattle. Brewer's posse, which included John Middleton, Fred Waite, Sam Corbet, and Florencio Gonzalez, also arrested Will and Ad Casey for the thefts and hauled them back to Lincoln forcing Ellen Casey to return.

Ellen Casey managed to appeal to John Chisum for assistance in getting her boys released. Tunstall's happiness in having his cattle back and Jessie Evans in the Lincoln jail was short lived, however. On the night of November 16th, or early on the 17th, Jessie and his companions were freed.

Various theories of just who was involved in the escape of Jessie Evans, George Davis, Tom Hill, Frank Baker, and Lucas Gallegos have been put forth. Lucas just happened to go along with the escape. He was being held on unrelated charges. Lucas had killed Sostero Garcia at San Patricio.

Certainly the Murphy-Dolan faction would have wanted their escape. Brady, who had been on the capturing side, was accused of being lax about it all and made no real effort to ensure the security of the prisoners. Brewer had also confided in Tunstall when the posse met him on the road that he felt it was just a matter of time before Jessie and the Boys escaped Lincoln.

Strangely, Tunstall was a prime suspect in aiding and abetting the escape. His motive likely being a payback for information given to him by the Boys. Evidence to this was the fact that he bought two suits for Jessie's men as well as the liquor.

The rescue posse who broke Jessie Evans and his cohorts out the Lincoln pit jail numbered anywhere from 25 to 30. The leader was Andrew Boyle, an avowed enemy of John Chisum. Also in the group were Buck Morton, Billy Mathews, Dick Lloyd, Charlie Crawford, and Billy the Kid.

Jessie Evans, Andy Boyle, and their large gang first stopped along the Ruidoso at Charlie Bowdre's place and either stole or was given a rifle. They next went to Dick Brewer's ranch. Dick was away and the gang helped themselves to breakfast and took eight of Brewer and Tunstall's horses. Jessie would later return seven of them. He also vowed that he would not steal from Tunstall any more.[71]

The next encounter the Boys had was with Francisco "Kiko" Trujillo and his brother Juan who were hunting. The bandits surrounded Juan while Kiko tried to make a run for it. Billy the Kid and Kiko drew their rifles on each other and a tense situation ensued. Kiko relented when the gang threatened to kill Juan if he didn't lower his rifle. Lucas Gallegos pleaded with Kiko that the Boys really would kill Juan, who was Lucas' friend, so Kiko complied.

Before the group left Juan and Kiko, they took Kiko's pistol, rifle, and saddle to give to their new member Lucas. Billy the Kid good-naturedly told Kiko not to worry, that he would pay him back.[72]

A few days later, Brady went into Tunstall's store and made overt threats towards Tunstall. Brady didn't appreciate Tunstall giving all the credit of the successful capture in Seven Rivers to Dick Brewer. Words were exchanged and Brady accused Tunstall of freeing the prisoners. As they argued Brady's hand went towards his revolver and McSween stepped in to cool the situation.[73]

News of Billy's possession of Tunstall's dapple gray horses reached Lincoln and once again Dick Brewer set off on the trail to Seven Rivers. Little is known about how Dick took Billy into custody, but Billy was brought back to Lincoln under arrest and deposited in the jail. How long he sat there isn't known exactly, either, but very soon he was freed and, inexplicably, began working for John Tunstall.[74]

It has been reported by both the Herreras and the Coes that Billy the Kid lived with them prior to going to work for John Tunstall.[75] While this would be a very short time period to occur, there is one anecdote related by Pedro Rodriguez who thought of Fernando Herrera as his grandfather.[76]

Pedro claimed to know an Apache named Chief Kamisa well into his later life. Chief Kamisa and a band of Apaches stole some of Fernando's horses. Fernando Herrera assembled a posse that consisted of his son Andres Herrera, Manuel Silva, George Washington (later to become one

---

[71] Nolan, *The West of Billy the Kid*; Utley.

[72] Eastwood, see Appendix "WPA – Billy the Kid/Trujillo"; Nolan, *The Billy the Kid Reader*, see the chapter entitled "The Mackyswins and The Marfes"; Utley.

[73] Fulton.

[74] Nolan, *The West of Billy the Kid*.

[75] Coe, Coe's footnote by Prof. Doyce Nunis reports that Billy could have likely wintered with George 1877-78; Sanchez.

[76] Eastwood, see Appendix "WPA – Pedro M. Rodriguez".

of McSween's hired help[77]), and Billy the Kid. The story goes that the Apaches surrounded the group and could have easily killed them except for Billy's antics of riding his horse in tight circles and shooting his pistol in the air. This startled the Apaches to behold such a spectacle and the posse made an escape. Later, Chief Kamisa returned to Fernando and made a bargain that settled the matter. The Apaches would no longer raid the cattle of the farms in that area. He said that the reason he felt compelled to return and make such a deal was because of the bravery of Billy the Kid. Such are the stories of Chivato – the name that the New Mexicans would come to call him.[78]

This likely happened in late 1877 after Doc and Charlie had established their own farms, as they likely would've been present in this excursion.

As the year 1877 came to an end, Tunstall had under his employment Dick Brewer as his ranch foreman, the elderly Gottfried "Godfrey" Gauss as cook, and Billy the Kid. Rob Widenmann was still firmly in Tunstall's good graces. Widenmann had been appointed a deputy U.S. marshal by John Sherman in order to add legality to the hunt for Jessie Evans and his fellow criminals.

Three other employees that would round out Tunstall's hired hands were Fred Waite, Henry Brown, and John Middleton.

Fred Waite was born September 23rd, 1853 at Fort Arbuckle, Indian Territory, Oklahoma. Fred was the eldest of ten children born to a prominent Chickasaw family. He was sent to Arizona, Illinois, and Missouri for schooling before returning to Indian Territory. He became involved in the Masons serving in several positions within the Lodge. Shortly after his father Thomas Waite died in 1874, Fred decided to head westward looking for adventure. He then surfaced in 1877 in Lincoln and began working for John Tunstall. Supposedly, Billy the Kid and Fred Waite had aspirations of partnering on a ranch.[79]

Henry Newton Brown was born in Missouri about 1859, but drifted to Texas before his arrival in Lincoln. Henry initially worked for the Murphy-Dolan outfit at Murphy's Carrizozo ranch but when the House failed to pay him his full wages, and in a timely manner, he became bitter towards them and went to work for John Chisum. Chisum arranged for him to work for Tunstall around the same time as Billy the Kid.[80]

John Chisum's cattle business took a turn on December 3rd, 1875 when he sold his Bosque Grande ranch along with 60,000 head of cattle to the livestock commission firm of Hunter, Evans, & Company. Chisum had many reasons for wanting to make this deal. First of all, his herd was becoming rather burdensome. The numbers were growing faster than he could sell. He also had numerous debts back in Texas that needed to be settled. Finally, his ranges were dwindling as more settlers arrived on the Pecos. It was the settlers, such as the Beckwiths and the Joneses, that participated in rustling his herds. Hunter & Evans offered to assist since the cattle was now their interest. Operationally, though, John and Pitzer Chisum continued to tend, protect, and drive the herds.[81]

John Middleton and Frank MacNab were both employees of Hunter & Evans and their job was to assist in the cessations of the rustling going on in the vicinity of Seven Rivers. John

[77] Rasch, *Warriors of Lincoln County*, see piece entitled "George Washington of Lincoln County".
[78] Eastwood, see Appendix "WPA – Pedro M. Rodriguez"; Sanchez.
[79] DeArment, see the piece "Old Habits Die Hard: A Note on Frederick T. Waite" by Marcus Huff.
[80] O'Neal.
[81] Ibid.

Middleton was born in Tennessee in either 1864 or 1865. He drifted to Texas and claimed to have fled due to the killing of a man. He was hired by Hunter & Evans largely because he was renowned as an expert marksman. He began working for John Tunstall in October 1877. Tunstall described him as "about the most desperate looking man I have ever set eyes on" but that he was actually a mild and composed man.

Although Frank MacNab didn't work for Tunstall, he did join the Regulators. Frank also fled from Texas. In the Panhandle he was incriminated in the killing of two Casner brothers. When more of the family began a series of vendetta killings, Frank managed to convince them that he wasn't involved. He began working for Hunter & Evans soon afterwards. Col. Dudley said of him, "His reputation was as bad as it could be; he was looked upon as an outlaw and a murderer."[82]

It appears that Henry Newton Brown, John Middleton, and Frank MacNab, who would all fight along with the Regulators, became acquainted with Chisum after Doc's departure from Chisum's outfit, but they all aligned themselves with Chisum, McSween, and Tunstall.[83]

---

[82] Nolan, *LCW: A Documentary History*; Rasch, *Warriors of Lincoln County*, see the piece "These Were the Regulators".

[83] Coe; Rasch, *Warriors of Lincoln County*, see "A Note on Henry Newton Brown" in.

INTERLUDE 4: THE MOST DANGEROUS STREET IN AMERICA

Lincoln, New Mexico, 1868-1882

In 1878 President Rutherford B. Hayes declared that the town of Lincoln, New Mexico was "the most dangerous street in America." In the *Daily New Mexican* on March 28th, 1881 Billy the Kid was quoted as saying, "At least 200 men have been killed in Lincoln County during the last three years but I did not kill all of them." Billy's stats might be questionable, but not by much.

From 1868 to 1882, in the short stretch of road that was the town of Lincoln, more than 50 people were killed. Lincoln was also host to two "wars" on its streets.

The first one was dubbed the Horrell War. The Horrells were the predominant family in an extended family that fled Texas to New Mexico. The Horrell clan stirred up quite a bit of animosity in Lincoln among the New Mexican families. The worst attack came on December 20th, 1873 when the Horrells retaliated for the killing of Ben Horrell by Constable Juan Martin by shooting up a wedding celebration. Isidro Patron, Isidro Padilla, Mario Balazan, and Jose Candelaria were killed and three people were wounded. Isidro Patron was Juan Patron's father. The Horrells were eventually driven out of Lincoln but not before Martin Chavez killed another of their party, Ben Turner. Martin became a local hero among the New Mexicans for this.

Of course, the more famous war was the Lincoln County War. The culmination of which was the battle that took place in Lincoln over five days from July 15th through the 19th of 1878. The grand finale of the battle was dubbed "The Big Killing". Charlie Crawford had been mortally wounded a few days earlier, but the burning of the McSween house and the desperate escape of Billy the Kid and the other Regulators resulted in the deaths of Alexander McSween, Harvey Morris, Vicente Romero, Francisco Zamora, and Bob Beckwith.

The statistics aren't all from gun battles, either. There was one stabbing, one poisoning, and six hangings or lynchings. William Wilson was famously hung twice. George Washington, the ubiquitous former buffalo soldier who worked as a handyman for Alexander McSween claimed to have accidentally shot his wife Luisa Sanchez and their infant child while trying to shoot a stray dog. His credibility was strained when he later tried to elope with Saturnino Baca's 18-year-old daughter Josefa Baca. Saturnino raised a posse and pursued them. When they were caught, George was lynched.

Doc Scurlock was involved in several violent episodes in Lincoln. One of his killings is credited as one of the four accidental shootings in Lincoln when he shot Mike Harkins in the carpenter's shop behind the Murphy-Dolan store while examining one of the newer self-cocking pistols.

Doc was also a member of the posse who intercepted Saturnino Baca and relieved him of his prisoner Jesus Largo who was then taken just outside of town and lynched.

[DISCLAIMER: For an excellent presentation of the violence in Lincoln see *True West* magazine's July 2019 issue titled "Billy the Kid Walks the Deadliest Street in America".]

LINCOLN COUNTY WAR

Alexander McSween and his wife Susan had migrated from Eureka, Kansas to Lincoln, arriving March 3rd, 1875. McSween was born in Canada, but his family was Scottish Presbyterian. It's likely that McSween went to St. Louis and attended the Law Department of Washington University. As Lincoln had no resident lawyer, McSween found himself quite useful.

He initially was hired by the Murphy camp, but it was clear that McSween didn't have much in common with those lads. McSween was of the Republican party, had never served in the military, and was a Presbyterian Scot. Almost to a man Emil Fritz, the first senior partner, Lawrence Murphy, James Dolan, James Riley, and Sheriff William Brady were Irish, Catholic, Democrats, had served in the Union Army as officers and soldiers, and were Masons. Fritz being the only non-Irish of the bunch – he was German. So, Alex split ties with The House and decided to try and compete with their rule of the land.

The power factions were really beginning to align in opposite directions of each other at this point. John Tunstall's family had money and he had come to New Mexico to do serious business. Through his association with Alexander McSween, who had formed an association with Chisum, the three men had undertaken the task of breaking the economic and political power held solely by the Murphy-Dolan faction, who had controlled matters for quite some time. Lawrence Murphy was the senior member, but by this time, he was suffering from cancer and not engaged in the day-to-day operations of things in Lincoln. That task fell to James Dolan.

Animosity grew to its boiling point over an incident concerning how McSween had handled the estate of Emil Fritz, a partner of L. G. Murphy & Co. Fritz died while away in Germany and a battle ensued over how the insurance money was to be settled. The Fritz family felt they were entitled to the insurance money outright and held McSween as the insurance representative responsible for ensuring that they received it. On the other side, Dolan felt that the Murphy firm was entitled to a piece of the settlement as Fritz still owed money to them.

McSween had traveled back east to settle the matter and negotiated a settlement less than the full amount of the $10,000 policy. After deducting his fees and travel expenses, he received $7,148.94 credited to his account. At the time, Dolan and Riley were rapidly sinking into financial straits and this money would certainly help cover debts and expenses.

Dolan showed himself to be a shrewd fellow in setting into motion what must have been his master plan. He and his cronies waited till Mr. and Mrs. McSween left Lincoln to meet John Chisum on December 18th, 1877. The three were going on a trip to St. Louis on business. Dolan left immediately for Mesilla. On the way he stopped in Las Cruces to meet with Mrs. Scholand, Fritz's surviving sister, who he convinced that McSween planned on skipping the territory with intentions of taking the money. Affidavits were signed and Dolan continued his trip to meet with District Attorney William Rynerson, a fellow conspirator planning the fall of the triumvirate.

Since Chisum wasn't involved in the Fritz affair, a different crime had been concocted for his downfall. United States Attorney for New Mexico Thomas B. Catron had a client named William Rosenthal. He alleged that he held debts for a company called "William, Chisum, & Clark" that was a meatpacking venture in Arkansas. The only fly in the ointment was that Chisum claimed he never agreed to the business in the end. Since he never signed anything, it wasn't his debt to square. Catron and Dolan didn't care, though. They just needed a pretext to arrest McSween and Chisum in one stroke.

In order to travel to St. Louis in those days, you first had to travel to the nearest train depot. That was all the way in Trinidad, Colorado. The last major stop before that was Las Vegas, New Mexico. The railroad was still a couple of years away from arriving in Las Vegas. Las Vegas was in San Miguel County. Dolan and Rynerson contacted the San Miguel County sheriff who was ordered to detain them in Las Vegas with the warrants to follow quickly.

This was done and after a couple of days, no warrants had arrived so, John, Alex, and Susan headed out for Trinidad. The warrants arrived and the sheriff and his posse chased the three down when they were just outside of Trinidad. Mrs. McSween was convinced to go on to St. Louis while the two men were rather rudely hauled back to Las Vegas.

Chisum would remain in the jail for the next two months. He practically chose to do this out of spite. Catron, under an obscure law, required Chisum to share his true assets. Chisum refused with the faith that since he truly hadn't signed anything, he would eventually be set free – it was just a matter of time. A time he was willing to serve.

McSween, on the other hand, was ordered to return to Mesilla and face Judge Bristol under the escort of San Miguel Deputy Sheriffs Adolph Barrier and Antonio Campos. They left on January 4th, 1878. Judge Bristol happened to be ill at this time and would notify everyone when he thought he'd be well enough to convene in Mesilla. The best estimate was the end of January. Because of this, McSween was allowed to go to Lincoln for the next few weeks. McSween and his two escorts arrived in Lincoln on January 8th where he was essentially under house arrest until he was brought to Mesilla.

Also in Lincoln, there was a victory for the McSween side. Murphy and Dolan's claim against the Fritz estate was disallowed by Murphy's replacement, Florencio Gonzales. Murphy, who was entering the last stages of his terminal illness turned everything over to Dolan and Riley who promptly mortgaged all of the House's assets.

Tunstall, still free and feeling that with Chisum and McSween writing letters exposing the Santa Fe Ring to the newspapers along with this victory over the House, he might as well write a letter to the *Independent* exposing Sheriff Brady for the mismanagement of public funds. This was published January 18th. All this really served to do, though, was bring Dolan's wrath back around to just how he was going to bring Tunstall into his still ongoing machinations. Dolan might have encountered a setback with Gonzales, but the war was far from over.

The same issue carried other news. Jessie Evans was doing his version of laying low by getting shot in the buttocks while stealing cattle in Mimbres Valley. The bullet passed through his flesh and exited through his thigh near his groin. Not life threatening, but a bit embarrassing due to the tenderness.

Deputy Sheriff Campos was sent back to Las Vegas and Barrier, McSween, Tunstall, Squire Wilson, and McSween's brother-in-law David Shield made it to Mesilla on January 28th. Shield was also an attorney and his family, his wife Elizabeth was Susan McSween's sister, shared McSween's large house. The McSweens lived in one wing, while the Shields lived in the opposite arm of the "U".

Dolan, along with Charlie Fritz and James Longwell were also present in Mesilla. They picked up Jessie Evans along the way, although he didn't make his appearance known till afterwards.

Bristol and Rynerson, after being rather openly antagonistic to McSween, agreed to a continuance until the meeting of the grand jury at Lincoln in April when Juan Patron and Florencio Gonzales would be present.

McSween was ordered to return to Lincoln, still escorted by Barrier, to be turned over to Lincoln Sheriff Brady until the bond of $8,000 could be arranged. It was said that Riley and Brady even cleaned the jail in preparation for receiving their prize prisoner.

Dolan remained behind just long enough to file a civil suit and convince Rynerson and Bristol to agree to executing a writ giving Sheriff Brady the authorization to begin liquidating McSween's assets. Even though Tunstall and McSween had deliberately kept much of their business affairs separate, the writ also gave Brady authority to attach Tunstall's property too.

On the way from Mesilla to Lincoln, it had become a logistical tradition to camp at Shedd's ranch. The same ranch where Jessie Evans had taken refuge when Doc and Charlie had tried to convince Jessie to return Brewer, Widenmann, and Tunstall's horses.

Both the Dolan and the McSween parties camped at Shedd's place and Jimmy Dolan, with a limping Jessie Evans providing close cover, couldn't resist confronting Tunstall for having the gall to publish his article. Dolan held his rifle cocked at the ready while he called Tunstall a "damn coward". He tried to taunt Tunstall into a fight, but when Tunstall wouldn't take the bait, Dolan promised he would get Tunstall soon. Barrier, trying to act as mediator, stepped between the two parties and tried to cool the situation. In a parting comment, Dolan told Tunstall that the next time he wrote the *Independent* to tell them that Dolan was with "the Boys".

The trip was tense, but the McSween party arrived in Lincoln on February 10th. McSween did manage to post bail. McSween's sureties were Tunstall, James West, John Copeland, Isaac Ellis, Refugio Valencia, and Jose Montano.

Sheriff Brady began to inventory and liquidate McSween's assets. Almost immediately Brady, George Peppin, James Longwell, John Long, and F. G. Christie took over Tunstall's store. Tunstall, Widenmann, Billy the Kid, and Fred Waite confronted them while conspicuously armed for a fight. Tunstall must have thought that Brady only had eyes on his store and not his cattle and horses. McSween had never been involved in any ranching business and Tunstall's livestock was decidedly a separate business. He convinced Brady to let him take the six horses and two mules in the coral to his ranch. Brady agreed and Widenmann took the animals to be placed under watch at Tunstall's by John Middleton, Godfrey Gauss, and William McCloskey.

One morning Billy the Kid and Fred Waite stopped Sam Wortley from delivering food to Brady's men occupying Tunstall's store. Billy challenged James Longwell to throw down, but Longwell refused.

Brady deputized Jacob "Billy" Mathews. Mathews then gathered a posse consisting of George Hindman, John Hurley, Andrew "Buckshot" Roberts, Manuel "The Indian" Segovia, Jessie Evans, Frank Baker, and Tom Hill and proceeded to go after Tunstall's cattle at his ranch.

Jessie was picked up by the posse at Blazer's Mill and went along under the loose pretext that Billy Bonney had horses that Jessie had loaned him and he wanted them back.

The posse was bolstered by additional men from the Pecos. Murphy and Dolan had a cow camp on the Pecos and their boss, William "Buck" Morton, along with several others joined Mathews' posse as a sub-posse under Buck.

Brewer, acting as spokesman, requested a parley with Mathews. Widenmann couldn't resist making a few remarks to Jessie Evans and there were taunts made between Widenmann and Jessie and his men. Brewer managed to keep everyone level-headed. Mathews and Brewer agreed to leave the cattle at Tunstall's until a court could decide their fate. Widenmann, Billy the Kid, and Fred Waite rushed back to Lincoln to inform Tunstall.

On February 13th, Tunstall decided to ride to Chisum's South Spring ranch to request additional manpower. Riley had confided in George Washington, who then told Tunstall that Dolan was assembling a small army. He sent Rob, Billy, and Fred back to his ranch. John Chisum was still in jail in Las Vegas and his brothers Pitzer and Jim refused to release any of their cowboys or get involved.

Tunstall, no doubt deflated and tired from the quick trip, returned to his ranch. He decided the best course of action was to take his men and return to Lincoln with the six horses and two mules that Brady had already given him permission to keep. He kept the elderly Gauss at his place to watch over Mathews' actions. He also enlisted a neutral party in the form of Martin "Dutch" Martz, who was a good cattle counter, to help oversee things as well. He sent McCloskey, who was friendly with both camps, to Paul's ranch to notify Mathews that Tunstall and his men wouldn't violently oppose them.

Tunstall's group set off on the morning of February 18th.[84]

The large Dolan posse arrived at Tunstall's ranch and Dolan didn't accept that Tunstall had left such proxies to turn over his property. The decision was made to pursue Tunstall.

---

[84] Fulton; Nolan, *LCW: A Documentary History* and *The West of Billy the Kid*; Utley.

It was nearing evening when the meandering group of Tunstall's men, mules, and horses had become spread out. Some of the men happened to go chasing after Turkeys.

Tunstall was gunned down by the Dolan posse that included Jessie Evans, Tom Hill, John Long, Frank Baker, Bob Beckwith, Tom Cochran, Jimmy Dolan, Pantaleon Gallegos, Tom Green, George Hindman, John Hurley, George Kitt, Charles Kruling, Charles Marshall, Billy Mathews, Felipe Mes, Ham Mills, Ramon Montoya, Thomas Moore, Buck Morton, J. W. Olinger, Pablo Pino y Pino, Samuel Perry, Buckshot Roberts, The Indian Segovia, E. H. Wakefield, and Charlie Wolz.

Tunstall had been accompanied by Dick Brewer, Robert Widenmann, John Middleton, Fred Waite, and Billy the Kid, but because they were separated from Tunstall at the time the posse overtook him, they were not eyewitnesses to the shooting.

Both sides had radically different versions of what exactly happened. The Dolan faction claimed they were trying to serve an order to retrieve cattle from the attachment to McSween's debts. In their version, Tunstall was resistant, belligerent, and pulled his weapon. This seems rather foolhardy for one man against such overwhelming odds. The putative view is what the Tunstall faction believed: Tunstall was murdered. Most likely, the three gunshot wounds that took his life were inflicted by Evans, Hill, Morton, and maybe Baker.

While Doc wasn't among the men accompanying Tunstall that day, he quickly made his allegiance known by joining the men who would avenge the death of John Tunstall and call themselves The Regulators. Also joining the ranks with Tunstall's employees were Charlie Bowdre, Frank MacNab, Sam Smith, and Jim French.[85]

Not much is known about Jim French's early history. Frank Coe said he was half-Cherokee. He went by "Jim", "Big Jim", and "Frenchy". He threw in with the Regulators and became very active.[86]

The Regulators felt that Brady and the Dolan faction were obstructing their pursuit of justice and managed to convince (or coerce) Justice of the Peace Wilson to their cause. Wilson then issued warrants for Tunstall's killers and swore in Brewer as a constable. Brewer then deputized the other Regulators. Thus, having sufficient legal credentials, they proceeded to take the hunt to the Dolan faction.[87]

Suspecting that many of the men would head to the Murphy-Dolan cow camp on the Pecos, the Regulators headed for that area. The first victims of their fury were five men. As they gave chase, the five split into two groups and the Regulators went after the party of three which included Dick Lloyd, Frank Baker, and Buck Morton. The pursuit turned into a running gunfight. Lloyd's horse gave out and the Regulators passed him by with their eyes on the prize of Baker and Morton. Eventually, Baker and Morton's horses also failed and the two were cornered and captured. The Regulators argued over whether to take the men in or to exact justice on the spot. Notably, Billy the Kid was for the latter, but Brewer managed to convince the group to take the two men as prisoners.[88]

They headed back home via Roswell in order to avoid a potential rescue attempt. While they were there, Buck Morton mailed a letter to a cousin who was a lawyer.

---

[85] Nolan, *LCW: A Documentary History*.

[86] Ibid.

[87] Nolan, *LCW: A Documentary History*; Fulton; D. Scurlock.

[88] Nolan, *LCW: A Documentary History*; Garrett; D. Scurlock.

In the letter, Morton elucidates his predicament.[89]

Dear Sir:

Some time since I was called upon to assist in serving a writ of attachment on some property, wherein resistance has been made against the law. The parties had started off with some horses which should be attached, and I, as Deputy Sheriff with a posse of twelve men was sent in pursuit of same, overtook them, and while attempting to serve the writ our party was fired on by one J. H. Tunstall, the balance of his party having ran off. The fire was returned and Tunstall was killed. This happened on the 18th of February. The 6th March I was arrested by a constable party, accused of the murder of Tunstall. Nearly all of the Sheriff's posse fired at him and it is impossible for anyone to say who killed him. When the posse which came to arrest me and one man was with me first saw us about one hundred yards distant, we started in another direction when they (eleven in number) fired nearly one hundred shots at us. We ran about five miles when both of our horses fell and we made a stand, when they came up they told us if we gave up they would not harm us: after talking a while we gave up our arms and were taken prisoners. There was one man in the party who wanted to kill me after I had surrendered, and was restrained with the greatest difficulty by others of the party. The constable himself said he was sorry we gave up as he had not wished to take us alive. We arrived here last night en-route to Lincoln I have heard that we were not to be taken alive to that place, I am not at all afraid of their killing me, but if they should do so I wish that the matter be investigated and the parties dealt with according to law. If you do not hear from me in four days after receipt of this, I would like you to make inquiries about the affair.

The names of the parties who have me arrested are, R. M. Bruer, J. G. Scurlock, Chas. Bowdre, Wm. Bonney (Godrich!) Henry Brown, Frank McNab, "Wayt", Sam Smith, Jim French, Middleton (and another named McClosky and who is a friend.) There are two parties in arms and violence expected, the military are at the scene of disorder and trying to keep peace. I will arrive at Lincoln the night of the 10th and will write you immediately if I get through safe. Have been in the employ of Jas. J. Dolan & Co. of Lincoln for 18 months, since 9th of March of 1877 have been getting $60 per month, have about six hundred dollars due me from them, and some horses etc. at their cattle camps.

I hope, if it becomes necessary, that you will look into this affair, if anything should happen I refer you to T. B. Catron, U.S. Attorney, Santa Fe, N. M. and Col. Rynerson District Attorney La Messila, N. M. they both know all about the affairs as the writ of attachment was issued by Judge Warren Bristol La Messila, N. M. and everything was legal. If I am taken safely to Lincoln I will have no trouble but let you know.

If it should be as I suspect. Please communicate with my brother Quin Morton Lewisburg, W. V. Hoping that you will attend to this affair if it becomes necessary, and excuse me for troubling you if it does not.

I remain yours Respectfully,

---

[89] Part IV, letter dated March 8th, 1878.

W. S. Morton"

There are many interesting aspects to this letter. To begin with, Morton states that he doesn't fear that he'll be killed. If he didn't fear this, why write the letter and make mention of the possibility that he would be killed? He also mentions that McCloskey was a friend. William McCloskey was a man who seemed to play both sides. He was known to take work wherever he could get it regardless of which side was offering it. Morton's mentioning him as a friend seems to indicate that he trusted him. The tone of the letter seems to convey that while Morton was lucky to escape his initial capture alive, he was still fearing for his life but that possibly he had a backup plan he was hoping would ensure his safety and included McCloskey.

The next day Morton, McCloskey, and Baker would be dead at the hands of the Regulators. The Regulators' version of the story held little water, but they certainly all stuck to their story. In their version, Morton managed to get McCloskey's gun and kill McCloskey. After that, the gang was forced to kill Morton and Baker as they attempted to escape.

A more likely scenario is that the Regulators didn't trust that McCloskey would remain trustworthy and decided it was best to execute the two Tunstall killers and in order to do that, they needed to first take out the vacillating McCloskey who couldn't pick a side.[90] Allegedly, Morton and Baker had a bullet hole for each one of the Regulators.

Brewer returned to Lincoln to see McSween. The other Regulators then headed for their haven of San Patricio. This small community comprised a large population of sympathetic New Mexicans. While in San Patricio, Billy the Kid found Kiko Trujillo and repaid him his guns back that he had taken after Jessie's jail break. Kiko said that the Regulators admitted that McCloskey was shot in the head prior to them executing Morton and Baker'.[91]

That same day, March 9th, 1878, New Mexico Territory Governor Samuel Axtell visited Lincoln to meet with both parties. He wound up meeting primarily with Murphy and Dolan. Even though he briefly met with Widenmann and McSween's partner, David Shield, he summarily discounted their views. He made a grand proclamation of removing Justice of the Peace Wilson from office and voiding any legal proclamations he had made. This made Brewer's constableship and, thus, the Regulators' authority as deputies revoked. He also made it clear that the only authority in legal matters in Lincoln were Judge Bristol in Mesilla and Sheriff Brady in Lincoln. Suddenly, the Regulators were outlaws.[92]

Also, that same day, in a different part of the county, Jessie Evans and Tom Hill were raiding a sheepherder's camp when Tom was killed and Jessie took a nasty shot in the wrist. Jessie went to Ft. Stanton for medical treatment.[93]

On March 11th, Jimmy Dolan broke his leg while dismounting a horse and was forced to use a crutch to walk.

The Regulators next victim in their path toward retribution was Sheriff Brady. It's not quite clear the actual details behind the motive to ambush Sheriff Brady and his deputies in the manner

---

[90] Rasch, *Trailing Billy the Kid*, note his comments about the killing as related in the piece entitled "Twenty-One Men".

[91] Eastwood, see Appendix "WPA – Billy the Kid/Trujillo"; Nolan, *The Billy the Kid Reader*, see the chapter entitled "The Mackyswins and The Marfes"; Utley.

[92] Nolan, *LCW: A Documentary History*.

[93] Ibid.

the Regulators did, either. One theory holds that there was a deliberate plan to create a ruckus at the end of town to draw out Brady and kill him. Another theory holds that the Regulators got wind of Sheriff Brady's intention to serve a warrant for McSween's arrest and they felt he would likely kill the isolated and unprotected McSween. Finally, there is the possibility that a smaller group of the more vengeance-bent Regulators were taking matters into their own hands against the wishes of the others. Kiko Trujillo claimed that McSween ordered the execution of Brady, but this seems a stretch to credibility.

Kiko, along with other New Mexicans including San Patricio Constable Jose Chavez y Chavez and Fernando Herrera, joined the Regulators. Kiko stated that Billy the Kid didn't want any of the New Mexicans to go to Lincoln to take on Brady because Brady was married to a New Mexican and Billy felt like the New Mexicans would be sympathetic to Brady. Chavez y Chavez protested because he wanted to go fight. Someone made the observation that Doc was also married to a New Mexican, so why did he get to go? In the end, Doc accompanied Fernando back to San Patricio.[94]

Jose Chavez y Chavez was born in 1851 in Valencia County. He relocated to Lincoln in his late teens and married Maria Lucero on January 10th, 1871. He served as constable for San Patricio, then became the justice of the peace before serving again as constable beginning in February of 1877. Kiko reported that Constable Chavez y Chavez was itching to go to Lincoln.

Either way, on April 1st, 1878, the Regulators, consisting of Frank MacNab, Jim French, Fred Waite, John Middleton, Henry Brown, Billy the Kid, and possibly Chavez y Chavez, hid behind an adobe wall and ambushed the Sheriff and his men.

Sheriff Brady, along with his deputies, George Hindman, Billy Mathews, George Peppin, and Jack Long, were walking abreast of one another down the street when Brady paused to chat with someone. After he passed by Tunstall's place, the ambush occurred. Brady was struck three times – in the head, back and side – and fell dead instantly. Hindman was struck but didn't die immediately. The other deputies ran for cover.

Billy the Kid and Jim French ran out into the street. It's not clear why exactly they ran out, but it might have been to retrieve the warrant for McSween's arrest off of Brady's body. Another suggestion was that Billy wanted to retrieve Brady's rifle which was once Billy's rifle until Brady arrested Billy and took it. While the two Regulators were exposed, Mathews fired and his shot grazed Billy's hip and entered French's thigh.[95]

A few days later, on April 4th, the Regulators would take a beating by a lone gunman – Andrew "Buckshot" Roberts. Doc was definitely present at Blazers Mill that day, although he didn't take a very active role in the shootout. Unless one were to believe Ab McCabe's account of it in a letter to Lilly Casey. Ab credits Doc with making the killing shot of Buckshot. Blazer's Mill ranks right up there with The Gunfight at the O. K. Corral in Wild West lore.

The Regulators included Brewer, Middleton, Bowdre, MacNab, Brown, Waite, French, Frank Coe, George Coe, Steve Stephens, John Scroggins, Ignacio Gonzales, Billy the Kid, and Doc. They had left their weapons outside, as requested by Dr. Joseph Blazer, while they went inside to eat.

---

[94] Eastwood, see Appendix "WPA – Billy the Kid/Trujillo"; Nolan, *The Billy the Kid Reader*, see the chapter entitled "The Mackyswins and The Marfes"; Utley.

[95] Nolan, *LCW: A Documentary History*.

Frank Coe was outside and intercepted Buckshot Roberts when he arrived. Frank parleyed with Roberts trying to convince him to give himself up to the Regulators without a fight, but Roberts refused to listen. He likely felt that he would be dealt with as the Regulators had dealt with Morton, McCloskey, and Baker and decided he would be better off putting up a fight.

When the Regulators inside grew restless, they proceeded to try and apprehend him. As Bowdre rounded the building, he and Roberts fired at each other. Bowdre's bullet struck Roberts in the gut and Roberts' bullet struck Bowdre in his belt buckle. Bowdre's gun belt was severed but Bowdre was otherwise unhurt. The bullet, however, ricocheted and struck George Coe's hand severing his trigger finger and ruining his gun. According to Coe, he rushed Roberts and Roberts managed to fire several more times. All the shots missed Coe but one did hit Middleton through the lung. Supposedly, Billy the Kid saw Roberts cartridge belt still on Roberts' horse and counted shots until he knew Roberts was out of ammo before joining the battle, but this is likely apocryphal.

There are two accounts of Doc getting shot in the battle. McSween doesn't mention Doc among the injured in a letter to Tunstall's sister, but Frank Coe reported that Doc was grazed. Doc's grandson Joe Buckbee in a letter to Philip Rasch said that Doc told him he was hit in his holster and the bullet zipped down his leg giving him a burn.[96]

Roberts was wounded and slowly dying, however he still had some fight left in him and he managed to get inside of Dr. Blazer's office under cover. One account avers that Blazer happened to have a rifle and plenty ammunition that Buckshot commandeered. The Regulators took cover, too. Brewer fired into the office and Roberts tracked his location by the gun smoke behind a pile of logs. Roberts waited for the smoke to clear and then shot. He plugged Dick Brewer right in the middle of the forehead. Brewer, the captain of the Regulators, fell dead. At this point, the Regulators fled the scene leaving the body of Brewer behind. Buckshot Roberts would struggle on until he fell into a coma and died the next day.[97]

The *Mesilla Independent* would carry the following on Saturday, April 13th, 1878.

> Lincoln County Items
>
> At a Coroner's inquest held on the body of Andrew L. Roberts, who was killed at Blazer's mill on the 4th inst. The jury found that the deceased came to his death from gunshot wounds at the hands of Richard Bruer, Charles Bowdry, "Doc" Scurlock, Waite, Middleton, McKnabbe, John Scroggins, Stephen Stephens, George Coe, Frank Coe and W. H. Antrim, alias "The Kid".
>
> Our readers will remember that in our report of the killing of Baker and Morton we stated that Morton, while a prisoner in the hands of Bruer and his party, registered a letter at Roswell, after which he was taken out and killed. The following is a true copy of the letter written on that occasion. It will be observed that Morton anticipated being killed. The letter was directed to H. H. Marshall, a prominent lawyer at Richmond, Virginia,

---

[96] Nolan, *LCW: A Documentary History*; Nolan, *The West of Billy the Kid*; Utley.

[97] Part IV, article dated April 13th, 1878; Nolan, *LCW: A Documentary History*; Rasch, *Gunsmoke in Lincoln County*, see the piece "A Second Look at the Blazer's Mill Affair".

and was received by him March 25th. The letter gives Morton's version of the killing of Tunstall, the act which precipitated the Lincoln County War.

The Regulators returned to the area of the Ruidoso and San Patricio to lick their wounds. On the way, the group met Dr. Appel who had been summoned to Blazer's Mill. Dr. Appel amputated George Coe's trigger finger at the second knuckle and treated John Middleton's wound; he would be out of the fight for some time.[98]

[98] Nolan, *The West of Billy the Kid*.

INTERLUDE 5: THE WORST IN THE BUNCH!

Lincoln, New Mexico, May 1878

Doc stood inside of Ben Ellis's place peeking out the window at the group of men riding down the street of Lincoln. Ever since Tunstall was killed, the Regulators had taken up refuge while in Lincoln at both the McSween house and the Ellis's house and store. Matter of fact, the iron clads had turned Ellis's place into a regular fortress. The roof had breastworks that gave both cover as well as a high view of the town.

A better part of the day was spent fighting the Pecos boys – now calling themselves the ridiculously lofty sounding title of Seven Rivers Warriors. Doc knew practically all of them by name, and had once been friendly with most. But things had changed dramatically since Tunstall's death. Doc had made amends with his former employer Mr. Chisum and was now as good as back on his payroll.

Sure, Alex McSween was the one dishing out the pay, but Alex and John were partners in business deals that Doc hardly knew all of the details of and, really didn't care to know. Still, the Pecos families had chosen the Murphy-Dolan party for sure now.

Yesterday evening they had killed Frank MacNab and severely wounded Ab down by the Fritz Spring. Frank Coe was taken as their prisoner and Doc had hoped that because they didn't kill him outright that it was a good sign that Frank was still alive. It was mighty good to hear that when Sheriff Copeland convinced Lieutenant Smith to take the entire posse of at least twenty-five fighting men up to the fort, that news spread that Frank had escaped.

This was after almost the entire day of fire fighting with the posse. Half of the Regulators were at the McSween house protecting him and his when the action started. Doc was there at the time with Alex and Billy. John Copeland was over at McSween's at the time, too. They were planning on how word could be sent around the Fitz ranch to San Patricio to petition J.O.P. Trujillo to swear out warrants for the men responsible for MacNab's death when the fighting erupted early this morning.

As soon as the Pecos boys were up the road, Alex decided that some of the group should accompany him to San Patricio. It was just too risky for everyone to remain in Lincoln. So, Alex, Billy, Charlie, and the others had taken off and left Doc and Rob Widenmann in charge. Rob and George Washington had been cleared of their involvement with Brady's killing so the two of them decided to abandon the McSween place, leaving it to the non-combatants while the rest fell back to the Ellis place.

Also with Doc, were Steve Stanley, John Scroggins, Ignacio Gonzales, and Will, Ben's son. Oh, and Sam Corbet was severely sick in the other room, so he had no choice but to stay.

Now Doc saw that Alex was smart to be warry of John Copeland's ability to bring a truce without getting the blue bellies involved. After ascertaining that the Regulators had split up with half heading to San Patricio, John was apparently being forced into assisting the Federals with the hunt.

John rode beside Lieutenant Goodwin in front of nearly ten cavalry. Lieutenant Smith had taken an equal number out of town.

John and Lieutenant Goodwin stopped at the McSween place and, not finding any of their prey there, were heading straight to Ellis's.

Doc looked at Rob. Knowing his tendency to let his temper get his mouth going, Doc said, "Let me do the talking, Rob."

Stopping in the street, John yelled, "Mr. Ellis! Mr. McSween in there?"

Doc waved back Ben and cracked the door. "John, it's me, Doc! I'm coming out to chat, alright?"

John glanced at Lieutenant Goodwin who nodded.

"Yeah, Doc, step out!"

Doc slid out but kept the door ajar.

John said, "Listen, Doc. We have everyone's name and Colonel Dudley wants them all – both sides – brought back to the fort. You're gonna have to go before Easton."

Doc and Alex had come up with a plan that Doc sure was hoping would work. The plan involved Doc surviving and he hoped that things didn't go south in this first part of the plan. The unknown in the equation was John Copeland's ability to stick to the script. It was time to see.

Doc said, "And what if we decide to contest that decision, John."

As if on cue, Goodwin, who was really calling the shots now, chimed in. "I don't think that would bode well for any of you, Scurlock. The entire fort is prepared to bring you in."

"How do we know that that doesn't include those Seven Rivers' boys joining in again?" Doc asked.

The officer replied, "Everyone will be incarcerated separately; you have my word."

"Well, sir, I can tell you that several names, including mine, was mentioned in certain oaths of vengeance. Who's to say that we don't end up like our dear friend Frank MacNab?"

"What do you want me to do, sign an oath, Scurlock?"

"Nope, I'll just take your word, but first, I have some more information to give you before I give the conditions of the verbal oath."

"Conditions?!" Goodwin began, but Doc cut him off.

"Ah, first the information, Millard."

Goodwin grumbled while Doc said, "All of us here will willingly go into custody with you, but you won't find us all here. And you're buddy Smith won't find anyone except Mr. McSween in San Patricio. The rest have fled and, trust me on this, they won't be found by ten of your forts. We like to keep a force in reserve, as you say."

Goodwin glowered at Doc and finally said, "And what, pray tell, are your conditions?"

"One: you let us bury Frank before we go. We'll do the digging."

"Alright."

"Two: you jail our contingent separate from theirs, but you place me in solitary confinement. And in shackles"

"What?! Why would I do that?" Goodwin exclaimed.

"Because, when everyone is finally released, I need those Pecos boys to believe that I'll be indefinitely detained so they don't try and immediately kill me. Trust me, they will."

Goodwin thought it over and said, "Fine."

"I mean it, Lieutenant, you have to make Colonel Dudley think I'm a wild-eyed killer. On your word as an officer and a gentleman."

"I said, fine. You have my word. Now turn over your weapons and bring everyone out."

Doc sat in the Fort Stanton stockade with his shackles on. It hadn't gone exactly as planned, but it was damn close. Everyone from both sides had been released except for Doc. That was three days ago.

Now, Doc sat listening to John Copeland wrangle over all of the details of Doc's release. All of Doc's firearms had been released to John. Now he was filling out the official request for a military escort back to Lincoln.

Since Easton had been shown the wisdom resigning his position, Dudley had agreed, but everything with the federals entailed paperwork.

Colonel Dudley allowed three soldiers to escort John and Doc back as far as Lincoln and then they were to promptly return.

It was a silent ride.

Once Doc, John, and the three cavalry soldiers reached the Ellis store, Doc dismounted. John handed Doc his rifle, pistol, and belt.

Doc asked, "We still got a deal?"

John turned to the three cavalry soldiers and said, "Before you boys head back would you mind bearing witness to me swearing in my new deputy?"

[DISCLAIMER: A lot of liberty has been taken with the dialogue and motives of McSween, Copeland, and the Regulators. In reality, McSween exchanged letters with Rynerson over the course of these days. The sequence of events is historically accurate except McSween secured Trujillo's warrants prior to Dudley's retaliatory action of securing warrants from Easton.]

THE BATTLES OF LINCOLN

Even though Lincoln County was a hornet's nest, the District Court still met on April 8th, 1878. Judge Bristol and the other officials stayed at Ft. Stanton and came into Lincoln each day under guard of soldiers. Dr. Joseph Blazer was elected jury foreman.

Since Brady's deputies were technically operating without grounds to do so, one of the first things Judge Bristol did was to appoint John Copeland as sheriff. Then Bristol promptly ordered Copeland to arrest Widenmann, Shield, George Washington, and George Robinson in connection with Brady and Hindman's murders. Assisted by soldiers from Ft. Stanton, the four were taken to the fort and held.

In connection with Tunstall's murder, principal indictments were brought against Jessie Evans, George Davis, Miguel Seguro, and John Long. Accessory indictments were brought against Jimmy Dolan and Billy Mathews. Of the principals, only Jessie Evans could be arrested.

For the murder of Sheriff Brady and Hindman, indictments were found for Billy the Kid, Middleton, Waite, and Brown.

In connection with Buckshot Roberts, Bowdre, Billy the Kid, Middleton, Brown, Waite, Steve Stephens, John Scroggins, George Coe, and Doc were indicted. None of the Regulators could be located.

Also, Doc and many other Regulators were indicted on charges of obstructing justice by occupying Tunstall's store in order to prevent the seizure of assets. This was transferred to Dona Ana County and was later dismissed.

In a victory for McSween, he was not under indictment for embezzlement, but there was still the civil suit and attachments to deal with. Since no indictments were brought against Widenmann, Shield, Washington, and Robinson, they were released.

Also, indictments were handed out for Dolan and Riley for cattle stealing.

After the decisive McSween victory, several citizens including Juan Patron, Florencio Gonzales, Saturnino Baca, Ben Ellis, Jose Montano, and even John Chisum, now out of Las Vegas jail, held a citizen's meeting to discuss all of the violence that had been plaguing the county.

They issued a formal statement that essentially condemned Governor Axtell's actions and thanked Sheriff Copeland and the new Ft. Stanton commander, Lt. Col. Nathan Dudley. Col. Hatch had ordered Dudley to replace Capt. Purington because he felt Purington had become too biased to the Murphy and Dolan faction.

As for Murphy and Dolan, at the end of April, Dolan and John Longwell escorted Murphy to Sant Fe for medical treatment. Murphy's health would deteriorate until he died on October 19th. At the early part of May, Dolan returned to Lincoln to meet with Edgar Walz, Thomas Catron's brother-in-law, who was also an attorney and represented Catron in settling Dolan and Riley's business affairs. While Murphy, Dolan, and Longwell were bound for Santa Fe, Riley was headed to Las Cruces to meet with Rynerson.

District Attorney William Rynerson was still doing everything in his power to thwart McSween. His latest effort was to enlist John Kinney to raise a posse called the Rio Grande Posse to join Dolan and Riley's cause.

Other good news for the McSween faction was the expected arrival of agents from the Department of Justice and the Interior Department to investigate the various murders, the actions of federal officials, and allegations against the Indian Agency.

The Regulators, now feeling like they had the upper hand, returned to Lincoln. At McSween's residence, Justice of the Peace for San Patricio Jose Trujillo appointed MacNab constable and he was also appointed the Regulators new captain.

McSween was offering a $250 reward for the capture of any member of the posse that killed Tunstall and Frank MacNab was boasting about the Regulators getting ready to ride down to the Pecos and clean it up. It wasn't long until the men of the Pecos decided to take action to neutralize the Regulators.

A letter written by Marion Turner of Roswell, then just a tiny village just north of Chisum's South Springs ranch, appeared in the *Las Vegas Gazette*. The letter, which many believe was drafted by Ash Upson in Turner's name, gives an interesting perspective on the state of affairs at the end of April 1878.

Rio Pecos, N. M.
April 28, 1878

Editor, *Las Vegas Gazette*:

As far as legal proceedings are concerned, the difficulties in Lincoln County were settled on the 15th of this month.

The charge to the grand jury by Judge Bristol was denunciatory to the action of McSween, and laudatory to the opposite party, the head of which is supposed to be Major Murphy and the firm of J. J. Dolan and Company.

The majority report of the grand jury sustains McSween whilst a minority report modifies, in some degrees, the majority report as affecting the rights of the contestants for supremacy as rulers of the interest, pecuniary and political, of this county are concerned.

Let me give you, as I understand it a brief summary of the condition of affairs, not for today, but for seven years past, with the money magnates of the county.

The firm of Fritz & Murphy, afterwards Lawrence G. Murphy& Co., were sutlers at Fort Stanton from 1870. They controlled the business of this country, as no farmer, stock raiser, artisan, or mechanic within a radius of 100 miles could secure employment, except through this firm, directly or indirectly.

They accumulated wealth. They were the mercantile aristocrats of the country.

In 1875 Alex A. McSween arrived at Lincoln. He came here with his wife penniless, hauled here in a farmer's wagon by Martin Sanchez, a rancher now living at El Bordo. He expressed his intention of making his El Dorado at Lincoln and he has accomplished his design.

It is not for me to say by what means, whether by the honest prosecution of his profession (the law) or by "ways that were dark and tricks that were vain," as he charged, he has accomplished his object; but it *is* true that he has so pursued his avocation that at the last session for the Lincoln County court (3rd judicial district) he has defeated the firm of Murphy, Dolan , and Riley, as by the decision of the grand jury but under the protest of Judge Warren Bristol and Prosecuting Attorney Wm. L. Rynerson.

This is the action of the court and jury which adjourned and was dismissed on the 24th of April, 1878. This county and the county of Dona Ana have been in a state of anarchy for the past two and a half years, the cause of which I understand as well as any man perhaps in the territory. I have been since 1872 a citizen of the county. My impression is that as there was a power (pecuniary) on the Rio Pecos, the perquisites of which both parties sought to procure, a struggle ensued in which bad blood was engendered. I also believe that both parties were unscrupulous, and used such means to accomplish each their object that they employed unlawful instruments, and that the result has been bloodshed and disaster – that it has cost the lives of good citizens against whose characters no breath of scandal has reached – against the lives of citizens who leave behind them friends who before this feud they would have sacrificed their lives to save.

There are two parties, designated as the "Murphy Party" and the "McSween Party." Both are charged with murder; the Murphy party with murdering Tunstall, Brewer, and others; the McSween party with murdering Major Brady, Morton, Baker, and others.

My firm belief is that although the adherents of these parties have been guilty of "killing their enemies," there was no murder in the matter, but a contest for "the best of the fight," which any good man will try to get. Let any man stand in the shoes of any one of these men and try to restrain his propensities. "Let him who is without sin cast the first stone."

M. Turner
Roswell, N. M.

It's quite obvious that the person referred to as the pecuniary power on the Pecos is John Chisum. George Peppin and Billy Mathews, still bitter from having their credentials pulled, along with John Hurley headed down to the Pecos to recruit men and it is no surprise that Marion Turner was one of the recruits.

Under the leadership of W. H. Johnson, another former deputy of Brady, a large posse was formed. It's two lieutenants were Marion Turner and Buck Powell. Other known members included Bob Beckwith, John Beckwith, Lewis Paxton, Joe Nash, John Long, Tom Cochran, Tom Green, Dick Lloyd, Charley Martin, Sam Perry, Milo Pierce, Jim Ramer, Wallace Olinger, Bob Olinger, Sam Cochran, "Dutch Charley" Kruling, and John Galvin.

On April 29th, the posse, dubbed the Seven Rivers Warriors, that also included numerous men who were in the posse responsible for the killing of Tunstall, headed to Lincoln for a confrontation with the McSween party. Their stated intent was to "assist" Sheriff Copeland in serving warrants.

The posse stopped at the Fritz Spring ranch located eight miles from Lincoln to water their horses and likely to feel out the state of affairs in Lincoln. That evening, Frank MacNab, Frank Coe, and Ab Saunders unwittingly blundered right into their midst.

The posse fired on the three men and mortally wounded McNab who tried to crawl to safety but was run down and killed with a shotgun by "The Indian" Segovia. Saunders was hit in the hip and ankle but survived. Frank Coe tried to ride to safety but his horse was shot in the head and fell on his rifle. He crawled to safety and quickly exhausted the rounds in his six-shooter. Frank parleyed with the men who took him into custody mainly because he had friends among the large group.

The next day, the Seven Rivers posse entered Lincoln. Most of them set up in the woods across from the Ellis store. The Regulators had commandeered the Ellis store as their commissary and used it as a safe haven along with McSween's residence while in Lincoln. Several of the posse continued on to the Murphy-Dolan store. Even though it had closed for business, the building was still used by the Dolan faction.

Some of the posse stopped at the Baca residence and requested permission to use it as a strategic location, but Captain Baca refused them.

Copeland, who happened to be at McSween's, was sent a message from the posse that they were there to assist him in serving the warrants for the named Regulators who were involved in the killings of Brady, Hindman, and Roberts. This only served to alert the Regulators to the danger and they all began to fan out through the town and take up defensive positions.

George Coe and Henry Newton Brown took up position atop the Ellis store. During the morning, George and Henry got a bead on a Seven Rivers Warrior in a clearing in the distance. The man seemed to be sitting on a rock or cow skull with his legs straight out in front of him. George and Henry decided to take a shot. Henry missed, but George, even missing his trigger finger, hit "Dutch Charley" Kruling through the meaty part of both legs.

Dutch Charley was taken along with Ab Saunders to the post for treatment. Frank Coe, still a prisoner, was being held in the Murphy-Dolan store and when the shooting started in earnest after George's shot, all the Warriors ran out to participate.

The shooting lasted off and on for four hours and during that time, Frank simply walked away to freedom.

Sheriff Copeland tried to mediate a cease fire, but was unsuccessful. He was seen as heavily biased towards the McSween side. In exasperation, he sent a request for help from Fort Stanton. Lt. Col. Dudley sent him Lt George W. Smith with over a dozen cavalry.

Lt. Smith rode between the parties and began to wave his hat. A truce was declared and both sides sent out representatives to parley. In the end, Copeland convinced Smith to take all of the Seven Rivers Warriors up to the fort until a decision could be made about what to do with both sides.

As there was a lull in the fighting and the Regulators could see that there were so many Pecos men around, it was decided that McSween, Billy the Kid, Middleton, and Bowdre should head to San Patricio. Once there, McSween bought dinner for the group and then Billy, John, and Charlie lit out for the mountains.

McSween, however, went immediately to Justice Trujillo and had warrants issued for the men responsible for killing MacNab and trying to kill Saunders and Coe.

Meanwhile, the men at Fort Stanton sent word to Blazer's mill to strongarm Justice of the Peace Dave Easton to issue tit-for-tat warrants for the McSween side. This was done and Copeland was now charged with arresting the men he was loyal to. It was said that before Murphy and Dolan headed for Santa Fe that they had thoroughly turned Dudley to their side. The glowing thank you that had been issued by the McSween side was for naught. Dudley basically usurped the sheriff's position and ordered Lt. Millard Filmore Goodwin and an escort of soldiers to accompany Copeland to Lincoln and San Patricio to arrest McSween and the rest of the Regulators.

They arrived in Lincoln and proceeded to arrest Doc, Widenmann, Scroggins, George Washington, Ignacio Gonzales, Isaac Ellis, his son Will Ellis, Steve Stanley, and Sam Corbet.[99]

Goodwin sent Dudley the following message. Dudley was brevetted Brigadier General for meritorious service during the Civil War so his soldiers sometimes used the title of General as a courtesy even though Dudley was only a Lieutenant Colonel at the time.[100]

> Lincoln, N. M.
> 2 May 1878
>
> General,
>
> I send you under guard Scurlock, Widenmann, Scroggins, Washington, Gonzales, Ellis Senior, Wm Ellis, Stanley, Sam Corbet is sick I leave him in Town. Sheriff Copeland will be responsible for him.

---

[99] Fulton, Nolan, *LCW: A Documentary History*; Nolan, *The West of Billy the Kid*; Utley.

[100] Part IV, letter dated May 2nd, 1878; Fulton; Nolan, *LCW: A Documentary History.*

Scurlock is a bad man the worst in the bunch! (irons would not hurt him.) Lieut. Smith takes half the men and goes to San Patricio across the Mountains. I take the rest and go around the road. We will meet at 12 to-night and without doubt take them all in.

ours respectfully,

M. F. Goodwin
2nd Lieut. 9th Cav.

Goodwin met up with Smith who had continued to San Patricio and arrested McSween. Everyone was brought back to Fort Stanton. It was claimed that while McSween, Doc, and the others were jailed, the Seven Rivers contingent was allowed to freely use Fort Stanton while being armed. Dudley wrote in his report that "all of whom were confined, Scurlock was shackled."

Dudley's plan was to send the entire group from both sides before Justice Easton, but Dave, tired of the politics, resigned his position. The only other Justice was Trujillo and Dudley knew that he was a McSween sympathizer. Dudley decided his best course of action was to turn it all back over to Copeland and let him sort out the whole mess.

On May 4th, Copeland released all the members from both sides except for Doc who was still held at Fort Stanton. Copeland basically instructed them to all go home and quit their feuding. The same day, while all of this was going on, Agent Frank Warner Angel, the agent appointed to begin investigating affairs in Lincoln, arrived in Sant Fe.

On the way back to the Pecos, the Seven Rivers Warriors took the horses that belonged to MacNab and Saunders as well as more horses that had belonged to Tunstall.

On May 7th, Copeland returned to the Fort to secure Doc's release. He requested a military escort back into Lincoln. Once there he immediately returned Doc's firearms and deputized him. The Regulators had a new captain.

Frank MacNab was buried beside Tunstall in Lincoln.[101]

Doc's first act as captain was to expand the posse by recruiting Josefita Chavez to lead a New Mexican contingent in an excursion to the Pecos. Not caring that Dolan and Riley's interests were now technically Catron's, the Regulators, on May 14th, raided the Dolan-Riley cattle camp in order to retrieve horses taken from McNab and Saunders and those stolen from Tunstall's ranch. In the process, the Regulators captured "The Indian" Segovia, the man responsible for MacNab's death.

It just so happened that one of the New Mexican Regulators was Kiko Trujillo and The Indian voiced his concern to Kiko that he thought the Regulators would kill him. Charlie came over and pulled Kiko away while the rest of the Regulators did take The Indian and execute him. Billy told Kiko that he was finally paying him the rest of what he owed him by finally returning his saddle. Doc, noticing Kiko's disgust at all the blood on the saddle, told Kiko that he could have his saddle; he would take Kiko's and clean it.[102]

---

[101] Fulton, Nolan, *LCW: A Documentary History*; Nolan, *The West of Billy the Kid*; Utley.

[102] Eastwood, see Appendix "WPA – Billy the Kid/Trujillo"; Nolan, *The Billy the Kid Reader*, see the chapter entitled "The Mackyswins and The Marfes".

The newspaper reported that the Scurlock party "proceeded, as usual, to get drunk and 'whoop up' the country at their leisure".[103]

Throughout June and the beginning of July, the Regulators were on the run throughout the territory. Axtell had once again made one of his proclamations revoking the authority of Copeland's position as sheriff and Doc's position as deputy sheriff. George Peppin had been appointed the new sheriff.

It was during this time that a family story tells of how the Regulators rode to the Scurlock house to inform Doc that a posse was on their way to arrest him. Having no time to prepare a getaway for the family, he hid his wife Antonia and their daughter Marie Elena in the cellar. To help disguise their hiding place he carefully left the cobwebs covering the cellar undisturbed and then fled ahead of the posse. This deception worked as the posse never looked in the cellar.[104]

Also during May or June, a new member joined the Regulators. "Big Foot Tom" O'Folliard would become Billy the Kid's most loyal follower. He was born in Uvalde, Texas about 1858. After both his parents died of smallpox, he went to live with his aunt until he decided to head to New Mexico where he gave his allegiance to the Regulators.[105]

Sheriff Peppin along with Jose Chavez y Baca proceeded to apply heavy handed measures in searching San Patricio for the Regulators. This tactic backfired when the New Mexican citizens branded Baca a turncoat and decided that the abuse to their families would not be tolerated. On July 11th a meeting was held at Juan de Dios Trujillo's place, the brother of Kiko. Present also were Doc, McSween and many of the Regulators. The majority of the attendees, however, were New Mexicans who decided to support the Regulators' cause. It was said that everyone cheered when Martin Chavez arrived and announced he had about twenty men to add to the Regulators.

That same day McSween, now feeling like he had significant support of the citizenry, is believed to have penned a letter to the Cimarron *News and Press* where he claims the Regulators had two hundred able-bodied men.[106]

There were several skirmishes, namely in the area around San Patricio and at Chisum's ranch, but the Regulators managed to elude capture. Kinney and his Rio Grande Posse now joined on the side of the Dolan faction.

On July 13th, 1878, Mrs. Brady complained to Col. Dudley that her son had been threatened by the Regulators, naming Doc Scurlock. Doc felt obliged to swear out a statement that her accusations were false.[107]

On July 14th, 1878, the Regulators, along with their swelled numbers of New Mexicans, would try to shift the momentum of the war by taking up positions in Lincoln. This would turn into what would be known as "The Battle of Lincoln" or "The Five-Day Battle". This would eventually culminate in "The Big Killing" and the death of Alexander McSween.

The Regulators would entrench themselves in the McSween house, the Montano store, and the Ellis store and home. Doc, Bowdre, Middleton, Stephens and eight to ten other men would take up position in the Ellis store and home covering the east entrance of Lincoln. Doc's father-in-law, Fernando Herrera, would take up position with Martin Chavez and twenty to

---

[103] Nolan, *LCW: A Documentary History*; D. Scurlock.

[104] Payne, "The True Doc Scurlock story" and "Doc Scurlock, Frontier Legend"; D. Scurlock.

[105] Rasch, *Trailing Billy the Kid*, see the piece entitled "The Short Life of Tom O'Folliard".

[106] Nolan, *LCW: A Documentary History*.

[107] Part IV, letter dated July 13th, 1878; Part V, sworn statement dated July 15th, 1878.

twenty five men in the Montano store. At one point, Martin was shot and the crucifix he was wearing saved his life when the bullet hit it. The crucifix was given to him by Padre Sambrano.[108]

Fernando would make the most remarkable shot of the several-day battle. The distance was reported as anywhere from 300 yards all the way up to 900 yards. Whatever the distance, it was still quite a considerable shot that hit Charlie Crawford. The shot hit Crawford's gun and ricocheted passing through him from one hip to the other. He would die several days later from the wound.[109]

Dudley convened a meeting with his officers and they all agreed to intervene in the civil dispute. Once the manning and fire power of the soldiers entered on the biased side of the Murphy-Dolan faction, there was little hope for McSween and the Regulators. Doc and the men in the Ellis house managed to escape the town and Peppin's posse pursued them. As Doc's gang fought back on the run they managed to wound John Jones and evade the rest.

Martin Chavez, Fernando Herrera and the men in the Montano store also made an escape. It's likely that these two groups abandoned their buildings because of Dudley's introduction of the fort's Howitzer and Gatling gun into the equation. Dudley's camp was set up right across the street from the Montano store.[110]

Members of these groups would return to the hills outside of Lincoln to take pot shots at the Dolan faction as they constricted their circle and set fire to McSween's house. It's likely Doc was amongst these men, but, having abandoned their strongholds, they were ineffective.[111]

Susan McSween escaped the McSween house and made her way to Dudley's camp to plead for him to help end the whole affair peaceably, but Dudley treated her brusquely. The two exchanged heated words and Dudley retreated into his tent.

As night closed in. Andy Boyle managed to get a fire started on the McSween house. Within the house the fire continued to spread and the group of men remaining in the house decided to wait till dusk and enact a desperate plan. One party of men consisting of Billy the Kid, Jim French, Jose Chaves y Chaves, Harvey Morris, and Tom O'Folliard would try to make it to the Tunstall store and draw fire so the other group could escape. Immediately, Harvey Morris was gunned down, but the others managed to make it to the Bonito and escape.

McSween and the others waited too long and were pinned down by Andy Boyle, Joe Nash, Bob Beckwith, John Jones, Marion Turner, and a man condescendingly referred to as Dummy. McSween, or maybe Yginio Salazar, tried to surrender, but it was useless. Alexander McSween, Francisco Zamora, and Vicente Romero were killed. Somehow, Bob Beckwith also suffered a fatal wound.

In the end of the conflict, the Dolan side would lose two killed and the McSween side would lose five killed. During the Five-Day Battle, Sheriff Peppin had numerous warrants that he attempted to serve to no avail. Two of these warrants were for Doc for the murder of Sheriff Brady and Deputy Sheriff Hindman. These warrants were later dropped.

The death of Alexander McSween was a severe blow to the cause of the Regulators. It signaled the end of the Lincoln County War, but the hostilities were far from over.

---

108 Cummings.

109 Fulton; Nolan, *LCW: A Documentary History*; Sanchez; D. Scurlock. Interestingly, Nolan's citation points to Burns and the Sanchez's point to Utley.

110 Fulton.

111 Nolan, *LCW: A Documentary History*.

Doc and the Regulators, including Fernando Herrera, raided the Mescalero Apache reservation on August 5th, 1878. The purpose was to continue to settle the score with the Dolan faction by stealing horses they had lost during the Five-Day Battle, but things got out of hand in the battle that ensued with the Indians. During this battle, Indian Agent Morris Bernstein, who attempted to stop the fighting, was killed.[112]

The herd was taken to Bosque Grande and sold. Sallie Chisum, John's niece, wrote in her diary about Billy the Kid bringing her candy. Doc and Charlie took the time to visit Pete Maxwell where they took jobs on his ranch at Fort Sumner. Doc was already putting into motion his plans of relocating and distancing himself from the troubles of Lincoln County.

While Doc and Charlie remained at Ft. Sumner, the rest of the Regulators went first to Puerto de Luna and then to Anton Chico where they had a confrontation with Miguel County Sheriff Desiderio Romero. Romero and his posse had no warrants for the Regulators and eventually desisted when the Regulators bought the posse rounds of drinks.

Before returning to Bosque Grande, the Coes took their leave of the Regulators and decided to move to Colorado. Billy vowed that he would continue to steal a living in New Mexico. The Coes would both eventually return and live out the rest of their lives in Lincoln County.

On August 30th, John Middleton penned a reply to Rob Widenmann from Bosque Grande giving him an update on affairs.

> Dear Rob
>
> Yours came to hand this morning. I was glad to hear from you. There is nothing can be done by your coming out here. The 7 Rivers Outfit has stolen your cattle they are at Black River now. We will all start from here day after tomorrow, will do the best we can. Old man Beckwith killed [Johnson] his son in law so much for him. If we don't get Tunstall's cattle we will get more in their place. 10 Buffalo men have joined us we are about 36 in number there was something flying R [round] about you killing B [Brady] but George [Washington] says it is not so. He helped us in the Plaza the last fight. I don't think he said it tho while he was a prisoner. Pep taken him to Stanton where Angel interviewed him. Everything is running pretty you stay where you are and take care of yourself. I don't want you to go like poor Tunstall and Mc has gone. We can manage what is here as well without you as with you. Old John has gone back on us & Ellis & Sons the same. We don't ask no favours God Dem them. Jesse Evans is doing all he can for us say nothing about this whatever you do. The reason I don't want you to come here is this Everything is stoled out of the country by Pep's posses and we intend to play the same game at this we will back ourselfs. Old Peps has resigned and gone they are Basted in completely. Jim Dolan is on the road to 7 Rivers with the Carasosa cattle camped at Elk Springs 3 nights ago aims to join the rest of the outfit at B River, we will get him if he don't watch. Take care of yourself. I want to see you again befoe we die.
>
> Your friend John Middleton

---

[112] Nolan, *LCW: A Documentary History*; Rasch, "Man of Many Parts"; D. Scurlock.

Old John is John Chisum and it isn't a stretch to see that the Regulators were likely paid by McSween as hired guns with the assumption that McSween was paying in the name of both McSween and Chisum. However, when McSween died, Chisum didn't feel like it was his task to continue to pay the Regulators. At this point, the feelings between the Regulators and Chisum would become strained.[113]

On September 1st, Doc, Antonia, and their two small children, Marie Elena and Viola Inez, relocated to the safety of Fort Sumner. Bowdre and Manuela, who was now thirteen or fourteen, took the opportunity to get married as they also relocated to Fort Sumner. Billy helped his two friends move. Once there, Doc went to work for Pete Maxwell and Charlie went to work for Thomas Yerby.[114]

The date has been given in several accounts as September 1st for the move, but it seems more likely that it was after the 7th. On September 7th, the Regulators raided Charles Fritz's ranch in retaliation for hosting the Seven Rivers Warriors on the day that MacNab was killed. They drove off 150 head of cattle and a remuda of 15 horses. In all likelihood, this herd was driven north in conjunction with Doc and Charlie's move.

While Doc and Charlie stayed in Ft. Sumner to begin their new jobs, Billy the Kid, Tom O'Folliard, John Middleton, Henry Brown, and Fred Waite drove the herd to the area of Tascosa, Texas to sell.

The Regulators would remain in the Texas panhandle for nearly two months. While they were there, they made quite an impact. One night they were attending a dance at Pedro Romero's house. Pedro, knowing the proclivity of drunken cowboys to resort to shooting, had a rule that anyone entering his premises must do so unarmed. During the night Billy and Dr. Henry Hoyt stepped outside to chat. On the way back to the house they decided to have a footrace back and Billy, upon crossing the threshold, tripped and went sprawling across the floor. The other four Regulators, thinking Billy was being attacked quickly surrounded him and suddenly had pistols in hand and ready to throw down. They were banned from all future dances.

In another episode, the Regulators rode out to the LX ranch to try and sell some horses. The ranch superintendent, William C. "Outlaw Bill" Moore, who came by the nickname because of his checkered past, didn't want to deal with them. He had made the comment that they were all rustlers and needed to be run out of the area. Billy, upon hearing what Outlaw Bill had said, asked him to come outside and talk. Billy challenged him about it and swore that if he heard Bill badmouthing him and the Regulators again, he would shoot him half in to.

While in Tascosa, they all participated in traditional cowboy feats of shooting and horse racing. One story related how Billy the Kid and Bat Masterson lost a shooting match to Temple Houston, the son of Texas hero Sam Houston.

In October, just prior to leaving, Billy presented Dr. Hoyt a gift of his favorite Arabian sorrel named Dandy Dick. It was branded BB on the hip. To protect Dr. Hoyt from accusations of horse theft, Billy wrote out a bill of sale. Dr. Hoyt was later to learn that the horse had belonged to Sheriff Brady and was the horse that he rode into Lincoln the day he was gunned down.[115]

---

[113] Fulton, Nolan, *LCW: A Documentary History*; Nolan, *The West of Billy the Kid*; Utley.
[114] Fulton; Nolan, *LCW: A Documentary History*; Rasch, "Man of Many Parts"; Sanchez; D. Scurlock; J.D. Scurlock.
[115] Nolan, *Tascosa*; Nolan, *The West of Billy the Kid*.

When it was time to return to New Mexico, Henry Brown, Fred Waite, and John Middleton announced they wouldn't be returning with Billy and Tom.

Fred Waite returned home to the Chickasaw Nation. He served on the Indian Police Force in 1887, serving as the Chickasaw Nation speaker of the house in 1889, and Secretary of the Chickasaw Nation in 1894. He died at his home in Ardmore, Indian Territory on September 24th, 1894 from complications associated with rheumatism.[116]

John Middleton went to Kansas and became a prosperous businessman in the mercantile industry. He shared correspondence with John Tunstall's father. Henry Brown accompanied Fred to his Chickasaw home but returned to Tascosa in the Spring of 1879. In the Spring of 1880 he was appointed deputy sheriff of the fledgling county of Oldham serving under Cape Willingham. Henry would go on to become the assistant city marshal of Caldwell, Kansas. He would ultimately be gunned down by a mob of incensed citizens after being captured after a bank robbery he participated in on April 30th, 1884. The other three members of his posse were lynched.[117]

While Billy and the boys were in Tascosa and Doc and Charlie were laying low at Ft. Sumner, things were still happening in Lincoln.

On November 13th, 1878, the newly appointed territorial governor Lew Wallace issued a proclamation of amnesty to all involved in the months-long Lincoln County War. Axtell had been removed after Agent Angel's report had alerted Washington officials that a new governor might be best. On October 7th, President Hayes issued a proclamation requesting all citizens to cease their violence and disperse to their homes before noon of October 13th. Then Gov. Wallace made his amnesty proclamation, but it had a few stipulations that left those with current indictments out of the deal.

In September Susan McSween had been enjoying the personal protection of Big Jim French, but she moved to Las Vegas with her sister. Rob Widenmann, on his way out of the country to visit Tunstall's family in England, brought Susan $500 from John Tunstall's father. She immediately used the money to hire attorney Huston Chapman.[118]

On November 23rd, Susan McSween returned to Lincoln with Chapman accompanying her. They were going to bring charges against Dudley, who she blamed for her husband's death as well as the destruction of her home. Dudley demanded an inquiry into the affair so he could exonerate himself.[119]

The *Mesilla News* reported on November 30th, 1878:

> Peace was dawning in Lincoln Co. when Gov. Wallace extended a pardon to absent thieves, cutthroats and murderers and virtually invited them to come back and take a fresh start (in their 'usual occupations.')
>
> The Governor has pardoned Scurlock, Bowdre, Bonny alias the 'Kid', Wait, and all the murdering gauge of Lincoln County. That's one way of restoring 'law and order'.

---

[116] DeArment, see the piece entitled "Old Habits Die Hard: A Note on Frederick T. Waite".

[117] Rasch, *Warriors of Lincoln County*, see the piece "A Note on Henry Newton Brown".

[118] Fulton, Nolan, *LCW: A Documentary History*; Nolan, *The West of Billy the Kid*; Utley.

[119] Nolan, *LCW: A Documentary History*.

Obviously, the details of why it didn't apply to many of the Regulators weren't fully understood.

On January 1st, 1879, George Kimbrell was appointed the new sheriff. The tides of animosity seemed to be turning in Lincoln. On January 18th, the *Mesilla News* reported a peace treaty between Mrs. McSween and J. J. Dolan. It was reported on February 4th, Dr. Blazer had commented that the "war element" was "fading" in Lincoln.

INTERLUDE 6: LAST ESCAPE

Tascosa, Texas, June 1881

Doc couldn't believe his eyes. Standing in his front door was Billy Bonney. While the better part of him didn't want to see Billy ever again, he still broke out into a large smile upon seeing his old compadre. Billy grinned from ear to ear and the two men shook hands and hugged.

"Jeez, Billy," Doc said scanning the yard, "you alone?"

"Just me, Doc."

Doc pulled Billy inside and closed the door and then the two looked each other up and down. Billy said, "I figured I owed you a thank you in person for what you did for me."

The last time the two had seen each other was almost two years ago in October of 1879. It was shortly after they had completed what Doc had vowed would be his last rustling job by taking a bunch of cattle from Old John and selling them to Padre Polaco. After that, Doc had loaded his small family into a wagon and prepared to move to Texas. Just before commencing the trip, Billy had come out to bid his farewells and bring Doc a parting gift of 50 pounds of flour. Doc later learned that Billy had stolen it from Pete Maxwell's pantry.

Billy and Doc had agreed to paint a tall story that their parting was akin to a break up of two lovers. That way, people would think that the two had parted ways, maybe not as enemies, but at least not as friends. And now, here was Billy, freshly escaped from the old Murphy-Dolan store.

The two adjourned to a private place and began to compare notes.

Billy began. "As soon as Pat left town, Sam Corbet come to see me. He slipped me a note and whispered 'from Doc'. All it said was 'privy'. That's when I knew that you'd come through on our plan. Every day they would take all of us prisoners over to the Wortley to eat. I made an excuse that I was sick and my stomach was upset and didn't feel like eating. After that damn Bob Olinger left, I told Bell I needed to go use the privy. But who put the gun there, Doc?"

"A school teacher."

"What?!"

"It was your moon-eyed fan Jose Aguayo."

"Jose?" Billy said amazed.

"He owed me for helping him to take my place as teacher of the Spanish kids in town. In return for getting his bona fides, he practically begged to do it."

Billy ran his fingers through his hair and said, "I'll be. I sure hated to have to kill Bell, but he went for his gun. I did enjoy paying Olinger back for what he did to John Jones, though. I took the shotgun that that sombitch had told me he would use on me and gave him both barrels from the upstairs window just as he come running across the street. You shoulda seen the look on old Godfrey's face when I did."

Billy only stuck around for a few days. Doc tried his damnedest to get Billy not to return. Just before Billy left, Doc told him he was leaving Tascosa as well. Doc and Antonia had just had their second son and it was time to find a city to live in where law and order was established.

Doc watched as Billy held his newborn son, John and played with Viola and Joe, Jr.

"Billy, Antonia and I have decided to move to Vernon," Doc announced.

The two friends gave each other a hug and Doc, Antonia, holding John, Viola, and Joe, Jr. waved as they watched Billy swing into the saddle and ride off. It would be the last time they saw Billy.

[DISCLAIMER: This is most assuredly a stretch to veracity. First of all, there are numerous versions of Billy's escape and absolutely none of them include Doc in any way. There are versions that include the gun hidden in the privy and versions that don't. It's impossible to say exactly how Billy did overpower James Bell, but a gun hidden in the privy by Jose M. Aguayo is just one among many theories. It is true that Jose was a teacher and it is also interesting to note that Sam Corbett was keeping the mail in Lincoln. But these are probably just coincidences with Doc being both a teacher and a mail keeper. After Billy escaped Lincoln he was reported to be in numerous places. Passing Henry Farmer's ranch where Sam Farmer, his son, and Ambrosio Chavez reported seeing him; at Ladislado Salas's; Yginio Anaya's; Yginio Chavez's, where Yginio helped Billy remove the shackles; and John Meadows' ranch. He was reported being seen in some rather dubious places such as Las Vegas; El Paso; John Miller's camp on the Penasco; heading to Fronteras, Old Mexico; killing Chisum cowboys near Roswell; Seven Rivers; the Red River near the Texas line; and even Denver. The most likely route was to Agua Azul, Las Tablas, Newcomb's cow camp, Conejos Springs, Buffalo Arroyo, and Taiban Arroyo. He is believed to have stayed around Ft. Sumner moving between various New Mexican sheep herders such as Francisco Lobato and Paco Anaya's.

John Joshua Scurlock's claim that Billy visited Doc in Tascosa represents the furthest east that Billy was reported to have gone after his escape. Certainly possible, but is it true? The question still stands that if it's true, what was Billy's intention of doing so?]

FROM NEW MEXICO TO TEXAS

In early February, Billy sent a message to Jessie Evans that he wanted to meet and bury the hatchet. On February 18th, 1879, Evans, Dolan, Mathews, Edgar Walz, and Billy Campbell met Billy, Doc, Tom O'Folliard, George Bowers, and Jose Salazar at the plaza in Lincoln. It was an ominous date – a year to the day that Tunstall was killed.

Tensions were high, especially between the Kid and Evans, but Walz managed to mediate between the factions and the men shook hands. Their agreement included terms of no more hostility and no giving of evidence against the other side. They also agreed to assist each other in eluding the law and, should anyone get captured, the assistance of helping to escape custody. The penalty for breeching their agreement would be death. Having come to terms, they proceeded to drink it up.

Huston Chapman happened upon the drunken group and words were exchanged between he and Campbell and Evans whereupon Campbell shot and killed Chapman. Dolan asked Walz to place a gun in Chapman's hand to make it look like he was armed, but Walz refused. Billy the Kid offered to do it, but he didn't. Instead, he quickly picked up Tom O'Folliard and skipped out to San Patricio.

This incident would play into the negotiations that Billy the Kid and Lew Wallace would undertake in the coming months in reference to The Kid's eye-witness testimony incriminating the killer and the accomplices.

Governor Lew Wallace arrived on the scene in Lincoln on March 5th. He spearheaded the creation of a wanted list that numbered thirty-five men from all the factions involved. Billy the Kid took the opportunity to send Wallace a letter suggesting that he would testify about the Chapman killing if the governor could arrange his pardon.

Needing a group to round up all the wanted men, Wallace turned to the New Mexican citizens for the brunt of the group and on March 13th he created the Lincoln County Mounted Rifles. The captain of the organization was Juan Patron with Ben Ellis acting as his 1st Lieutenant. One of the first members was none other than Fernando Herrera. Curiously, Jose Chavez y Chavez was also made a member.[120]

One of their first excursions was to Ft. Stanton to find Doc and Charlie. Wallace received word that they were there and sent the Mounted Rifles to surreptitiously approach Pete Maxwell's place. Fernando felt bad about his mission, but he talked Doc into going into custody. Charlie, who was working at Thomas Yerby's ranch escaped their dragnet and Doc didn't divulge his whereabouts.[121]

On March 17th, Billy the Kid and Lew Wallace met in person at Squire Wilson's house. It was just the three men present. Neither Billy or Wallace made a firm commitment to the plan which entailed a staged arrest of Billy so it wouldn't appear that he was turning himself in. Billy then would testify in the Chapman affair in exchange for a pardon of the murders of Brady, Hindman, and Roberts.

There was a problem, though. After their meeting, Billy Campbell and Jessie Evans escaped from custody at Ft. Stanton.

On March 21st, Sheriff Kimbrell made the staged arrest of Billy and Tom O'Folliard in San Patricio. Doc , Billy, and Tom were kept in the pit jail at first, but they were moved to house arrest at Juan Patron's.[122]

This arrangement was likely made due the fact that the Widow Casey was also a prisoner. Of all people that Ellen Casey had ran afoul of, it was Padre Sambrano. He had a run-in with the Caseys over an allegedly stolen trunk of money and then was subsequently assaulted by Ellen Casey, Ad Casey, W. A. Alexander, William Jones, and John Jones. It was over this incident that Ellen Casey, Ad Casey, and Alexander were being held prisoner at the Wortley at the same time that Doc, Billy, Tom, and Dan Dedrick were being held prisoner in Juan Patron's house.

Apparently, Padre Sambrano bought land from Ellen Casey that was paid in gold and/or silver and jewelry. Then, she decided, much as she had with Tunstall over her cattle, that she wanted her money back. Not much is known about the outcome of this incident, though.[123]

Billy made his testimony on the 14th or April. Lew Wallace had no real desire to ensure that Billy was given amnesty, though. He went back to Santa Fe on the 18th leaving Rynerson to refuse the deal on the 20th of April.

Billy and Doc hung around through May and part of June hoping that their names would be cleared, but seeing that no one was fighting for their cause, they decided to simply ride out of Lincoln on June 17th.[124]

---

[120] Fulton, Nolan, *LCW: A Documentary History*; Nolan, *The West of Billy the Kid*; Utley.

[121] Sanchez.

[122] See Part IV, request dated 12 Nov 1880 for compensation.

[123] Cummings; Sanchez.

[124] Fulton, Nolan, *LCW: A Documentary History*; Nolan, *The West of Billy the Kid*; Utley.

The *Mesilla News* reported on June 21st:[125]

> A private letter from Mr. Ellis from the town of Lincoln, N. M. dated June 18, 1879, says: That on the night of the 17th inst. 'The Kid' very suddenly disappeared: Mr. Ellis thinks it unnecessary to be at the trouble and expense of attending the court in Mesilla. We suppose 'The Kid' had the same feeling, or perhaps he was anxious to save the county and territory the heavy costs of a trial.
>
> Mr. Ellis says however that if the sheriff should recapture 'The Kid' in time to be present at this court he (Ellis) may attend also.
>
> Doc Scurlock also thought there was very little use in his appearing at court in Dona Ana Co, to answer to indictments or other charges, so he skipped with 'The Kid.'

On July 13th Jimmy Dolan married Carolina "Lina" Fritz, the niece of one-time partner Emil Fritz. The couple then left for a two-month honeymoon in Texas. Padre Sambrano performed the ceremony.

Padre Sambrano died June 8th, 1884. He was descending the bank of a canyon while either driving his wagon and two horses or riding on horseback when the horse or horses spooked. When they bolted, Padre was knocked to the ground but his foot became entangled in the leather straps of the stirrup or wagon rigging. He suffered a terrible head injury and was dragged for many yards. This happened on June 1st, 1884 and he held on for a week before dying. The canyon, just outside of Lincoln, was initially called Canon del Padre Sambrano, but is known today as Priest Canyon.[126]

Other things that happened in July and August were the clearing of Col. Dudley of the allegations brought against him. On August 26th, 1879 John Jones killed John Beckwith and then on the 29th, Bob Olinger killed John Jones.

Doc returned to Ft. Sumner and resumed working for Pete Maxwell. Having heard of the booming town of Tascosa, Doc thought it might provide a good opportunity to relocate and get away from New Mexico. He, however, needed to pull one more job to raise money to fund the move. Doc's final act with his Regulator friends was with Billy, Bowdre, O'Folliard, and two unidentified Hispanics. The group stole 118 head of cattle from Chisum on the Bosque Grande and drove them to Yerby's ranch. They rebranded the cattle and sold them at Alexander Grzelachowski's ranch at Alamogordo. There was reputedly a dispute among the gang over the division of the spoils from this transaction.[127]

On August 17th, 1879, Doc's oldest daughter, Marie Elena died. This was likely another blow to the Scurlock family that helped Doc and Antonia to rethink the direction of their life. Marie Elena Scurlock was most likely buried in the Fort Sumner cemetery.[128]

---

[125] Part IV, letter printed June 21st, 1879; Nolan, *LCW: A Documentary History*; Rasch, "Man of Many Parts"; D. Scurlock.

[126] Cummings.

[127] Garrett; Fulton; Nolan, *LCW: A Documentary History*; D. Scurlock.

[128] D. Scurlock. Dan asserts that Marie Elena was buried at Ft. Sumner. Tim Sweet, whose family built The Billy the Kid Museum at Ft. Sumner has a record of the burials at the Old Ft. Sumner cemetery and Marie Elena is not listed.

On October 11th the couple was blessed with their first son, Josiah Gordon Scurlock, Jr. The birth of their new child so soon after the loss of their daughter would seem to have convinced Doc that it was time to try and put his life in New Mexico behind him.[129]

Prior to the Scurlocks departing, Antonia, who had become concerned that Charlie wasn't taking the same wise path as Doc, pulled her sister Manuela aside and gave her a prophetic warning that if she didn't convince her husband to quit his association with Billy and the other boys, bad things might happen to her husband.[130]

As Doc left the scene another Alabama-born man, who happened to be born just five months after him and in the neighboring Chambers County, would enter the stage and finish the drama of both Charlie Bowdre's and Billy the Kid's life – Patrick Floyd Jarvis Garrett.

While Lew Wallace was still in Lincoln, John Chisum penned the following letter to him.

Fort Sumner
April 15, 1879

To his Exelency
Gov Lue Wallis
Lincoln, N.M.

Sir:

If 10 good men was stationed at a large Spring 12 miles East of this place, It would prevent Robers from coming in off the plains on to the Pecos and give protection to this place and the Citizens below. Roswell is so far below that the Robers can come in and rob as low down as Bosque Grande a distance of 50 miles and get out unmolested before Troops can reach them.

If 20 men was stationed at Popes Crossing on the Pecos, it would prevent them from crossing up the Pecos, having these two points guarded you then have possession of the two main keys to the Settlements on the Pecos River. Pat Garrett who resides hear would be a very suitable man to take charge of the Squad East of this place if authorized to do so.

I hope Gov you will not think I show any disposition to meddle or dictate. I know the County well, and I am satisfied you are more than anxious to give the Citizens protection and I am equally anxious to see the Robers kept out hence I make these suggestions. Robers cannot very will reach the Pecos by any other rout on the account of water.

I remain yours
Respectfully
John S. Chisum[131]

---

[129] D. Scurlock.

[130] Sanchez.

[131] Metz.

Doc had made many enemies during the past several years and he would spend the rest of his life avoiding his daring deeds with Charlie Bowdre, Billy the Kid, and the other Regulators. For one thing, he would drop the moniker of "Doc" and go by his family-given nickname of "Joe". He would also refuse to speak of the events of the Lincoln County War to virtually everyone except a few family members; and even then, his tales were nothing on the order of a detailed memoir, which would have been invaluable to historians.

It was in October or November of 1879 that Doc got rid of all his guns except for one squirrel rifle and moved to Potter County, Texas. He also sold his share of a mine to Bill Gill for $500. Gill would later sell the gold mine for $75,000. This mine would become the Helen Rae mine.[132]

Bill Gill was Doc's brother-in-law. He married Antonia's sister Altagracia Herrera.[133] Lily Casey Klasner recounts one story about Bill. Like Doc and Charlie, Bill went through L. G. Murphy & Co. to procure a ranch as well as equipment to operate a blacksmith shop on the ranch. When Bill's account with the House got to be what they considered too high, they attempted to take his blacksmith tools as compensation. Bill, however, reported that everything had been stolen. In reality, he took the equipment and hid it in Chavez Canyon where they couldn't find it. Will Casey found the equipment one day and alerted his father Robert. Robert knew that all of the equipment belonged to Bill Gill.[134]

Doc, Antonia, daughter Viola, and son Joe, Jr. moved their small household to the Panhandle of Texas and the LX Headquarters ranch in Potter County, Texas. Doc got a job taking care of the horses and wagons used by the mail carriers. The ranch's headquarters had grown into a small community and Doc also served as a translator between English and Spanish for court proceedings. On the 1800 census Doc and family are reported to be in the pseudo-town of Wheeler, as the community was known, where Doc is recorded as "keeping mail station" and Antonia as "keeping house".[135]

His work for the court likely brought him into contact with the one-armed Cecil B. Vivian. Doc and Vivian shared a passion for reading and exchanged books with each other.[136]

Vivian was born in Louisville, Kentucky October 11th, 1848. He initially was the bookkeeper for the LS ranch but was elected as the county clerk for Oldham County. He was known as a teller of tall tales and loved to gamble. No one knew for sure how he lost his arm because he seemed to tell the story different as various times. One version said a corn grinder, another said in a shootout, and yet another that he lost it to a steer while roping it. There was no doubt that he was intelligent, witty, and well-read.[137]

There are a couple of noteworthy things about Doc's time at the LX ranch and the "town" of Wheeler, Texas.

To begin with, there was corruption already occurring in his current organization – the U.S. Post Office Department. The Wheeler Post Office was reported to be "an attractive building,

---

[132] Payne, "The True Doc Scurlock Story" and "Doc Scurlock, Frontier Legend".
[133] Sanchez.
[134] Klasner.
[135] Nolan, *Tascosa*.
[136] See Part VI, Doc's books.
[137] Nolan, *Tascosa*; McCarty.

sturdily constructed of tan-colored native stone and situated on a hill overlooking a beautiful valley near the Canadian".[138] In reality, there wasn't too much more to Wheeler even though it was reported to the U.S Post Office Department that Wheeler was a large, flourishing town, in order to receive more Federal funds. The LX ranch foreman, Outlaw Bill Moore, the same man who Billy had threatened to shoot in to, was likely involved in this deception, but the real scandal became a national affair dubbed the "Star Route Scandal" and Wheeler just happened to be one of the small, fabricated "towns" strewn across the Panhandle to take center stage. Charges were preferred against Arkansas Senator Stephen W. Dorsey, who happened to be involved in the cattle business in Texas and New Mexico. Even though the prominent attorney and orator Robert Ingersoll was able to win an acquittal for Senator Dorsey, it was estimated that over $400,000 had been fleeced from the Postal coffers.[139]

Somehow Doc avoided being tied to this scandal.

The second problem stemmed from his association with his prior organization – the Regulators. This was during the heyday of Tascosa, Texas and there were some very influential cattlemen who ran several local ranches that each have their own, rich histories. George W. Littlefield's LIT ranch, Lucien Scott's LS ranch, and W.H. Bates and David T. Beal's LX ranch being three prominent ranches in the vicinity of Tascosa. John Chisum and Charles Goodnight also held serious influence within the Panhandle. Goodnight, together with other cattlemen in the Panhandle had created the Panhandle Stock Association. This organization unified many interests of the businessmen, but one of the primary issues to be dealt with was cattle rustling.

Billy the Kid, Charlie Bowdre, Tom O'Folliard, and others, including Dave Rudabaugh, Tom Pickett and Billy Wilson continued to be a nuisance to the cattlemen, though. The Panhandle Stock Association, along with Chisum, and the other ranchers in the area of Tascosa decided to throw their support behind the newly elected Lincoln County Sheriff Garrett, who was elected in November 1880 replacing George Kimball. Pat wouldn't take his new office till January, but he was given the position of deputy sheriff with the understanding that he could begin his hunt for the Kid and his gang immediately.

Billy the Kid's new associate Billy Wilson had been identified as the man passing a counterfeit hundred-dollar bill to none other than Jimmy Dolan. This was the catalyst that brought in Agent Azariah F. Wild from the U. S. Treasury department to investigate. Wild, as will be recalled, was the man who wrote that "Joseph Scurlock" had killed men in Louisiana and Texas. He arrived in Lincoln in October to begin his investigation.

Wild was flustered that none of the officials in the territory seemed to be willing to go after Billy Wilson and his gang. He even went so far as to buy dingy mining clothes to go under cover and gather intelligence.

Finally, Wild assembled a group that were willing to go after the bunch. He recruited Sheriff Kimball, Deputy Sheriff Garrett, Captain Joseph C. Lea of Roswell, Ben Ellis, John Hurley, and Frank Stewart. Frank was a former LX ranch employee who was now working as a detective for the association of concerned cattlemen from the Panhandle.

U. S. Marshal John Sherman, Jr., the same man who had deputized Rob Widenmann, made the group deputy U. S. marshals.

---

[138] Price & Turner.

[139] McCarty; Price & Turner

Meanwhile, back in the Panhandle, each ranch decided to send a select group of men they felt were capable types for a posse. Outlaw Bill Moore sent Charlie Siringo, Jim East, Lon Chambers, Lee Hall, and Cal Polk from the LX ranch.

At the beginning of December, Pat Garrett was at the Tom Wilcox ranch when he received a note from Charlie Bowdre that he wanted to meet Pat and parley. The two met just outside of Ft. Sumner at a fork in the road. Garrett had a letter from J. C. Lea that promised leniency to any of the gang that defected and returned to honest ranching. Charlie promised Pat that he would disassociate himself from the Kid if Lea could produce something that was more reassuring.

On December 12th Billy the Kid wrote another letter to Lew Wallace professing his innocence and hurling accusations against Garrett and Chisum. Wallace responded on December 15th by posting a $500 reward for the capture of the Kid.

Pat Garrett met Frank Stewart in Las Vegas and then went to White Oaks to meet up with Charlie Siringo where the three posses were combined into one posse. Not every member of the posses went on the hunt for Billy and his gang. The final choice Pat made for the posse were Frank Stewart, Lon Chambers, Lee Hall, Jim East, Tom Emory, Luis Bozeman, and Bob Williams. Three of the men were LX men and Stewart had been an LX man.

The posse's next stop was Puerto de Luna where they picked up Juan Roibal, Jose Roibal, Charles Rudolph, and George Wilson. They then continued on to Ft. Sumner arriving December 19th.

At Sumner, Pat noticed that Juan Gallegos was acting suspicious and apprehended him. Under scrutiny, Juan revealed that Billy the Kid, Tom O'Folliard, Charlie Bowdre, Billy Wilson, Dave Rudabaugh, and Tom Pickett were at the Wilcox ranch. Pat convinced Juan to become a double agent and report back to Billy that Pat's posse had left Ft. Sumner.

The ruse worked. Pat and his men set up in the old adobe Indian hospital where Doc had lived and where now Charlie and Manuela were living. Lon Chambers and Lee Hall were placed as sentries outside. That night, Billy and his gang came straight into Pat's waiting posse who opened fire hitting Tom O'Folliard and Dave Rudabaugh's horse.

Tom had no choice but to surrender while the rest rode off back to the Wilcox ranch. Tom was brought inside where he soon died.

Billy next sent Emanuel Brazil, Tom Wilcox's partner, into Ft. Sumner to spy on things and ascertain what Pat's next move would be. Brazil, however, had no intentions of siding with Billy. Instead, he went directly to Pat to inform him of Billy's plan. Pat decided to play along, though. He sent Brazil back with instructions to return to him as soon as Billy and the boys lit out.

Around midnight of the 20th of December, Brazil returned to Pat to tell him that Billy's gang had departed. The next morning Pat's group set out and tracked Billy's party to the old rock house at Stinking Springs.

They set up on both sides of the house and on the morning of December 23rd, Charlie Bowdre, mistaken for Billy the Kid, came out to feed their horses and was greeted by a hail of fire. Charlie fell back into the house but Billy placed a gun in his hand and told him that since he was as good as dead, he should go out and take out as many as he could. Instead, Charlie stumbled towards Pat and fell down and died.

The four remaining men tried to pull the horses inside so they could mount and make a run for it but Pat shot one of the horses which fell dead in the doorway.

With no recourse, after several hours, the four surrendered.

They were taken to Las Vegas and then to Santa Fe. Billy was finally moved to Mesilla to stand trial where Judge Bristol sentenced him to hang on May 13th, 1881.

Billy the Kid was taken to Lincoln and kept in the upstairs floor of the Murphy-Dolan building.[140]

The interesting thing about the pursuit and capture of Billy the Kid, as it relates to Doc Scurlock, is that the brunt of the men who made the capture were from the LX ranch where Doc was currently living and working, yet, no historian of Billy the Kid or the Lincoln County War seems to even mention this fact. It raises so many questions. Was Doc even consulted about his views on the pursuit of Billy and Charlie? Did Doc try to help or hinder in any way? Did Doc simply keep his mouth shut and lay low while all of this was going on? After the capture, when the men returned to the LX, what did Doc do then? And what about Henry Brown? He was back in Tascosa serving as deputy under Cape Willingham. What must have the two thought when they received the news that Billy was jailed in Lincoln waiting to be hanged? So many questions with so few answers.

Family legend asserts that after Billy the Kid escaped from custody and killed Bob Olinger and James Bell on April 28th, 1881, he hid out at Doc's residence near Tascosa, Texas. Doc's second son, John Joshua Scurlock, was born May 21st and Billy supposedly visited Doc for a few days after John's birth. John Joshua would boast throughout his life that Billy had held him as a babe. While Billy was there Doc told him that he thought it would be a good idea to stay away from New Mexico and try to quit the life of an outlaw. Billy refused and said that he needed to return to see a girl there. One wonders how Doc reacted when he got the news that Billy had been killed by Pat Garrett in Pete Maxwell's bedroom, of all places, on July 14th, 1881.[141]

It would seem that Doc would move yet again to try and lose the two hellhounds of rustling and mail scandal dogging his trail.

Soon after the news of Billy's death, in 1881, Doc taught school near the town of Vernon, Texas. He also dabbled in medicine, treating the locals. There were many French and German settlers and Doc became conversant in their languages. While living close to Vernon, he also started a wheat farm and built a sod dug-out for the family to live in.

Two poems survive that were written on The Vernon Ice, Light & Water Company stationary and are dated May 14th, 1893. The first poem is presented here and the second poem is presented at the end of Doc's biography. Both are presented in their entirety:[142]

The Ship
By Josiah Gordon Scurlock

On a summer day as the waves were rippling
By a soft and gentle breeze,
Did a ship set sail with a cargo laden
For a port beyond the seas

---

140 Nolan, *Tascosa*; Metz.

141 Payne, "The True Doc Scurlock Story" and "Doc Scurlock, Frontier Legend"; Rasch, *LCW: A Documentary History*; D. Scurlock; J.D. Scurlock.

142 Part V, poems dated May 14th, 1893.

There were sweet farewells, there loving signals,
For her fate was yet unlearned
Though Mary knew it not, twas a solemn parting
Of a ship that never returned

Did she never return? No, she never returned
And her fate is yet unlearned,
Though for years and years there were loved ones waiting
For the ship that never returned

Said a feeble lad to his anxious Mother
I must cross the wide, wide sea
For they say per chance in a foreign climate
There is health and strength for me
Twas a gleam of hope in a day of danger,
And her heart for her youngest yearned
So she sent him f[orth with] a smile and blessing,
On a ship that never returned

Did she never return? No, she never returned
And her fate is yet unlearned,
Though for years and years there were loved ones waiting
For the ship that never returned

Only one more trip said a gallant seaman,
As he kissed his loving wife
Only one more bag of golden treasure
And will last us all through life
Then we'll spend our days in our cozy cottage
And enjoy the rest we've earned,
But alas, poor man who sailed commander
On a ship that never returned

Did she never return? No, she never returned
And her fate is yet unlearned,
Though for years and years there were loved ones waiting
For the ship that never returned

It was also in 1893 that the family once again moved and Doc sold his property to W. T. Wagner. Later, this land would become a rich oil field. The Scurlock family moved to Johnson County, Texas near Ft. Worth. Here, Doc grew cotton and corn on his farm. He also taught Spanish and various other courses at Mehan Business College.[143]

---

[143] D. Scurlock; J.D. Scurlock.

On June 7th, 1894 Doc and Antonia's daughter Viola died. She was 5 years old. The circumstances are unknown.[144]

In 1899 Doc relocated to a farm in Granbury, Texas. He would reside in this location until 1913.

On June 1st of 1903 Doc lost his mother Esther Ann (Brown) Scurlock. Unfortunately, the records are completely silent on the relationship Doc had with his mother and father so we can only speculate on how their deaths were received by Doc.

On November 27th, 1912, Doc lost his beloved bride, Antonia. She was buried in Acton, Texas. After Antonia's death, Doc and the family moved to Mabank, Texas, southeast of Dallas.[145]

In 1913 Doc witnessed a shooting and reported it in a letter to his daughter Linda and her husband Ed Buckbee on September 3rd, saying:[146]

> Oh! I liked to have forgot to say, I saw a man shot the other night. First man I've seen shot in a long time. Two Mexicans quarreled and one of them shot the other three times, once through the breast, once through the stomach, and once through the thigh. If he had had any common sense he would have died in two or three hours, but it has been seven days now, and today he got up and walked about the tent, so guess he decided to live so he can hunt the other fellow up.

In Mabank, Doc worked as a bookkeeper for the S.L. Humas Company, a farming concern. It was during these years living in Mabank that a reporter from the *Dallas Star* learned of who Doc was and approached him for a story about his association with Billy the Kid and their deeds during the Lincoln County War. Doc refused the interview.[147]

Doc was also teaching Spanish while living in Mabank. An ad that ran in the May 11th, 1916 issue of the *Mabank Banner Newspaper* read:[148]

> Will Teach Spanish
>
> J. G. Scurlock informs us that he will open a Spanish class in Mabank in the near future. Mr. Scurlock has had unusual advantages in his long residence in Mexico, where he was for a long time employed in the translation of official records.
>
> His English education has been no less proficient, thereby better fitting him for the work in hand. Owing to the great number of Spanish speaking people in our state, and the near relation between our state and that of Mexico, it is very wise for anyone who has the time and means to avail themselves of this unusual opportunity.
>
> Mr. Scurlock has appeared before the teacher of Spanish in the Dallas public schools and satisfied him of his ability to teach the language.

---

144 Part V, Doc's Bible.

145 Ibid.

146 Part V, letter dated September 3rd, 1913.

147 Payne, "The True Doc Scurlock Story" and "Doc Scurlock, Frontier Legend"; Rasch, "Man of Many Parts"; D. Scurlock; J.D. Scurlock.

148 Part IV, advertisement dated May 11th, 1916.

In October of 1916 his daughter Lola was admitted to St. Paul's Sanitarium for an operation. Doc wrote a note about it on the 12th informing his family that she likely wouldn't make it. Lola passed away on October 27th, 1916. The cause of death was listed as septicemia, but it's not known exactly what precipitated this.[149]

In 1919 Doc moved to Eastland, Texas. He would live out the rest of his life here. The first couple of years in Eastland he opened a confectionary store. This allowed him much time to read and he used the Eastland Library quite extensively to read the classics and other intellectual works. He must have loved to read about philosophy and religion, too, because he soon became interested in the Theosophical Society and their teachings. He joined the society on January 8th, 1919. His certificate was signed by the famous Theosophist Annie Besant.[150]

In April of 1920 Doc received the news that his grandson had died. This was certainly distressing news and he penned a very touching letter conveying the news to daughter Linda and her family:[151]

> Eastland, Tex 4/20/20
> Ed, Linda & children
>
> Dear Children:
>
> I just received a letter from Amy this morning bringing the news of little Wilbur's death. It was a great shock to me, and I fain would say something that would in some measure console you for your great loss, but we all know that words of consolation and sympathy sound very meaningless in a case of this kind. About all we can say is that it is a trial that we ought to be prepared to meet, for it is the one thing that we must all meet sooner or later. It comes to us all Young or Old, High or Low. When our child is born, we know but one thing as to its future and that is it must die. Now I can but believe that whatever is, is best. We can't understand always, but time shows us that all is for the best. What the final outcome of it all is to be, no one knows. There are and yet will be many guesses, but no one knows. But whatever it may be you may be assured it will be best, for the Supreme Intelligence that governs the universe makes no mistakes.
>
> If I was in shape so I could I would come and spend a few days with you but don't see how I can just now. I have just finished taking a course of treatment for my kidney trouble and rheumatism and am much impaired in health, but my bank account is at low ebb, so I must go to work again.
>
> Let me hear from you soon. I will come to see you just as soon as I can get off. Be brave and bear your sorrow with fortitude is all that I can advise.
>
> Your Affectionate Papa

---

149 Part V, postcard dated October 12th, 1916.

150 Part VI, certificate dated January 8th, 1919; Payne, "The True Doc Scurlock Story" and "Doc Scurlock, Frontier Legend"; Rasch, "Man of Many Parts"; D. Scurlock. Note Rasch's comments at the end of "Man of Many Parts", "If there is any validity to the Theosophical belief that a man's actions in his present life determine his lot in his reincarnation, 'Doc' should have an interesting career the next time around."

151 Part V, letter dated April 20th, 1920.

In 1921 Doc went to work for the State Highway Department until he finally retired in 1925. The year after he started, in 1922, his older brother Sampson Van Buren Scurlock died. Sampson was the last of his nuclear family members left in Alabama. Of his five siblings remaining alive who had migrated westward with Doc's father, all survived Doc.[152]

After retirement, Doc spent time visiting each of his kids, sometimes months at a time. In 1926 he went to live with his daughter Martha Ethilnda "Linda" Scurlock Buckbee. He did continue to make extra money by tutoring, writing book reviews, and writing book reports for students at the University of Texas.[153]

Josiah Gordon Scurlock died of a heart attack on July 25th, 1929. He was 79 years old.

His death certificate causes some confusion because of his son William Andrew Scurlock who is listed as the informant. Apparently, William gave the year of Doc's birth as 1849 instead of 1850. William knew Doc was 79, however, because he got Doc's age right, but the math doesn't work out for an 1849 birth year.[154]

The census record of Tallapoosa County, Alabama of 1850 list him as 1 year old. However, in a letter dated May 16th, 1869 by Priestly Norman Scurlock, his father states he is 19 years old, which would be consistent with 1850. His tombstone shows a date of January 11th, 1850. The most compelling piece of evidence is by Doc himself. In the family bible, in Doc's own writing, he lists his own birthday as January 11th, 1850.[155]

The Funeral was conducted in daughter Linda's residence with a horse-drawn carriage being used for the hearse.

Doc was buried in Eastland, Texas and his family had the body of his wife Antonia moved from Acton, Texas so the two could be laid to rest beside one another.

After Doc died, his son John Joshua took his family to Lincoln. While there, family legend holds that the Scurlocks went to a church service and Frank Coe was there and invited John Joshua to come and visit. It was said that Frank couldn't quit going on about how much John Joshua resembled Doc at a younger age. The family visited with Frank Coe who regaled the Scurlocks with stories about Doc's exploits during the Lincoln County War. Marie, John's daughter, recalled how Frank told stories and fed the family with vegetables from his garden. Frank died not too long after this visit in 1931.[156]

Doc and Antonia had ten children: Marie (who died young), Viola Inez (died early), Josiah Gordon, Jr., John Joshua, Amy Antonia, Martha Ethlinda (Linda), Prestley Fernando, Delores (Lola), William Andrew, and Josephine Gladys.

---

152 Havelka; J.D. Scurlock.

153 Rasch, "Man of Many Parts".

154 Part VI, documents pertaining to Docs's passing.

155 Part III, Priestly Scurlock letter dated 16 May 1869; Part V, Doc's Bible records; Part VI, death certificate and tombstone; and Part IX, census records.

156 Payne, "The True Doc Scurlock Story" and "Doc Scurlock, Frontier Legend".

Pulling Hard Against the Stream
By Josiah Gordon Scurlock

It's in this world I've gained my knowledge
And for it I've had to pay
Although I've never been to college
Yet I've heard the poets say
Life is like a mighty river
Rolling on from day to day
And we as ships are launched upon it
Some get wrecked and cast away

Then do your best for one another
Make this life a pleasant dream
Help a weary careworn brother
Pulling hard against the stream

There's many a bright good hearted fellow
Many a noble minded man
Who find themselves in water shallow
Then assist him if you can
Some succeed at every turning
Fortune favors every scheme
While others far the more deserving
Have to pull against the stream

Then do your best for one another
Make this life a pleasant dream
Help a weary careworn brother
Pulling hard against the stream

As in this life we journey onward
Striving hard for wealth or fame
As favored ones, we're never thinking
Of those struggling in the stream
But the darkest night must have an ending
Though the sky be overcast
And the longest lane will have a turning
And the tide will change at last

Then do your best for one another
Make this life a pleasant dream
Help a weary careworn brother
Pulling hard against the stream

Mica Pharris is the great, great granddaughter of Doc Scurlock; Mica possesses the largest collection of Scurlock family surname records, especially those about Doc.

David Garrett is the great great grandnephew of Doc Scurlock; David has researched both the Scurlock and the Garrett surnames in Alabama including Pat Garrett's family.

REFERENCES:

(Note: All source materials from Scurlock family research or articles written on Doc's life were supplied by Mica Pharris.)

Alabama Historical Quarterly, Vol. 18, No. 2, Summer issue 1956; Alabama State Department of Archives and History; Wetumpka Printing Co.

Babits, L. (1998), *A Devil of a Whipping: The Battle of Cowpens*, The University of North Carolina Press (pg. 139 references the pension of Rhoda Ann Simmons' father.)

Bell, B. (1996), *The Illustrated Life and Times of Billy the Kid*, Tri Star – Boze Publications

Buckbee, J., (Numerous family notes, letters, newspaper articles, and correspondence. Includes copy of "Doc Scurlock: man of many parts" article written by Rasch, Buckbee & Klein.)

Burns, W. (1925), *The Saga of Billy the Kid*, Double Day and Company

Coe, G. (1934), *Frontier Fighter: the autobiography of George W. Coe, who fought and rode with Billy the Kid*, Houghton Mifflin

Cummings, B., (1995), *Frontier Parish: Recovered Catholic History of Lincoln County, 1860-1884, No. 4*, Lincoln County Historical Society Publications

DeArment, R. (2001), *Outlaws and Lawmen of the Old West: The Best of NOLA*, NOLA

Douglas, C. (1939), *Cattle Kings of Texas*, published by Cecil Baugh, Dallas, Texas

Eastwood, R., *Nuestras Madres: A Story of Lincoln County, N.M.*, CreateSpace Independent Publishing Platform

Elrod, J. (2014), County Museum to Welcome Doc Scurlock Family this Saturday, *Microplexnews.com*, 7 Oct 2014

Fulton, M. (1980), *History of the Lincoln County War*, University of Arizona Press

Garrett, P. (2007 edit.), *The Authentic Life of Billy the Kid*, Palladium Press, 2007 (This edition contains notes by Maurice G. Fulton)

Gomber, D.(1998), Doc Scurlock, Drew Gomber's Western Destinies, *Vision Magazine*, page 9

Haley, J. (1929), Horse Thieves. *Southwest Review*, 15(3)

Havelka, H. (1999), Farmer, Rancher, Road Hand . . . Gunslinger?, *Transportation News*, Novemeber 1999

Keleher, W. (2007), Violence in Lincoln County, 1869-1881, Sunstone Press

Klasner, L. (1972), *My Girlhood Among Outlaws*, The University of Arizona Press

McCarty, J. (1946), *Maverick Town: The Story of Old Tascosa*, University of Oklahoma Press

Mehren, L. (1968), Scouting for Mescaleros: The Price Campaign of 1873, *Arizona and the West*, 10 (2)

Mullins, R., Inventory of Robert N. Mullins Collection, RNM, VI, Bio/Top, (entry for "Huggins, Newt (Alexander)")

Neal, R. (1998), *Tidewater to Texas: The Scurlocks and Their Wives*, BookCrafters

Nolan, F. (2007), *The Billy the Kid Reader*, The University of Oklahoma Press

Nolan, F. (2009), *The Lincoln County War: A Documentary History, Revised Edition*, Sunstone Press

Nolan, F. (2017), *Tascosa: Its Life and Gaudy Times*, Texas Tech University Press

Nolan, F. (1998), *The West of Billy the Kid*, The University of Oklahoma Press.

O'Neal, B. (2018), *John Chisum: Frontier Cattle King*, Eakin Press

Payne, V. (1989), The True Doc Scurlock Story, *Eastland County Newspapers*

Payne, V. (2007), Doc Scurlock, Frontier Legend, Buried in Eastland, *The Texas Messenger, Vol. 13, No. 4, Winter*

Price, M. & Turner, G. (2007), *The Cruel Plains*, Rogers Publishing & Consulting

Rasch, P., Buckbee, J., & Klein, K. (1963), Man of Many Parts, *The English Westerners' Brand Book*, January 1963

Rasch, P. (1969), A Second Look at the Blazer's Mill Affair, *Frontier Times*, December-January 1969.

Rasch, P. (1995), *Trailing Billy the Kid*, The National Association for Outlaw and Lawman History, Inc.

Rasch, P. (1997), *Gunsmoke in Lincoln County*, The National Association for Outlaw and Lawman History, Inc.

Rash, P. (1998), *Warriors of Lincoln County*, The National Association for Outlaw and Lawman History, Inc.

Sanchez, E. & Sanchez, P. (2015), *Nuestros Antepasados*, AuthorHouse (A valuable source on the Lincoln County War as told from the New Mexicans' perspective.)

Scurlock, D. (2001), Physician, Gunfighter, and Family Man, *Dona Ana County Historical Society, Vol. III, No. 1*

Scurlock, J. D. (1999), From the Lincoln County War to the Eastland Library: Josiah Gordon Scurlock, Cisco Press – Eastland Telegram – Ranger Times, Sunday Mar 14, 1999

Scurlock, P. (Letter written to nephew William on May, 16th, 1869.)

Scurlock, T. (Numerous letters preserved by Theodcius Scurlock from mother, brother, and various other family members; physician's business book which he also used as a diary.)

Sides, H. (2006), *Blood and Thunder: The Epic Story of Kit Carson and the Conquest of the West*, Anchor Books

The Handbook of Texas Online, entry for "Chisum, John Simpson", Texas State Historical Association (TSHA), pulled 17 Apr 2019

Utley, R. (1989), *Billy the Kid: A Short and Violent Life*, University of Nebraska Press

PART II – YOUNG GUNS AND DOC

YOUNG GUNS AND DOC

The two movies Young Guns and Young Guns II were the only movies to ever prominently feature Doc Scurlock as a main character. The Young Guns movies are doubly bad for historians; first, because they are riddled with discrepancies and even wholesale inventions, and secondly, because they're so darn good. If a movie flops and no one sees it to pick up bad history, then historians don't really have a tough battle in teaching people accurate history, but when a movie is a box office success grossing over $45 million, then historians find themselves facing an uphill struggle to correct a lot of folks' ill-formed ideas of what actually happened.

Still, both movies draw on the historical facts and it's obvious that writer John Fusco was beginning with the history and twisting things to make them more Hollywood. And one can only hope that people who are truly curious about the history of Billy the Kid and the Lincoln County War will take enough interest to dig deeper than just watching a couple of movies for their history.

Kiefer Sutherland's portrayal of Doc fell into that category of drawing on the real history and keeping what worked then changing things to fit the template of what sells in the theaters. This chapter will take a look at Kiefer Sutherland's role in Young Guns to correct erroneous things in the movies and to act as a way to dig a little deeper into what we actually know about what Doc was really like.

Was Doc Scurlock really a poet-reciting Romantic who begrudgingly tolerated Billy the Kid just because the two had united their fates in pursuit of justice for their friend John Tunstall's murder? Is there any truth to the semi-educated, well-read, well-spoken, level-headed Alabaman who was born in squalor but possessed enough intellect to become "refined"?

Appearance

Let's begin with how close Kiefer Sutherland looked like Doc. We know from a newspaper account that he was "between five feet eight or ten inches high, light hair, light complexion, front teeth out, writes a very good hand, quick spoken, and usually makes a good impression on first acquaintance". Photos also show that around 1898, some twenty years after the Lincoln County War, that Doc had rather large ears and he also wore a mustache. Kiefer isn't too far off the mark, but, to be more accurate, he should have sported a much thicker mustache and blacked out his two front teeth.

If Doc grew his mustache to help conceal his loss of teeth, it's very likely that he was self-conscious of his smile. In all but one of the pictures of Doc, it's impossible to see his teeth because he isn't smiling. In the one picture where he is smiling, the photo isn't clear, but he appears to be joking around with his three siblings in the picture.

Upbringing and Home

In one scene of the first movie, Dirty Steve makes a gibe at Doc upon seeing the dilapidated hovel where they catch Henry Hill. Never mind that this scene never even happened in real life. Steve makes a comment that the place looked like the hole where Doc grew up. Was Doc born into poverty in Alabama?

On the contrary, Doc's father was a well-respected member of the community who had means. He was outspoken on the need for children to learn how to read and write. Priestly Scurlock was the community school teacher. He evidently had enough money to send Josiah to medical school in New Orleans. Josiah was taught his well-cultured habits from a very early age and was just like his father in passing on the same wisdom to his family.

As to what the house where Doc grew up really looked like, unfortunately, the land may have had sections submerged. The Scurlocks lived about five miles southwest of the town of Dadeville, Alabama on the fertile lands along the Tallapoosa River. In 1920 the Cherokee Heights Dam was built on the Tallapoosa River northwest of Dadeville. The lake and the dam were later named for the president of the Alabama Power Company at the time of the dam's construction, Thomas Wesley Martin. Large areas of the land south of the dam were submerged by the Martin Dam.

Friendship with Tunstall

When Young Guns begins, Doc accompanies Tunstall into Lincoln because he is employed by Tunstall. In reality, Doc didn't work for Tunstall like Billy the Kid did. Doc and Charlie Bowdre's ranches were close to the Coe's and Saunder's ranch as well as Dick Brewer's ranch.

Before Tunstall even arrived in Lincoln, Doc and his neighbors had already banded together and formed a lynch mob in the Jesus Largo and Chihuahua killings. This early vigilante excursion could be seen as the proto-Regulator seed that would eventually grow to become around fifty-men strong by the Battle of Lincoln.

Doc's Love Interest and His Reason to Fight the Murphy-Dolan Faction

In the movies, Doc pines for the China girl Yen Sun. Doc and Charlie both married daughters of Fernando Herrera in reality. I don't know why the movie didn't depict Antonia and Manuela, but it's interesting that the movies use Doc's attraction to Yen as his rasion d'etre to fight against the Murphy-Dolan gang, though. I suppose it simplified things and made Doc appear more of a Romantic. In reality, Doc and his neighbors had sufficient reason to challenge the corruption in Lincoln because they were victims of it.

Murphy and Dolan had a full-scale monopoly on the politics, economics, and government of Lincoln. They owned the cattle contracts with the military and the reservations, they owned the general store and the bank. Many ranchers who had taken out loans felt that they were being swindled by the high interest rates and ruthless tactics used when payments were late or loans were defaulted.

It wasn't just the Anglo ranchers, either. The Spanish-speaking community of New Mexicans were also steadily growing unhappier at how things were going in the aftermath of Tunstall's murder. The Regulators like Doc, Charlie, and Billy, who either spoke Spanish or had married into a Spanish-speaking family, had an easier time earning the confidence of the Spanish-speaking community in support of their cause.

Poetry

Yes, Doc enjoyed poetry and reading a wide variety of other literature. It's hard to know just how much he dabbled in writing because only two poems survive in their entirety (presented for the first time in this volume). These weren't written until 1893, well after the events of the Lincoln County War.

Doc's Involvement in the Brady/Hindman Killing

In the first movie, Doc is shown participating in the ambush on Brady. In reality, there's no reason to believe that Doc was present. It's likely that some of the Regulators including Billy the Kid believed that Brady was carrying a warrant for McSween's arrest and decided, without the consent of McSween or Brewer, to take care of Brady before the warrant could be served.

Doc's Involvement in the Blazer's Mill Shootout

The movie, besides placing this event before the Brady/Hindman killing when it was actually after, shows Doc taking a bullet in the hand. Although Doc was definitely present at this shootout, he wasn't the one to get shot in the hand. It was George Coe who had his trigger finger shot off when Buckshot Robert's bullet ricocheted off Bowdre's belt buckle. George Coe isn't even depicted in the movie.

The Dirty Underwear Gang of Liberty, Missouri

No, Doc never road with any such gang as his character claims to Yen in the first movie.

Doc's Involvement in the Five-Day Battle

The ending of the first movie culminates in the Battle of Lincoln. There are so many discrepancies that it's hard to list them all. As relates to Doc, though, he was never positioned in the McSween house. Doc was at the Ellis place on the east end of town. When Col. Dudley and the military arrived, Doc and the Regulators who were with him, including Charlie Bowdre and Dirty Steve, made a break for safety. There was a brief skirmish that resulted in the wounding of John Jones.

Bowdre did not die in the battle as the movie depicts. Charlie would die later at Stinking Springs. In Young Gun II, Doc is shown getting killed at Stinking Springs, but, of course, Doc was already living in Texas at that time.

Doc After the Lincoln County War

Doc made his exit from Lincoln not long after the Five-Day Battle by first relocating to the safety of Ft. Sumner and then moving to Texas in October or November of 1879. In essence, Doc shouldn't have even made an appearance in Young Guns II.

Doc Heading East to Teach

While Doc never went as far as New York, he did teach. Doc relocated to several towns in Texas and worked numerous jobs including teaching Spanish and assisting college kids with their essays and writing.

Doc's Beliefs

While there is no place in the movies where Doc discusses his philosophical or religious beliefs, I wanted to end this endeavor with a couple of interesting perspectives on Doc's life.

Doc joined the Theosophical Society in 1919 which is a very telling piece of evidence for some of his inner beliefs. The Theosophical Society was essentially a movement that embraced Eastern and Western religions and attempted to promote open-mindedness in religious exploration. It was started by Madam Blavatsky, but at the time Doc joined, Annie Besant had become one of the dominant members. Thus, suggesting that if he would go through the effort of joining, he must have had views that were reflected in their teachings.

Another surprisingly informative insight into Doc was this excerpt from the letter he wrote to his daughter conveying the horrible news of his grandson's death.

> Now I can but believe that whatever is, is best. We can't understand always, but time shows us that all is for the best. What the final outcome of it all is to be, no one knows. There are and yet will be many guesses, but no one knows. But whatever it may be you may be assured it will be best, for the Supreme Intelligence that governs the universe makes no mistakes.

Notice that this isn't a very Biblical message. This view was actually formulated, and caused much influence, by the universal genius Gottfried Leibnitz. Leibnitz was the man who co-created Calculus, but separately, from Newton.

Leibnitz's formulation went something like this. God has the idea of infinite universes but can only create one, unique universe. Because he is all-loving and an all-good deity, he chooses to create the best of all possible universes. Therefore, we live in the best possible creation.

It's also interesting that Doc references God as the Supreme Intelligence. This terminology is used by Deists. The movement of Deism came to fruition along with the prevailing discoveries of Science in the Age of Enlightenment. Deism holds that God is a perfect being who creates the universe and then lets it run without too much intervention, whereas Theism holds to the Biblical view that God does interact with his creation to guide and steer it through prophets, teachers, miracles, and revelations.

Deism was a huge influence on the Masonic movement, but there is absolutely no proof that Doc was ever interested in joining the Masons Lodge. This could likely be that most of the members of the local Lincoln Masonic Lodge were from the Murphy-Dolan faction.

Among Doc's personal affects retained by descendants are some of his books. These include a Spanish Language text book that he likely used to teach, but there was also a Bible and a book on Evolution.

In the end it's tough to say what Doc's personal views on Religion, Science, and Philosophy actually were, but the evidence points to a man who was both curious and intelligent.

Doc and Billy's Relationship

Was Doc annoyed by Billy but bound to him through a common fate, at least till the end of the Lincoln County War? Doc and Billy went through quite a bit together and were obviously very close friends, maybe even like brothers.

It's not known for sure how long Doc and Billy had known each other because one of the unprovable things about Doc and Billy is the Scurlock family story about Doc and Charlie trying their hands at mining before deciding to try the cattle business. But, because their mining wasn't lucrative, they opened a cheese factory on the Gila River somewhere between Arizona and New Mexico to raise capital for ranching. Supposedly, though, this cheese operation was where they first met Billy the Kid. He worked for them for what must have been a very short time.

Regardless, Doc and Billy did spend quite a bit of time together. Probably the longest stretch of time was when they were both under house arrest at Juan Patron's in 1879.

From March 21st through June 17th Doc and Billy spent every day together. It was said that they played a good amount of cards and that the local New Mexicans stopped by to visit and serenade them. They likely talked about all manner of subjects as well.

Billy was a sharp guy. I'd like to think that rather than being annoyed, Doc and Billy had many interesting conversations and enjoyed each other's company, as good friends do. It's too bad Doc didn't record for posterity some of these details.

PART III – DOCUMENTS PERTAINING TO DOC'S GENEALOGY

14 Sep 1794 – Will of Joshua Scurlock (great grandfather of Josiah Gordon Scurlock)

"In the name of God, Amen, this fourteenth day of September one thousand seven hundred and ninety four, I, Joshua Scurlock of the state of Georgia and Hancock County being sick and weak but of sound mind and memory thanks be to the Almighty God for it.

I do make and ordain this to be my last will and testament. In manner and form following, first and chiefly I give my soul to God, who give it me and my body I commend to the Earth to be decently buried in a Christianlike burial at the discretion of my executors. Nothing doubting but at the general resurrection I shall receive the same again by the almighty power of God – as touching worldly estate wherewith it hath pleased God to bless me.

I give and devise and bequeath and dispose of the same in manner and form following.

Item, I give and devise to my daughter Argatha Watts five shillings sterling to her and her heirs forever.

Item, I give and bequeath to my son Thomas Scurlock five pounds sterling to him and his heirs forever.

Item, I give and bequeath to my daughter Elizabeth Scurlock my best feather bed and furniture to her and her heirs forever.

Item, I give and bequeath to my son Daniel Scurlock my next best feather bed and furniture to him and his heirs forever.

Item, I give and bequeath to my dearly beloved children namely William Scurlock, Thomas Scurlock, Presley Scurlock, Joshua Scurlock, Daniel Scurlock, Sarah Parker, Lucy Norman, and Elizabeth Scurlock all the remainder and reserve of my estate which I have not above mentioned to be equally divided between them after my just debts and funeral expenses are paid to them and their heirs forever.

Sixthly and lastly I nominate, constitute and appoint my two sons William and Daniel Scurlock to be my full and whole executors of this my last will and testament.

In witness whereof I have herewith set my hand and seal this day and year above written.

Joshua Scurlock his mark

Signed sealed in the presence of

John Hamilton
William Hamilton
John Hamilton, Jr.

State Georgia, Hancock County

This day appeared before me John Hamilton, William Hamilton, John Hamilton, Jr. three [...] to the above will, who being duly sworn on the holy Evangelicals of Almighty God do depose and say that they saw the within named Joshua Scurlock sign, seal, publish and declare the within to be his last will and testament and that at the time of his so doing he was of sound disposing mind and memory and [...] to the best of their knowledge and that at his request in his presence in the presence of each other they subscribed their names [...] the same this 18th day of August 1795

[Myles?] Greene"

44

In the name of God amen this Fourteenth day September
one thousand seven hundred and ninety four I Joshua-
Scurlock of the State of Georgia and hancock County
Being Sick and weak but of Sound mind and Memory
thanks be to Almighty God For it:

I do make and ordain this to be my last will and
Testament In manner and form following, first and
Cheifly I give my Soul to god who gave it me and
my Body I commend to the earth to be decently buried
In a christian Like burial at the discretion of my Executors
Nothing doubting but at the general resurrection I shall
Receive the same again by the mighty power of god —
As touching worldly estate wherewith it hath pleased
God to bless me

I give and devise and bequeath and dispose of the same
In manner and form following

Ithem, I Give and devise to my daughter argatha
Watts five Shillings Sterling to her and her heirs forever

Ithem, I Give and bequeath to my son Thomas Scurlock
Five pounds Sterling to him and his heirs forever

Ithem I Give and bequeath to my daughter Elizabeth
Scurlock my best Feather bead and furniture
to her and her heirs forever

Ithem I Give and bequeath to my son Daniel -
Scurlock my next best Feather bead and furniture
To him and his heirs forever

Ithem I Give and bequeath to my dearly beloved children
Namely William Scurlock James Scurlock —

Presley Scurlock Joshua Scurlock Daniel Scurlock
Sarah Parker Lucy Norman and Elizabeth
Scurlock all the remainder and residue of my Estate
Which I have not above menconed to be equally divided
Between them after my Just debts and funeral Expences
are paid to them and their heirs forever.

Sixthly and lastly I nominate constitute and appoint
my two sons William and Daniel Scurlock to be my
Full and whole Executors of this my last will and Testament
In Witness whereof I have hereunto set my hand and seal
this day and year above written

Signed sealed in the
Presents of
John Hamilton
William Hamilton
John Hamilton Junr.

his
Joshua J Scurlock (Seal)
mark

State Georgia
Hancock County

This day appeared before me John Hamilton & William Hamilton & John Hamilton Jun. three Subscribing witness to the above will, who being duly sworn On the holy Evangelists of Almighty God do depose and say that they saw the within named Joshua Scurlock sign seal publish and Declare the within to be his last will and Testament and that at the time of his so doing he was of sound disposing mind and memory and understanding to the best of their knowledge and that at his request in his presence in the presence of Each other they subscribed their Names as witness the same
this 18th day of August 1795

Myles Greene R.P.H.C.

15 Apr 1837 – Land Record of Priestly Norman Scurlock (father of Josiah Gordon Scurlock)

The Scurlock family lived on this property in Tallapoosa County, Alabama until Priestly moved to Texas in 1874. In 1920 the Martin Dam was erected and caused much of the land along the Tallapoosa River to rise resulting in much land being submerged, but an overlay of the land grant of 1837 with the current area shows that the Scurlock land should mostly be above the waterline. On the 1860 census the Scurlocks are listed adjacent to the Willis family. Priestly's son Sampson Scurlock married Mary Willis and there is still a Willis Road in the area.

Josiah Gordon Scurlock was most likely born at home on this property.

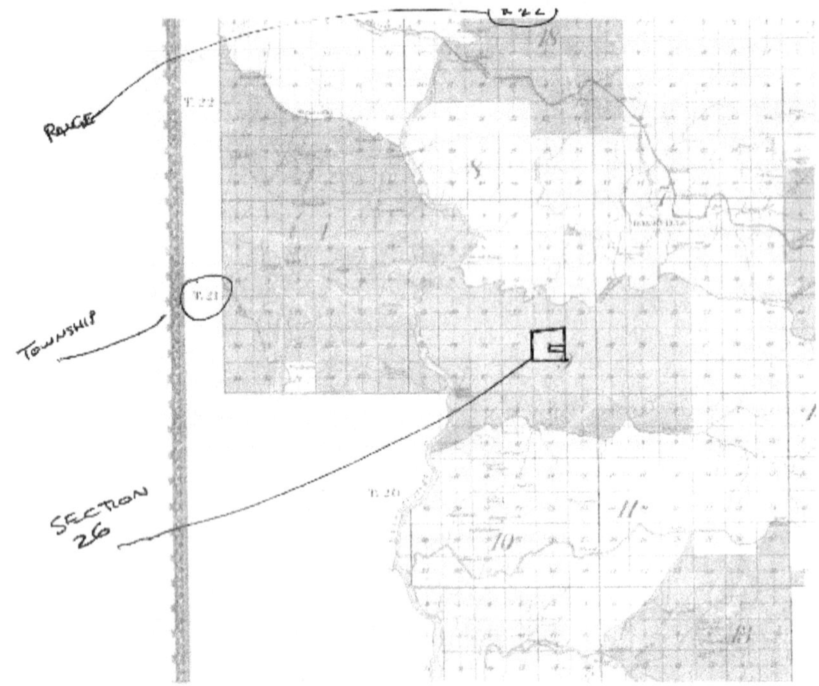

Pan Image Up
Pan Image Down

View Image Full Size
Return to Thumbnail List

Pan Image Left
Pan Image Right

Filename
States\Alabama\Counties\tallapoosa\\Tallapoosa1835a.sid
Name
Description

NORTH HALF OF THE S.E. QUADRANT
SECTION 26 IN
TOWNSHIP 21 OF
RANGE 22

424 **THE UNITED STATES OF AMERICA.** Ed

CERTIFICATE No. 10723

To all to whom these Presents shall come, Greeting:

WHEREAS Presley N. Hurlock of Tallapoosa county Alabama

has deposited in the **GENERAL LAND OFFICE** of the United States, a Certificate of the REGISTER OF THE LAND OFFICE at Montgomery whereby it appears that full payment has been made by the said Presley N. Hurlock according to the provisions of the Act of Congress of the 24th of April, 1820, entitled "An Act making further provision for the sale of the Public Lands," for the North half of the South East quarter of Section twenty six, in Township twenty one of Range twenty two in the District of Lands subject to sale at Montgomery Alabama, containing seventy nine acres, and ninety one hundredths of an acre,

according to the official plat of the survey of the said Lands, returned to the General Land Office by the **SURVEYOR GENERAL**, which said tract has been purchased by the said Presley N. Hurlock

NOW KNOW YE, That the **United States of America,** in consideration of the Premises, and in conformity with the several acts of Congress, in such case made and provided, *HAVE GIVEN AND GRANTED*, and by these presents *DO GIVE AND GRANT*, unto the said Presley N. Hurlock and to his heirs, the said tract above described: **TO HAVE AND TO HOLD** the same, together with all the rights, privileges, immunities, and appurtenances of whatsoever nature, thereunto belonging, unto the said Presley N. Hurlock and to his heirs and assigns forever.

In Testimony Whereof, I, Martin Van Buren PRESIDENT OF THE UNITED STATES OF AMERICA, have caused these Letters to be made PATENT, and the SEAL of the GENERAL LAND OFFICE to be hereunto affixed.

GIVEN under my hand, at the CITY OF WASHINGTON, the fifteenth day of April in the Year of our Lord one thousand eight hundred and thirty seven and of the INDEPENDENCE OF THE UNITED STATES the sixty first.

L.S.

BY THE PRESIDENT: Martin Van Buren

By A. Van Buren Sec'y.

Saml. S. King acting Recorder of the General Land Office ad interim

Overlay of land location with current map.

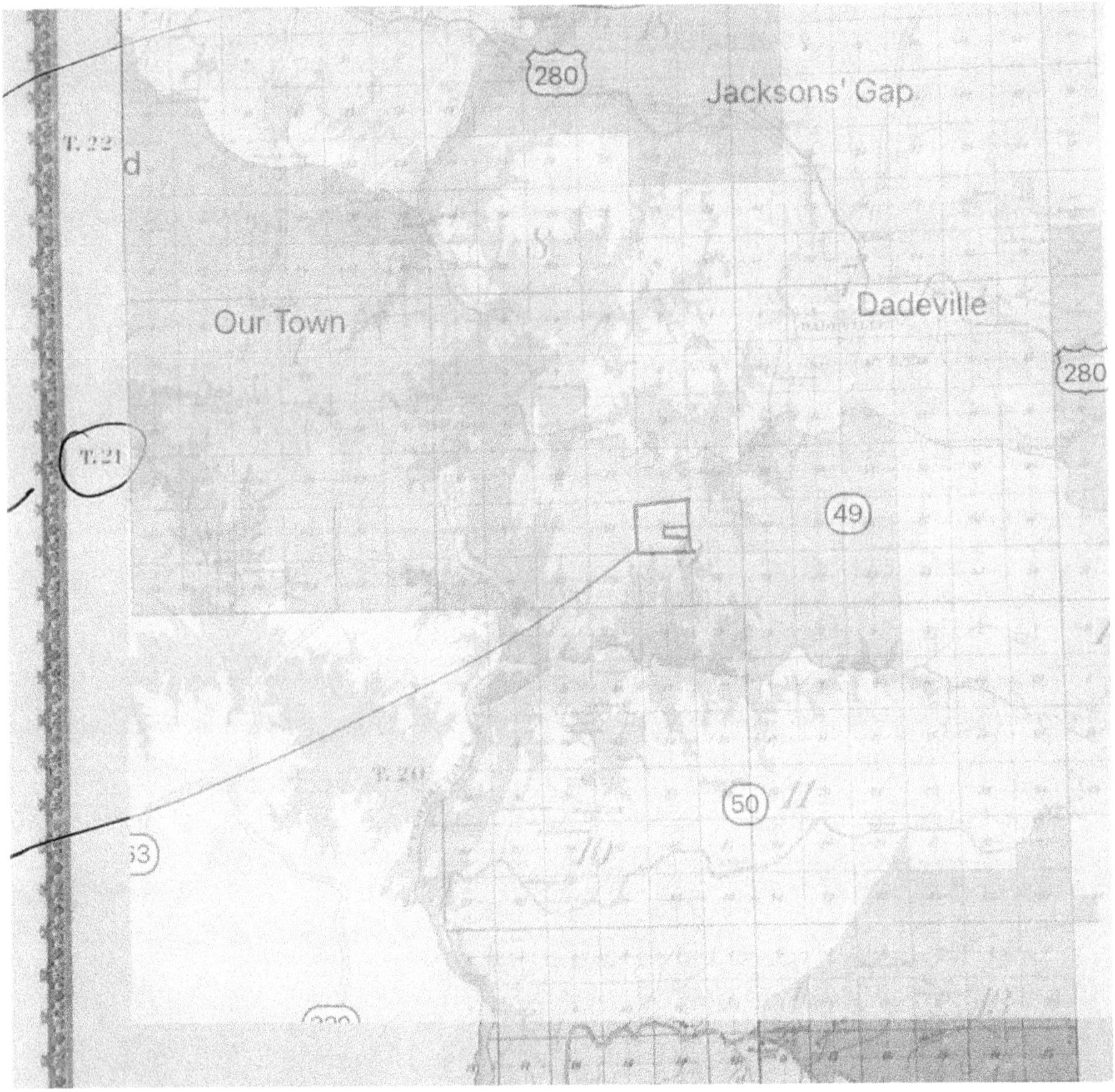

15 Aug 1840 – Will of William Scurlock (grandfather of Josiah Gordon Scurlock)

"Georgia, Muscogee County

Be it known to all to whom these presents shall come that heretofore to wit on the fifteenth day of August in the year of our Lord eighteen hundred and forty, William Scurlock of said county and state in his last sickness in the habitation or dwelling house of John Scurlock where he had been resident about one month made the following nuncupative will in words, that is to say, he, the said Scurlock, then and there gave and bequeathed a certain Negro girl slave of light complexion named Rachel about seven years of age to his daughter Caroline Matilda Files now (formerly Caroline Matilda Scurlock together with all her future natural increase to her and her heirs forever). He also then and there gave and bequeathed to his beloved wife Rhoda Scurlock all the balance of his real and personal estate of whatsoever kind or nature the same may be to her and her heirs forever.

Georgia, Muscogee County

Personally appeared in open court Benjamin [Poles?] and John Scurlock and Gracey Scurlock who being duly sworn deposeth and said that they were present at the last sickness of William Scurlock at the residence and dwelling house of John Scurlock in the county and state aforesaid and that he did without returning to his residence and that they heard him declare and publish in substance the above and foregoing as his last will and testament and that the said Scurlock called upon them to take notice thereof and bear witness to the same and that each were in his presence and that he was at the time of sound disposing mind and memory and that he published and declared the same freely without any compulsion so far as is known or believed.

John Scurlock his mark
Gracey Scurlock

Sworn to and subscribed in open court this 26th day of January eighteen hundred and forty one

Ishom [McIntire?]"

Georgia
Muscogee County } Be it known to all to whom these presents shall come that heretofore to wit on the fifteenth day of August in the year of our Lord eighteen hundred and forty William Scurlock of said County and State in his last sickness in the habitation or dwelling house of John Scurlock where he had been resident about one month made the following Nuncupative Will in words that is to say he the said Scurlock then and there gave and bequeathed a certain Negro Girl slave of light complexion named Rachel about seven years of age to his daughter Caroline Matilda Fels now (formerly Caroline Matilda Scurlock together with all her future natural increase to her and her heirs forever. He also then and there gave and bequeathed to his beloved wife Rhoda Scurlock all the balance of his real and personal estate of whatsoever kind or nature the same may be to her and her heirs forever.

Georgia
Muscogee County } Personally appeared in open court Benjamin Pohs and John Scurlock and Gracy Scurlock who being duly sworn deposeth and saith that they were present at the last sickness of William Scurlock at the residence and dwelling house of John Scurlock in the County and State aforesaid and that he died without returning to his residence and that they heard him declare and publish in substance the above and foregoing as his last will and testament and that the said Scurlock called upon them to take notice thereof and bear witness to the same and that such was in his presence and that he was at the time of sound disposing mind and memory and that he published and declared the same freely without any compulsion so far as we know or believe.

Sworn to and subscribed in open Court this 26th day of January eighteen hundred and forty one

John Scurlock

his
Gracy X Scurlock
mark

Ashon McLester Clk. C.O.

Priestly Norman Scurlock 2nd Creek War of 1836 record.

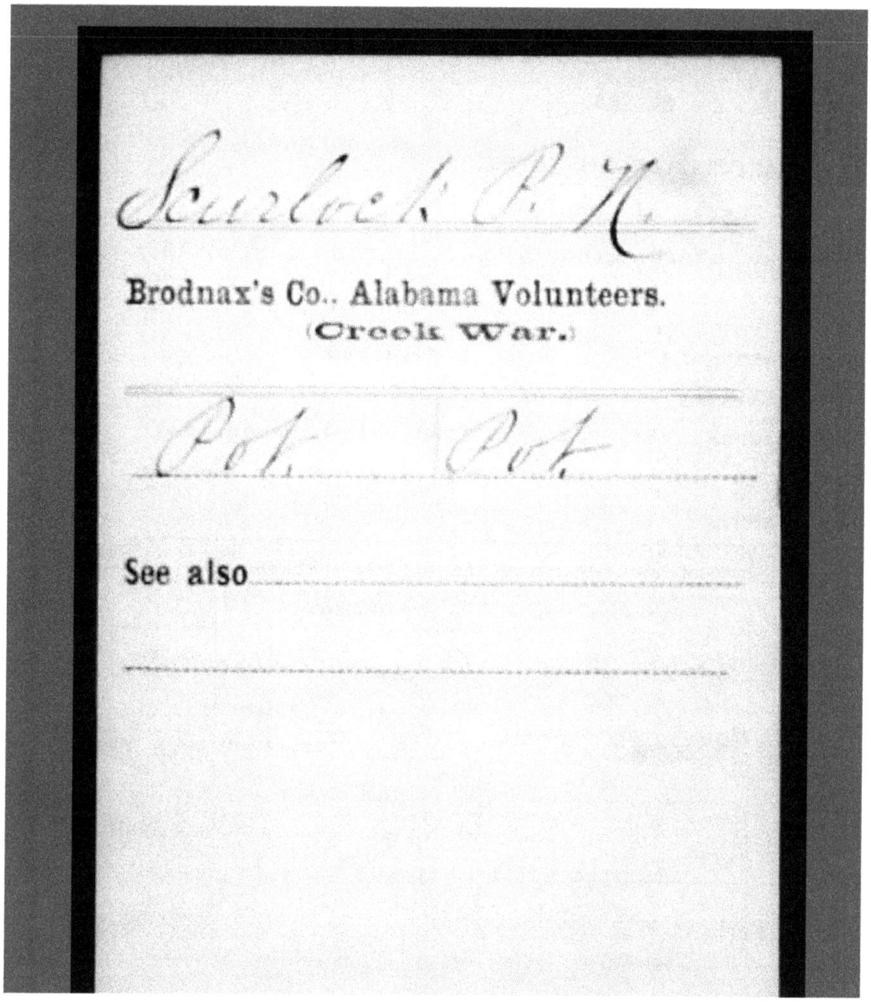

Scurlock P. N.

Brodnax's Co., Alabama Volunteers.
(Creek War.)

Pvt. Pvt.

See also

Revolutionary War Record for William Scurlock showing service under Col. Cleveland.

O. W. and N. Division. 3—525.

DEPARTMENT OF THE INTERIOR,

S. File 16,523

Bureau of Pensions,

Washington, D. C., ..., 190...

In reply to your request of ...., received .... for a statement of the military history of William Scurlock a soldier of the REVOLUTIONARY WAR, you will find below the desired information as contained in his (~~or his widow's~~) application for pension on file in this Bureau.

Dates of enlistment or appointment.	Length of service.	Rank.	Officers under whom service was rendered. Captain.	Colonel.	State.
1779	3 mos.	Pvt	Ab. De Moss.	Benjamin Cleveland	N.C.
Spring 1780	3 mos.		Ab. De Moss.	Benjamin Cleveland	
1780	6 mos.		William McDonald William Sloan	Cleveland	

Battles engaged in, ✓

Residence of soldier at enlistment, 1. Enlisted at Wilkes C.H., N.C.

Date of application for pension, Feb. 27, 1833 - Cl. al.

Residence at date of application, Scurlock's District, Baldwin Co., Ga.

Age at date of application, b. Prince William Co. Va. 1762 - d. Sept. 1, 1840

Remarks: Soldier married fall 1790 Rhoda —. Seven children four of whom were living in 1856. Widow died Mar. 13, 1851 at her daughter's, Kitty Collins, in Coosa Co., Ala.

Very respectfully,

Commissioner.

31793b5m10-07

12 Sep 1856 – Letter from Kitty Scurlock Collins (Doc Scurlock's aunt) to the Pension Dept.

"In state of Alabama, Coosa County – September 12th, 1856

To the officers of the Pension of at Washington City

Dear Sirs,

Yours of the 8th of April last has just been to hand in which you wish to know how many of William Scurlock's children there were that is living share my Father's Family Bible that my mother brought to my house after the death of my Father and as it may be of some advantage to me in obtaining the Pension that is coming, I will you whole of the Record as it stands Recorded in his Bible my Father William Scurlock & his wife Rhoda was married in the fall of 1790 and had seven children. There is three of them Decsd. The rest were living the last I heard from them. My Mother came to my house after the death of my Father and remained there until her death. My Father died September 1st, 1840 and my Mother lived until the 13th March 1851 and for the trouble that my Mother was to me in her old age. The rest of the Children gave me the right to draw the pension that is coming to my Father & Mother. It appears from your letter that my father drawed up to the 4th of September 1833 it appears that there was a seven years lacking three days that he should be entitled to a [...] at time and my Mother from the 1st of [...] the 13th of March 1851. I [...] you on your receiving of this letter if there is anything that is necessary that I should do in as plain a manner as you can. Direct your letter Wetumpka, Coosa, State of Alabama.

Most Respectfully
Your obedient servant

Kitty Collins"

Sir Sale ... County

September 12th 1856

To the offices of the Pension of at Washington City

Dear Sirs

Yours of the 8th of April last has Just come to hand in which you wish to know how many of William Scarlock's Children there wer that is living I have my Farthers Family Bible that my Mother Brought to my House after the Death of my Farther and as it may be of some advantage to me in obtaining the Pension that is Comming I will you whole of the Recrd as it stands Recorded in his Bible my Farther William Scarlock & his Wife Rhoda was Married in the fall of (1790) and had seven Children there is three of them Died the Rest were living the last I herd from them My Mother Came to my House after the Death of my Farther and Remained ther until her Death my Farther Died September 30th 184 and my Mother lived until the 13th March 1851 and for the trouble that my Mother was to me in her old age the rest of the Children gave me the Right to Draw the Pension that is Comming to my Farther & Mother it appears from your letter that my Farther Drawed up to the (4) of September 1833 it appears that there wer a ... years lacking three days that he should be

intitled to a at time and My Mother
from the 13th of January 1840 to the 13th of Mach
1851 I wish you on your receiving this letter if
there is any thing that is nessasary that I should
doe inorder to enable me to draw the Money you
would be so good as to informe m what is required
that I should doe in as plain a manner as you
Can. Direct your letter Wetumpka Coosa Co.
State of Alabama

Most Respectfully
your obedient Servant

Kitty Collins

Civil War records for three of Doc's brothers. 1860's

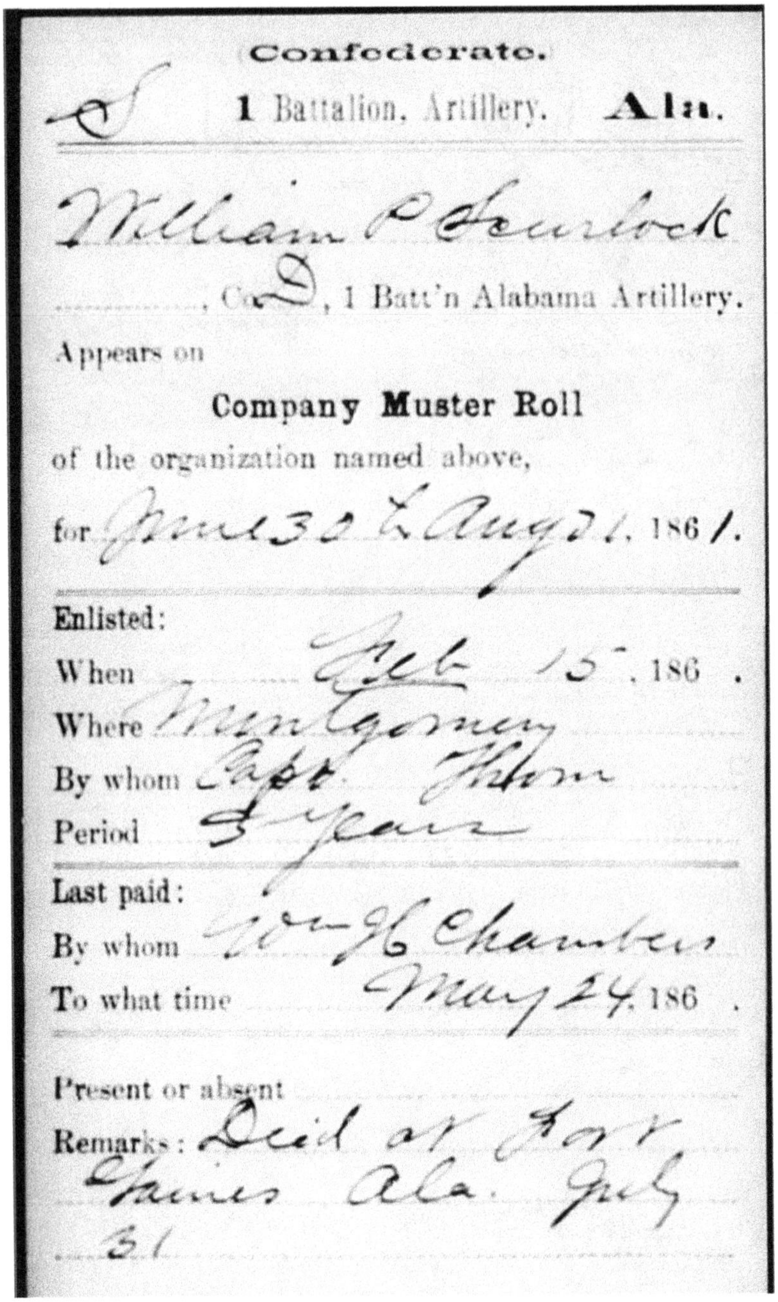

Confederate.

S 1 Battalion, Artillery. Ala.

William P Scurlock

........., Co. D, 1 Batt'n Alabama Artillery.

Appears on

Company Muster Roll

of the organization named above,

for June 30 to Aug 31, 1861.

Enlisted:

When Feb 15, 186 .

Where Montgomery

By whom Capt. Thom

Period 3 years

Last paid:

By whom Wm H Chambers

To what time May 24, 186 .

Present or absent

Remarks: Died at Fort Gaines Ala. July 31

Dear Sir:

In an act passed by the Legislature at the recent special session, there is required to be prepared a permanent roll of the pensioners of the State, giving as full information as possible as to the service of the soldiers who are on the pension roll and of the husbands of widows who are drawing a pension from the State.

In order to accomplish the purpose intended, you are respectfully urged to co-operate promptly with the Department by answering as fully as possible all the questions asked on the blank hereto attached, and should there be other information which you feel disposed to give or suggestions which you think would be helpful and protective to those for whom the fund was created, you may add this in separate letter and enclose with this blank filled out. The pension fund was created as a benefit to only those who rendered service and to the widows of such. It may be possible that there are some whose names should not be on the pension roll because faithful, loyal service was not rendered. If you know of such you are requested to so inform the Pension Commission.

There are numbers of instances where inquiries have been made of the Pension Department to know the name of any one who served in a particular Company or Regiment. These are usually in cases where some soldier or the widow of a soldier cannot make proof of the soldiers service and is endeavoring to locate some comrade who served in same command to use as a witness. With the facts furnished by your answers it will enable us to give this information and thereby no doubt enable some worthy ones to be placed on the rolls of this State and of other states who are now kept off the rolls for want of proper proof of service or knowledge of where the same could be obtained. Again your personal statements regarding your service might prove a matter of protective information to your wife if she survive you, on her making application to be placed on the roll as your widow. It would be also a source of recorded information to your children. The law requires further that a report be made to the Governor showing all the acts and operations of the Pension Commission under the pension law and a list of all the pensioners of the State, with as full statement as practicable of soldier's service, and this report is to be published. You will readily see, then, the urgent need why your statements should be as full as possible.

In giving your present address be careful to give post office, county and state, and if living on rural route state number, and if in a city give street address.

Write your answers plainly. If you are unable to write, get some one to fill out the blanks for you.

Thanking you for an immediate compliance with this request by promptly filling out answers to the questions submitted, I am,

Yours very truly,

CHAS. E. McCALL,
Chief Examiner of Accounts.

Give your full name Sampson V. Scurlock

Your complete postoffice address Masena, Alabama, Bibb County

Your number on pension roll .... In what county did you live when you were first placed on the roll? Jefferson County

In what other states have you lived, and when? Lived in no other State

.... When did you move to Alabama? Borned

Where were you born? Place Tallassee, County Tallapoosa State Alabama

When were you born? Month June, Day 17, Year 1841. Where did you enlist? Tallassee When did you enlist? March 1861

In what branch of the service? 1st Artillery

What was your rank? Pvt. Soldier, letter of your Company? B

What was the number of your Regiment? 1st Bat. Was it an Alabama Regiment? Ala. Bat.

If not, give name of state

What was the name of your Captain? Capt Julius A. Law

What was the name of your Colonel? at time enlistment no Colonel

By what other name was your Company called? no other name

By what other name was your Regiment called? no other name

Name some of the battles in which you took part Kennesaw Mt. Ga. Jonesboro, Ga Franklin Tenn.

(Over)

FORM A

439-115-7M

For Use of Soldiers who are in Indigent Circumstances

THE STATE OF TEXAS

County of Harris

I, Daniel Norman Scurlock do hereby make application to the Commissioner of Pensions for a pension to be granted me under the Act passed by the 33rd Legislature of the State of Texas, and approved April 7, 1913, on the following grounds:

I enlisted and served in the military service of the Confederate States during the war between the States of the United States, and that I did not desert the Confederate service, but during said war I was loyal and true to my duty, and never at any time voluntarily abandoned my post of duty in the said service; or (that I was in the service of the State of Texas during the war, to protect said State against the Indians and Mexicans for more than 6 months). That I was honorably discharged ~~or surrendered~~ Paroled at Meridian Miss. & Was captured at Blakley, Ala & was taken Ship Island & then taken to Meridian & paroled

(Give date and cause.)

that I have been a bona fide citizen of this State since prior to January 1, A. D. 1900, and have been continuously since a citizen of the State of Texas. I do further state that I do not hold any National, State, city or county office which pays me a salary or fees of $300.00 per annum, nor have I an income from any other employment or other source whatever which amounts to $300.00 per annum, nor do I receive from any source whatever money or other means of support amounting in value to the sum of $300.00 per annum, nor do I own in my own right, nor does any one hold in trust for my benefit or use, nor does my wife own, nor does any one hold in trust for my wife, estate or property, either real, personal or mixed, either in fee or for life, of the assessed value of over one thousand dollars, exclusive of a home of the value of not more than $1000.00; nor do I receive any aid or pension from any other State, or from the United States, or from any other source, and that I am not an inmate of the Confederate Home, and I do further state that the answers given to the following questions are true:

1. What is your age? 69. Will be 70 in May 1916
2. Where were you born? Alabama.
3. How long have you resided in Texas? Since 1874.
4. In what county do you reside? Harris Co.
5. How long have you resided in said county, and what is your postoffice address? Since 1874. 1411 Chaise St. c/o Mrs M.L. Reive, Houston Texas.
6. Have you applied for a pension under the Confederate pension law and been rejected? If rejected, state when and where No
7. What is your occupation, if able to engage in one? laborer What is your physical condition? Had Silappe lately which left me in poor health
8. In what State was the command in which you served organized? Alabama
9. How long did you serve? Give, if possible, the date of enlistment and discharge. Oct 1863 to close of war.
10. What was the letter of your company, number of battalion, regiment or battery? Co "A" 62nd Ala Regt, Jas. Armstrong Captain
11. If transferred from one command to another, give time of transfer, name of command and time of service. No.
12. What branch of the service did you enlist in—infantry, cavalry, artillery or navy? Infantry.

(TX)

32440

16 May 1869 – Transcription of Priestly Norman Scurlock's only surviving letter. It was preserved because of Priestly's lesson to his nephew William on the family history of the Scurlocks. William was his brother Daniel Norman Scurlock's son.

In reference to Priestly's letter and the fact that he was the father of Josiah Gordon "Doc" Scurlock, he mentions Doc almost as an afterthought. At the time of the letter, Doc would have been either in Louisiana attending medical school or else he may have already gone to Mexico. In either case, it seems that since Doc was not present around the homestead, Priestly almost forgot to mention him.

"Elmore Co., Ala. May 16th 1869

Dear William,

I am glad you have waked up and thought of me, for sure enough it has been a long time since I heard from you, and I have hopes that you and Mit will keep it up as long as I live. I have not been a quarter of a mile from my house in 19 months; nothing but chills and fever; but the quantities of Quinine that was uselessly and murderously administered to me, almost destroyed my nervous system and put my head in such condition that I shall never see any more satisfaction. I have now got so I can work a little. Never use Quinine in your family if you can help it. We are all well at this time, and since you have mentioned your family, I will name mine for you. William Priestly, eldest son, who died on Dauphin Island aged 22 years, S. Van Buren, aged 28, Daniel Norman aged 23, Joshua Baldwin 15, (I should have Josiah Gordon before Josh) age 19, and John Dargan age 7. Girls: Rhoda Ann 32. Has been married twice has three children, Martha Augusta Barrow; and, Charles Edward Armstrong and Clara Cornelia.

The ordeal you spoke of is not quite past for we are now drinking the dregs and there appears to be an ocean behind yet; so so far as the justice of our cause is concerned he that doubts it ought to be Damned. I have been born a cessationist and can never be anything else. It is an inherent right born with as a part of our nature, as it is said of worm, tread on it, and [it] will turn. You spoke of retribution, that's all a fub, the party of our Government is gone and there is not the power nor the virtue to restore it. So you must begin to accommodate yourself to circumstances and be prepared for any contingency. Glad to hear from Dan. Sorry to hear of Dosh's trip, it's no go for a wise man.

I should have written to you sooner, but I wanted to see your Aunt Kitty as she is family oracle herself, but I have not seen her nor can't soon, but will do so, and add all she knows respecting our family history, for I am now going to write to you occasionally as long as I live and you will answer (I forgot part of my family history). My three youngest girls, there's Nancy Catherine 17, beautiful – a flame; Mary Caroline 13, Martha Lucena 10. So you see I have a considerable family yet. Sam has been married twice, has one child. At last advices your Aunt Kitty's family were well but taking draughts of the aforesaid revolutionary dregs.

Now for your family history. My Great-Grandfather came from Wales. William Scurlough, this way the name was originally spelt. He had three sons – William, Joshua and Mial. He accumulated considerable property, which, according to the English law of primogeniture, fell to William, his eldest son, for this was before the Revolution. Joshua was my grandfather. He married an Adams by whom he had two children – Thomas and Agnes. Thomas had sons, Dudley and Beverly, who went to Kentucky. I know nothing of their progeny. Joshua went to Georgia, married, had 3 children who all died and he followed the year. Washington re-married in Virginia, and he never communicated. I know nothing of his progeny. He (Thomas) also had a daughter who married a Thompson. Agnes married a Watts. She had three sons. Tom Thornton and Ludwell. Lud was hung in Butts Co., Ga. For killing Denton Daniels. My Grandfather next married Bettie Norman. Had children as follows: William (William joined the Revolution Army at the age of 16 and served under the command of Genl. Nathaniel Green in South Carolina), Joshua, James, Priestly and Daniel; daughters: Sarah, Bettie and Lucy. Father had sons: Daniel, John, William and Priestly; daughters: Kitty, Winifred and Caroline. They had a daughter Elizabeth who died in infancy, also a son Joshua, older than your father. He was burned up in a house. At some future time I will give you the names and ages of all your cousins with as many interesting particulars as I can gather. Uncle Josh had 4 sons and 3 daughters. Henry went to Mississippi, married and died. Napolean, (physician) was accidentally killed at Prairie Bluff while on a night visit to a patient. James and Walter are still in Florida. So is their sister Harriet Pope. Of their progeny I know nothing. Lucy died in the first bloom of womanhood. Uncle James went to Tennessee and reared a large family of sons and daughters. William and Josh, his sons, have been to see my father in Ga. Joshua was a Captain in the Florida war and was twice at my father's in Muscogee, Ga. Father thought Josh died in Florida, as he never called according to promise on his return. Daniel and Washington I never saw. Your preacher is a great grandson of Uncle James. Uncle Priestly had 2 sons at home, Jeff and Sam. Jeff died childless. Of Sam I know nothing. Eli and Jim Townsend were his two bastard sons. Jacob Parker had 2 daughters – Sarah and Mary. Next married Tom Hambrick – had sons, Joe, John, Jim, Bill and Burrell. Next married Wm. Ryan – had children; Hampton, Rysden and Elizabeth. Aunt Betty married Billy Wyatt. Had sons and daughters; John, William, James, Samuel, Jessie, Ezekiel, Wesley, Mary and Mahaney. Aunt Lucy married her cousin, Martin Norman. Had one child and both died. Would follow up the different ramifications further, but will wait until next time.

You spoke of having an interesting family, and let me [...] is by giving them a good education [...] as you can do at home, a good portion of which will [...] from your wife, and if I am rightly informed she is well qualified to second your exertion in elevating your children to an honorable station in life. William, cherish that wife as the most estimable jewel this earth affords. Tell Mit I haven't forgot her and that I shall owe her an answer [...] kind. I intend to give her a good one and if it was in my power I would relieve her, but if I [...] do no more. I write [...] a letter as possible when I replenish my stationary. Tell [...] to write and let me know if she got Jo's letter.

William, write as often as you can and tell me what you know of your Aunt Caroline and her family. Tell Dan to write me and to get all the information of her that you both can, also both of [you] give me some information of your Uncle William's family whether he left any children. I have fairly run through my [...] haven't said the [...].

Your affectionate,

P. N. Scurlock"

Elmore Co Ala May 16th 1869

Dear William

I am glad you have waked up & thought of of me, for sure enough it has been a long time since I heard from you, and I have hopes that you & Mit. will keep it up as long as I live. I have not not been a quarter of a mile from my house in 19 months, nothing but chills & fever, but the quantities of Quinine that was recklessly & murderously administered to me, almost destroyed my nervous system & put my head in such a condition that I shall never see any more satisfaction, I have now got so I can work a little, never use Quinine in your family if you can help it we are [illegible] at this time, and since you have mentioned your family I will name mine for you; William Prestly eldest son who lives in [illegible] aged 22 yrs. S Vanburen, aged 28. [illegible] Norman, aged 23. Joshua Beldon aged 15. (I should have Josiah Gordon before Joshua) aged 19 & John Dargan aged 7 yrs. Rhoena [illegible] aged 32 has been married twice has 3 children [illegible] Augusta [illegible], and Charles Edward Armstrong (and Character) — The ordeal you speak of is not quite past for we are now drinking the dregs & there appears to be an Ocean behind yet; so far as the justice of our cause is concerned [illegible] doubt it ought to be Damned, I have been born one (a secessionist) & can never be any thing else, it is an inherent right born with us a part of our nature, as it is said of worm, tread on it, and it will turn, You [illegible]

of retribution, that's all a fub, the Beauty of our Govern-
ent is gone, and there is not the power nor the Virtue to restore it, so you must begin to accommodate yourself to circumstance and be prepared for any contingency. Glad to
hear from Dan, sorry to hear of Tosh's step, it's no go for
a wise man — I should have written to you sooner, but
I wanted to see your Aunt Kitty as she is family oracle herself, but I have not seen her nor can't do so, but will
do so, and add all she knows respecting our family history, for I am ~~now~~ going to ~~you~~ write you occasionally as long
as I live & you will answer (I would [illegible] of the family
history. My 3 youngest girls there names Catherine age
17 beautiful, a flame, Mary [illegible] Martha
Lucena age 10. So you see I have a [illegible] able family yet. Sam has been married [illegible] children
at last advices your Aunt Kitty [illegible] best talking
draughts of the aforesaid [illegible],
Now for your He[illegible]
My Great Grandfather came from Wales [illegible]
this way the name was originally [illegible] 3 Sons
William, Joshua & Abijah. he accumulated a
considerable property, which according to the English
Law of Primogeniture fell to William the eldest son
for this was before the Revolution. Joshua was my
Grandfather, he married an Adams [illegible] he had 2
children Thomas, and Agnes, Thomas had Sons
Dudley & Beverly to Kentucky and I [illegible] their

[illegible] was Virginia.

[illegible] went to Georgia & married had 3 children who all [illegible] and followed in the same year, Washington remained in Virginia [illegible] never communicated I know nothing nor his progeny, he also had a daughter who married a Thompson, Agnes a Watts who had 3 sons Tom, Thornton & Caldwell, Lud ~~[illegible]~~ Dinah Daniel. The Grandfather next married Betty Norman, had Children as follows, William, Joshua, James Presley, & Daniel, Daughters Sarah, Betsey, Lucy, Father had sons Daniel, John, William & Priestly, daughters, Kitty, Winifred, Caroline, they had a daughter Elizabeth who died in infancy, also a son Joshua ~~older than your Pa~~ who was [illegible] in a [illegible], at some future time I will give you the names & ages [illegible] all our [illegible] with as many interesting particulars as [illegible], Uncle John had 4 sons 3 daughters, Henry went to [illegible] & died, Napoleon [illegible] was accidentally killed at Prairie [illegible] while on a night visit to a patient, James & Walton [illegible] Harriet Pope, of their progeny [illegible] Lucy [illegible] the first bloom of womanhood Uncle [illegible] a large family of sons & daughters, [illegible] had [illegible] to Georgia [illegible] my father Joshua was [illegible] my grandfather in [illegible] Co [illegible] Joshua died in Florida as [illegible] according [illegible] Daniel & [illegible] I never saw, your Preacher is a great grandson of [illegible] James [illegible], Uncle Presly had 2 son at home Jef & Sam, Jef died childless, Sam I know nothing, Eli & [illegible] Townsend were ~~[illegible]~~, Uncle Daniel married, but died childless, Aunt Sarah had husband, Jacob Parker, had 2 [illegible] revolutionary, at the age of [illegible] when the war was about half through [illegible] of the Southern army he was detached to Green and [illegible] end of the war, I had forgot till I had closed but [illegible] next time

[illegible]

Jo. John, Jim, Bill & Burrell, Married Wm Ryan, had Chil[illegible] Hampton, Rysden, & Elizabeth, Aunt Betsey Married Wyatt, had sons & daughters John, William, James, Samu[illegible] Jesse, Ezekiel, Wesley, & Mary Mahaney. Aunt Lucy [illegible] her Cousin Martin Forman, had a child & both died

I would follow up the different many Ramifications further but I will wait till next time

you spoke of having an interesting family, and let me [illegible] education [illegible] you can do at home, a good portion of which will devolve upon your wife, and if I am rightly informed she is well [illegible] to second your exertion in elevating your children to an honorable station in life, William, Cherish that wife the most [illegible] Jewell this earth affords

Tell [illegible] that I haven't forgot her and that I [illegible] owe her an answer her kind, I intend to give her a good one and if it was in my power I would relieve her, but if I can do no more I will [illegible] a [illegible] letter as possible when I replenish my stationary, tell her still to write & let me know if she got Jo's letter

William write as often as you can and tell me what you know of your aunt Caroline & her family, tell [illegible] to write me & to get all the information of her that you both can, also both of give me some information of your Uncle William's family whether he left any children, I have fairly run through my & having [illegible] the [illegible]

Your affectionate

P. N. Scurlock

March 1910 – Transcription of letter written by William Lafayette Scurlock, the recipient of the previous letter from Priestly Scurlock, to his niece Minnie Scurlock Cook. It appears that both Priestly and William begin their genealogies with the Reverend William Scurlock and don't include William's father Thomas and grandfather Michael, the immigrant. Of course, William Lafayette was getting his history from his Uncle Priestly. (William Lafayette Scurlock was Josiah Gordon Scurlock's first cousin).

"Dear Niece:

Yours of Feb 20th received some time ago. I would have answered sooner, but have been too unwell; to tell the facts, I am almost an invalid. I have not been a mile from Corrigan for several months. Physically I am broken down, a mere wreck, so to speak, and you will have to excuse me for negligence. Lissie did not go to Shreveport last year, but went to Dallas to my son John's widow's. She did not go up the H. E. & W. T. RR any further than Nacogdoches.

Now, I will tell you all I know about our ancestral line. The first Scurlock to come to America was named William and was from Wales. He settled in Spotsylvania Co., Virginia. He had three sons, William, Mial, and Joshua. Joshua was the father of my Grandfather, who was named William. Joshua, my Great Grandfather and William his son, my Grandfather, fought through the Revolutionary War, and were at the battles of King's Mountain, Cowpens, and Hangingrock, once called Judgment Day with the Tories. My Father, Daniel Scurlock was born 4th of June 1799. Was in Creek Indian War in Alabama, He died young, died in January 1838.

I had an uncle, Priestly N. Scurlock, who was in the Mexican War in 1846 & 47. He died in Washington Co., Texas in 1877. He intended to come to see me, but I received the news of his death, when was looking for him. He had an extraordinary education for people raised in his time. He taught school all his life.

My mother's maiden name was Turk. I never knew but little about them. Her mother's maiden name was Johnston (Irish). Came from Belfast, North Ireland. They were all Baptists and Presbyterians. I have heard my mother speak of him, (her Grandfather) William Johnston, so often. She says he was one of the most accomplished gentlemen she ever saw. He had a son, Uncle Albert Johnston, who used to live in Marshall, Texas; and from there he moved to Panola County. He died at, or near Carthage, 30 or 35 years ago. Your Uncle Dosh (T. J. Scurlock) thought was never such a man as Uncle Albert Johnston. After he (Dosh Scurlock) got back from the war, he stayed a while with us down here, and said he had to see Uncle Albert. He bought him a horse here and put out for Marshall, Texas.

My Mother's Grandfather, William Johnston, was with General Greene at Eutaw Springs. Your Uncle Dosh was assassinated about 50 or 60 miles from Tuxpan, Mexico, but I have forgotten the name of the place. If you will write to J. Tissier, Tuxpan, Mexico, he can give you all information about his death. Dosh lived some time after he was shot, and sent for Tissier. We got something over two hundred dollars apiece during your Father's lifetime. And last year I got $6.54 apiece from J. Tissier; it was for box surgical instruments $20.00, One saddle 5.00, One pistol 15.00, One lot drugs 10.00, $50.00 in Mexican money. It was exchanged at Laredo. Got money order for $24.16 and notified Claude and he ordered me to keep it for tax on your land here. I am tired and will close. Lizzie and Woodson send love to you and family. With love to all the family I close.

Your uncle,
W. L. Scurlock"

Letter written by Doc's niece Susan Jospehine Scurlock McCord, the daughter of Sampson Van Buren Scurlock, date unknown. Susan died in 1952 and this was likely recorded by her in the years prior to her death. This shows how little the Scurlocks of Alabama knew about Doc's life. Susan also seems to make an error on the marriage date of Sampson and his wife Mary. It's also doubtful that Esther Ann Brown's father Nathan Brown was Jewish. Doc is known as Joe in the family.

"Back in the 18th century a Jewish lad came to America, his name was Brown. I don't know what his given name was but he married Ann Holsomback and that they raised a family. Their children was Easter Ann Brown, John Brown. The Scurlocks was English. Priestly Norman Scurlock married Easter Ann Brown and they raised a large family. There was Billie, Sam, Josh, Johnnie and Joe, Rhoady Ann, Mary Ann, Nannie and Loucine. Billie was killed in the Civil War. Sam married and stayed in Ala, so did Nannie. The rest left Ala and went to Texas. Rhoady married James Armstrong. Nannie married James Dunn. Mary Ann married Jack Smith. Loucine married in Texas. I don't know her married name. Josh and Johnnie both in Texas. Joe married a Mexican girl in Mexico. Sam married Mary Elizabeth Willis and they raised a large family. They were married November the 19, 1864. Their children Mary Elizabeth, Loudella, Susan Josephine, William Bee, Georgia, Nannie, Simon, Dan and Joe. This is all I can give on the Scurlock family."

Back in 18th century a grand
Jewish ... came to america his name
was ... Brown I dont know what his
given name was but he married —
ann Holtom Hosenback and
tha raised a family
thare children was Easter ann
Brown John Brown the Scurlock
Was English Priesly Woman Scurlock
maried Easter ann Brown and
tha raid a larg fammely thare was
Billie, Sam, Josh, Johnnie and Joe,
Rhoady ann Mary ann Nannie
and Loucine Billie was killed in
the Civil War Sam maried and
Stayed in ala so did Nannie
the rest Left ala and went to texas
Rhoady maried 1 James Armstrong
Mainie Maried 1 James Dunn
Mary ann Maried Jack Smith
Loucine Marred in texas

2

I doant know her Maried name
Josh and Johnie batte in texas
Joe maried a mexican Girl in
mexico Sam Marrie
Mary Elizybeth Willis and tha
Raisd a large Family tha we
maried November the 19 1867
Thare Children Mary Elizybeth
Loodella Susie Josefine Willi Ben
Georgia Nannie Simon Dan
and Joe this is all I can give over the
[illegible] Surlocks Family

PART IV – DOCUMENTATION OF DOC DURING HIS LIFE

Santa Fe Weekly New Mexican, Tuesday, 7 Oct 1873. It doesn't mention Doc, but recounts the death of Alexander "Newt" Huggins. The fifth line reads, "They have killed Huggins, . . . scalped him and cut his nose off".

From a letter of P. Schwartze, Esq., dated Sept. [illegible] at Roswell, N. M., we extract the following: "The Indians have left the Fort Stanton reservation, and are committing depredations around here. They have killed Huggins, (buckboard driver who used to drive a year ago) scalped him and cut his nose off. This occurred near John Chisum's place. They also killed a man down at Seven Rivers and scalped him. They have been seen within a few miles of this place, and we are in dread of their paying us a visit. We have some good stock here, but keep it under lock and key; they have left pretty much the Mexicans that are down here afoot, and have fought a party of twenty-five men for two nights, but did not get away with any of their stock, etc."

***Santa Fe Daily New Mexican*, Saturday, 15 May 1875**

"From the *Arizona Citizen* we copy:

We received information too late for last week's issue, that a young man by the name of J. G. Scurlock, usually known as Doc Scurlock, a little previous to the 11th instant, stole three horses, two saddles and a gun from parties living in New Mexico, and made his way to Arizona. He is described as being 22 years of age, between five feet eight or ten inches high, light hair, light complexion, front teeth out, writes a very good hand, quick spoken, and usually makes a good impression on first acquaintance."

Santa Fe *Daily New Mexican*, 11 Sep 1876

FATAL ACCIDENT AT LINCOLN.—On Saturday evening of last week, the 2nd inst., a correspondent informs us, while J. G. Scurlock and Mike G. Harkins were examining a self-cocking revolver in L. G. Murphy & Co.'s carpenter shop, in Lincoln, Lincoln County, New Mexico, the pistol was discharged, the ball striking Harkins under the left nipple, killing him instantly. Immediately afterward a Coroner's inquest was held and a verdict rendered in conformity with the above facts. Mr. Scurlock was examined before Judge Wilson and discharged. The two were warm friends, and none can regret the unfortunate accident more than Mr. S. A post mortem examination was held by Doctors Cabello and McLean. The corpse was afterwards embalmed and buried in Major Murphy's burying ground, Major Brady reading the Church of England burial service at the grave.

It is reported that Lucas Gallegos was found dead, in Lincoln county, on the 2d inst., with a bullet hole through him, but at the time of our correspondent's writing this report could not be traced to a reliable source.

The bottom article from the Santa Fe *Daily New Mexican* is dated 12 Sep 1876. Although it doesn't mention Doc by name, it was he who accidentally shot and killed Mike Harkins.

DAILY NEW MEXICAN : SEPTEMBER 12, 1876, SANT

which has been occupying the attention of the bullies and bruisers of the country for many weeks past. Nobody killed. Allen has been arrested.

☞ There are dozens of pear, apple and plum trees in this neighborhood that can beat the Mesilla News' last count.

☞ The military hay stack is assuming mammoth proportions, as well as their winter's wood pile.

☞ Col. John H. Riley has just returned from a visit to St. Louis, where he has been attending the letting of the Government contracts for furnishing the Indian Agencies in New Mexico with beef, and informs us that Col. Wm. Rosenthall of this city got the contract for the Territory.

Accidental Killing.

By advices from Lincoln, we learn of the accidental killing of a young gentleman named M. J. Harkins, who was very favorably known in Lincoln county. Lately he was in charge of Mr. J. H. Rileys, business in the neighborhood, of what is known as "Blazers Mill," and we have a right to saying that his untimely death will be deeply regretted.

It may be a consolation to his friends to know that an unusual amount of attention was paid to the care of his remains, and that he now rests in a place consecrated to the last home of good men.

Three cases against Doc from 9 Oct 1876 (Cases 220, 226, and 230).

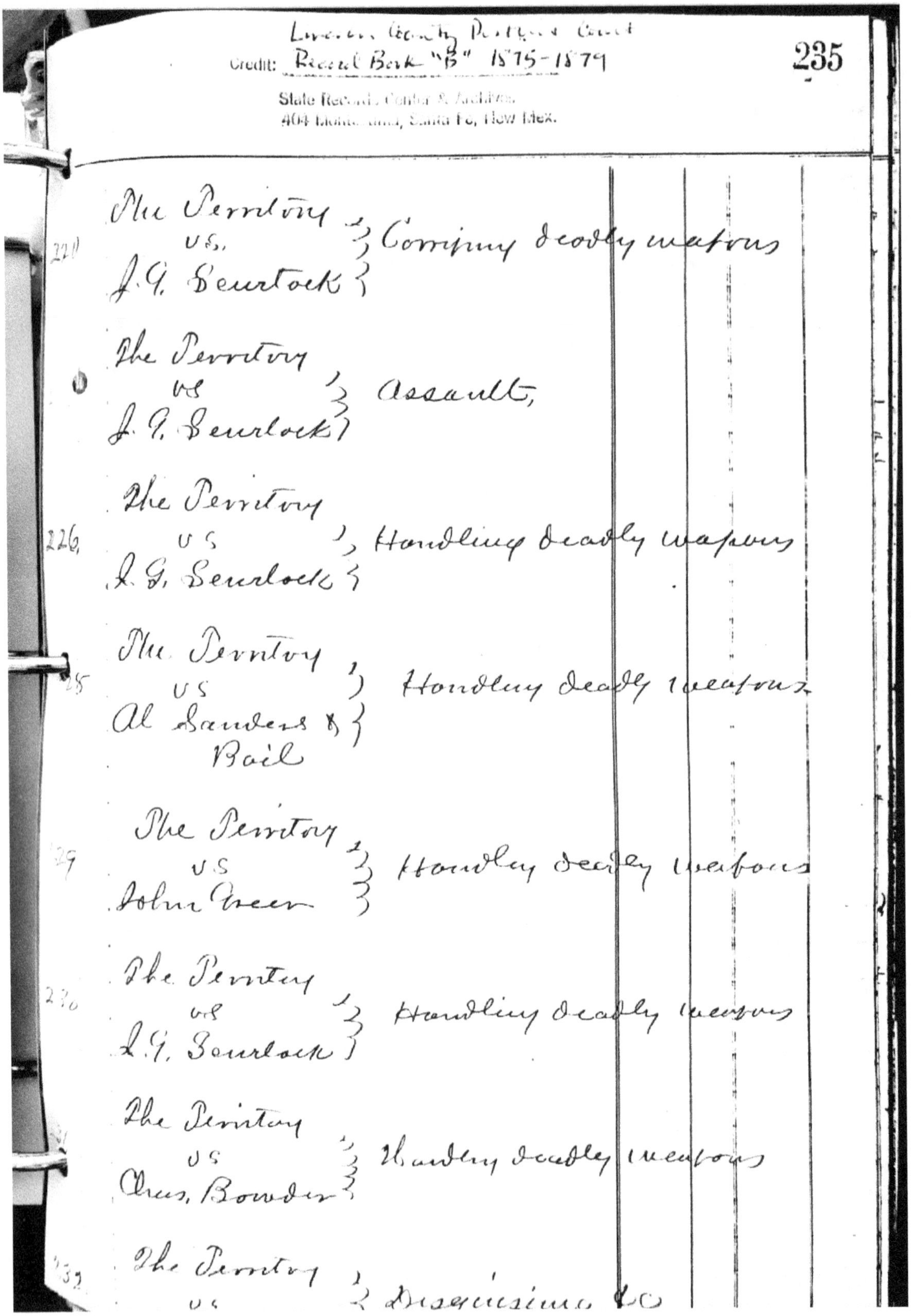

Lincoln County Probate Court
Credit: Record Book "B" 1875-1879
235
State Records Center & Archives
404 Montezuma, Santa Fe, New Mex.

220 The Territory vs. J.G. Scurlock } Carrying deadly weapons

The Territory vs J.G. Scurlock } Assault,

226 The Territory vs J.G. Scurlock } Handling deadly weapons

228 The Territory vs Al Sanders & Bail } Handling deadly weapons

229 The Territory vs John Green } Handling deadly weapons

230 The Territory vs J.G. Scurlock } Handling deadly weapons

231 The Territory vs Chas. Bowdre } Handling deadly weapons

232 The Territory vs } Disturbing &c

220

THE TERRITORY OF NEW MEXICO

VS.

J. G. Scurlock,

Carrying deadly weapons

INFORMATION

BY THE

DISTRICT ATTORNEY.

Filed in open court this 9th day of October 1876

John S. Crouch
Clerk.

WITNESSES.

Jose Montaño

Florencio Gonzales

Juan B. Patron

Credit: Lincoln County District Court Criminal Case #220 (1876)

Criminal Case #220

1of2

Case #220
2 of 2

Territory of New Mexico, } In the District Court at the October Term,
County of Lincoln } A. D. 1876

Be it remembered that ~~John D. Bail~~ A. J. Fountain acting, Esq., District Attorney for the 3d Judicial District of the Territory of New Mexico, who prosecutes for the Territory in this behalf, in his own proper person comes here into the said District Court, and before the Court itself at the term aforesaid for the county aforesaid and for the said Territory gives the court here to understand and be informed that J. G. Scurlock, late of the county of Lincoln Territory of New Mexico, on the 8th day of ~~April~~ Oct. in the year of our Lord one thousand eight hundred and seventy Six, at the county of Lincoln aforesaid did unlawful carry on and about his person, within a settlement of this Territory, a certain pistol called a revolver the same then and there being a deadly weapon, he the said J. G. Scurlock not then and there carrying the said pistol called a revolver in the lawful defense of himself, nor in the lawful defense of his property nor his family (the same being then and and there threatened with danger) nor by order of legal authority, nor on his own landed property, nor in the execution of an order of Court

contrary to the form of the statute in such case made and provided, and against the peace and dignity of the Territory of New Mexico.

A. J. Fountain
Acting
District Attorney 3d Judicial District
for the Territory of New Mexico.

p. 172

226

THE TERRITORY OF NEW MEXICO

VS.

J. G. Scurlock

Handling deadly weapons

INFORMATION

BY THE

DISTRICT ATTORNEY.

Filed in open court this 9th day of October, 1876

John Sherman

Clerk.

WITNESSES.

George Gwin

Pantaleon Gallegos

p. 172

Lincoln County District Court
Criminal Case #226 (1876)

Criminal Case # 226
p. 2 of 2

Territory of New Mexico, } In the District Court at the October Term,
County of Lincoln } A. D. 1876

Be it remembered that ~~John D. Bail, Esq.,~~ A. J. Fountain Acting District Attorney for the 3d Judicial District of the Territory of New Mexico, who prosecutes for the Territory in this behalf, in his own proper person comes here into the said District Court, and before the Court itself at the term aforesaid for the county aforesaid and for the said Territory gives the court here to understand and be informed that J. G. Scurlock, late of the county of Lincoln Territory of New Mexico, on the first day of September in the year of our Lord one thousand eight hundred and seventy six, at the county of Lincoln aforesaid did then and there, unlawfully handle a certain pistol, called a revolver, loaded and charged with gunpowder and divers leaden bullets, the same then and being a deadly weapon, in a threatening manner at and towards one Michael ~~Hawkins~~ Harkins, he the said J. G. Scurlock not then and there handling the said pistol as aforesaid in the lawful defense of himself his family or property, nor by order of legal authority,

contrary to the form of the statute in such case made and provided, and against the peace and dignity of the Territory of New Mexico.

A. J. Fountain
Acting District Attorney 3d Judicial District for the Territory of New Mexico.

230

THE TERRITORY OF NEW MEXICO

VS.

J. G. Scurlock

Handling deadly weapons

INFORMATION

BY THE

DISTRICT ATTORNEY.

Filed in open court this 9th

day of October 1876

John Newcomb

Clerk.

WITNESSES.

Marcus ~~[illegible]~~ Boell

E. E. Carey

R. M. Gilbert

E. B. Peters

Credits Lincoln County District Court Criminal Case No. 230 (1876)

p. 1 of 2

Criminal Case # 230
p. 2 of 2

Territory of New Mexico, } In the District Court at the October Term,
County of Lincoln } A. D. 1876

Be it remembered that ~~John D. Bail, Esq.~~ A. J. Fountain acting District Attorney for the 3d Judicial District of the Territory of New Mexico, who prosecutes for the Territory in this behalf, in his own proper person comes here into the said District Court, and before the Court itself at the term aforesaid for the county aforesaid and for the said Territory gives the court here to understand and be informed that J. G. Scurlock, late of the county of Lincoln Territory of New Mexico, on the 15th day of May in the year of our Lord one thousand eight hundred and seventy six, at the county of Lincoln aforesaid did then and there unlawfully draw a certain gun called a rifle on one Martin Baca, and that he the said J. G. Scurlock did then and there unlawfully handle the said gun (the same being then and there a deadly weapon) at and towards the said Martin Baca in a threatening manner,

contrary to the form of the statute in such case made and provided, and against the peace and dignity of the Territory of New Mexico.

A. J. Fountain
Acting District Attorney 3d Judicial District
for the Territory of New Mexico.

Lincoln New Mexico, 16 Aug 1877

"EDITORS INDEPENDENT.

We are having a terrible time with the lawless element from your County and with others of the same class amongst us. On the 6th inst. a portion of the outfit including Frank Freeman and Charles Bowder came into this town and kicked up a row. Their animosity was particularly directed against John S. Chisum who was at the house of Mr. McSween. They fired a number of shots into McSween's house and endangered the lives of all who were there; afterwards they started to Major Murphy's, when fortunately Major Brady the Sheriff arrived on the ground with a warrant issued for their arrest by Judge Wilson. They tried to kill the Sheriff but Freeman was secured and taken before Judge Wilson who committed him in default of $1000, bail. Freeman had previously shot and wounded a Sargent from Fort Stanton. Freeman succeeded in making his escape while enroute to Fort Stanton.

The Sheriff and posse then got after the gang and found them on the Ruidosa where a fight took place the particulars of which have not yet been received here, except, that Frank Freeman was killed, and others including Doc. Scurlock were captured.

The troops are out after the outlaws. Nelson from the Gila is here with the band; he says he is going to help the outfit burn the town. I tell you we are now having a death struggle with these outlaws; but right and Justice is bound to prevail. We are tired of being run over by outlaws and are determined to maintain out rights henceforth. Sheriff Brady deserves great credit for the prompt action in this matter. He is now on the track of the gang outlaws and you may look out for them your way soon as it is getting too sickly for them here."

Lincoln County Correspondence, Hondo, 16 Aug 1877

"EDITORS INDEPENDENT.

On Tuesday morning four horses were stolen from Martin Sanches ranch at the crossing of the Hondo some 30 miles east of Lincoln. Two belonged to Dow the Mail Contractor, one belonged to Jacob Harris, and one to Cosme Sedillos. Sheriff Brady and his *posse* had a fight with outlaws on the Ruidosa. Freeman was killed by the posse and Scurlock and another was captured. The Country is alive with outlaws from Grant and Dona Ana Counties. A man named Nelson is said to be in the lead.

OBSERVER."

***Mesilla Independent*, Saturday, 8 Sep 1877. While Doc isn't mentioned by name, this article tells more of the story of Bowdre and Freeman's drunken rampage through Lincoln which resulted in the arrest of Doc and George Coe. Philip Rasch cites this article in Man of Many Parts.**

THE MESILLA VALLEY

INDEPENDENT.

Vol. I. Mesilla, New Mexico, Saturday, September 8, 1877. No. 12

Professional Cards.

THE BANDITTI IN LINCOLN COUNTY.

Upon arriving at this place the sheriff deployed his men on each side of the creek, his presence was soon discovered by Freeman who rushed out and fired at Brady—and missed—he then sprang on his horse which stood ready saddled, in an instant the horse fell riddled with bullets. Freeman still unhurt endeavored to make his escape through a corn field firing as he retreated; he was pursued and killed. Bowdre escaped by wading down the bed of the stream, others of the party were captured and taken to Lincoln where they were examined and committed for trial.

***Mesilla Independent*, Saturday, 22 Sep 1877**

"THE BANDITTI AGAIN

Mr. Richard Brewer, a well known citizen of Lincoln county arrived at Las Cruces on Thursday from his ranch on the Ruidosa. He reports that in the early part of the week the notorious Jesse Evans and a companion in crime whose name we did not learn, stole four fine horses from Mr. Brewer's rancho. Two of the stolen animals belonged to Mr. Brewer, and two were the property of Mr. Widenman. The animals were taken in daylight and in Mr. Brewer's presence. Mr. B., having obtained assistance followed the thieves who came in the direction of San Nicholas; upon arriving at the place Brewer left his posse with directions to continue following the trail and he came into Las Cruces and obtained a warrant for the arrest of Evans and his companion. On Thursday night one of the *posse* sent word in to Mr. Brewer that Evans and his companion had been captured at San Augustine with the stolen stock in their possession. A word about San Augustine that we have long intended to say may as well be said right here. That place has the reputation of being the headquarters the haunt and the rendezvous of the worst gang of cut-throats that ever cursed any civilized community with its presence. The mountains and canons in its vicinity afford hiding places for stolen stock, and lurking places for the banditti that have been plundering the citizens of Dona Ana and Lincoln counties. Our authorities have for some time had an eye on this den, and it is about time they took steps towards breaking it up. A thorough search of the canons on the east side of the Organ mountains would not prove unprofitable to persons who have had stock stolen from them in Dona Ana and Lincoln counties during the past year.

LATER – Mssrs. Scurlock and Bowdry who accompanied Mr. Brewer, arrived in town this morning, they report that they went to San Augustine and found the four stolen horses at the house of W. F. Shedd in possession of Jessie Evans, Nicolas Provencio, Frank Beker, Tom Hill and three others of the band. They demanded the horses; the thieves refused to deliver them saying in effect that they had been at too much trouble to get them. Finding it impossible to take the animals, the two men came in town and reported; and thus the matter stands.

These Banditti are well armed and mounted. They are here in our country openly defying the laws. It appears that they cannot be arrested, *and they know it*. There is no telling who may be their next victim."

The previous article documents what might be considered one of the early seeds of what would become the Regulators. Also, you must regard the posse of Doc, Bowdre, Ab Saunders, Joe Howard, and John Jones in the Meras, Gonzales, Chihuahua and Largo killings. Further documenting this event is the register from Doc, Charlie, and Dick staying at the Corn Exchange Hotel in La Mesilla, New Mexico on 22 Sep 1877.

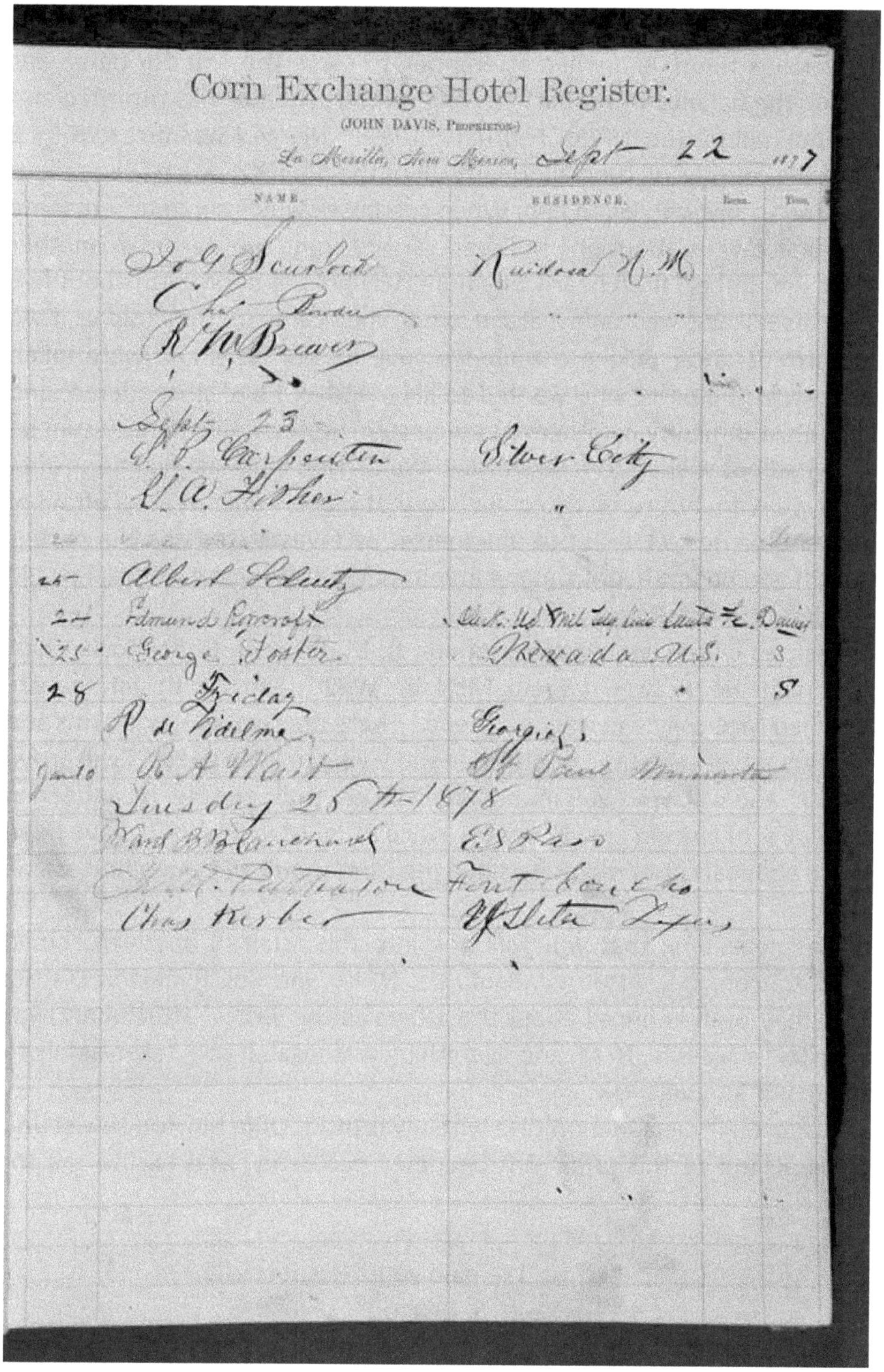
Corn Exchange Hotel Register.
(JOHN DAVIS, PROPRIETOR.)
La Mesilla, New Mexico, Sept 22 1877

NAME.	RESIDENCE.
Jos G Scurlock	Ruidoso N. M.
Chs Bowdre	"
R M Brewer	
Sept 23	
S. P. Carpenter	Silver City
G. A. Hether	"
Albert Schultz	
Edmund Ryecroft	
George Foster	Nevada U.S.
Friday	
R de Ridelman	Georgia
R A Wait	St Paul Minnesota
Tuesday 25 th 1878	
Ward B Blanchard	El Paso
Chas Kerber	Ysleta Texas

South Spring River, N. M. 8 Mar 1878. Morton's letter to his cousin.

"Dear Sir:

Some time since I was called upon to assist in serving a writ of attachment on some property, wherein resistance has been made against the law. The parties had started off with some horses which should be attached, and I, as Deputy Sheriff with a posse of twelve men was sent in pursuit of same, overtook them, and while attempting to serve the writ our party was fired on by one J. H. Tunstall, the balance of his party having ran off. The fire was returned and Tunstall was killed. This happened on the 18th of February. The 6th March I was arrested by a constable party, accused of the murder of Tunstall. Nearly all of the Sheriff's posse fired at him and it is impossible for anyone to say who killed him. When the posse which came to arrest me and one man was with me first saw us about one hundred yards distant, we started in another direction when they (eleven in number) fired nearly one hundred shots at us. We ran about five miles when both of our horses fell and we made a stand, when they came up they told us if we gave up they would not harm us: after talking a while we gave up our arms and were taken prisoners. There was one man in the party who wanted to kill me after I had surrendered, and was restrained with the greatest difficulty by others of the party. The constable himself said he was sorry we gave up as he had not wished to take us alive. We arrived here last night en-route to Lincoln I have heard that we were not to be taken alive to that place, I am not at all afraid of their killing me, but if they should do so I wish that the matter be investigated and the parties dealt with according to law. If you do not hear from me in four days after receipt of this, I would like you to make inquiries about the affair.

The names of the parties who have me arrested are, R. M. Bruer, J. G. Scurlock, Chas. Bowdre, Wm. Bonney (Godrich!) Henry Brown, Frank McNab, "Wayt", Sam Smith, Jim French, Middleton (and another named McClosky and who is a friend.) There are two parties in arms and violence expected, the military are at the scene of disorder and trying to keep peace. I will arrive at Lincoln the night of the 10th and will write you immediately if I get through safe. Have been in the employ of Jas. J. Dolan & Co. of Lincoln for 18 months, since 9th of March of 1877 have been getting $60 per month, have about six hundred dollars due me from them, and some horses etc. at their cattle camps.

I hope, if it becomes necessary, that you will look into this affair, if anything should happen I refer you to T. B. Catron, U.S. Attorney, Santa Fe, N. M. and Col. Rynerson District Attorney La Messila, N. M. they both know all about the affairs as the writ of attachment was issued by Judge Warren Bristol La Messila, N. M. and everything was legal. If I am taken safely to Lincoln I will have no trouble but let you know.

If it should be as I suspect. Please communicate with my brother Quin Morton Lewisburg, W. V. Hoping that you will attend to this affair if it becomes necessary, and excuse me for troubling you if it does not.

I remain yours Respectfully,
W. S. Morton"

The original letter which has a provenance of Jarvis Garrett to Robert McCubbin.

[illegible]

South Spring River N. M.

Mch. 8 1878.

[illegible]

Some time since I was called upon to assist in serving a writ of attachment on some property where resistance has been made against the law.
The parties had started off with some horses which should be attached, and I as deputy Sheriff with a posse of twelve men was sent in pursuit of same we overtook them and while attempting to serve the writ our party was fired on by one J.H. Tunstall the balance of his party having ran off. The fire was returned and Tunstall was killed, this happened on the 18th of February. The 6th March I was arrested by a Constable party accused of the murder of Tunstall. Nearly all of the sheriff's posse fired at him and it is impossible for any one to say who killed him. When the posse which came to arrest me and one man who was with me, first saw us

Major Maurice J. Fulton
N.M.M.I.
Roswell
N.M.

Territory of New Mexico, County of Lincoln, Apr 1878.

"In the District Court at the April Term A. D. 1878

Be it remembered that W. L. Rynerson . . . comes here into the said District Court . . . and gives the Court here to understand and be informed that Atanacio Martines and Doc Scurlock, John Middleton and William Bonny alias "Kid" and Samuel Smith, and Samuel Corbett and Frank Coe and George Coe and George Washington and George Robinson and Ignacio Gonzales and Jesus Rodriques and Esiquio Sanches and Roman Bargan and Frank McNab and "Wayt" and --- Edwards and divers others persons whose names are to said District Attorney unknown each and all of said persons being late of the County of Lincoln Territory of New Mexico on the twentieth day of February in the years of our Lord one thousand eight hundred and seventy eight at the County of Lincoln aforesaid in the Territory aforesaid did assemble together with intent then and there unlawfully with force and violence to take from one William Brady Sheriff of said county certain property to wit one house and lot known as the Lincoln County bank and McSween Store building there situate and one iron safe and divers goods chattles in said store building . . . and unlawfully and forcibly did obstruct the Sheriff William Brady in the execution of his office as Sheriff and then and there did unlawfully and forcibly take from the said William Brady . . . the possession of the property aforesaid . . .

W. L. Rynerson
District Attorney
3rd Jud Dist"

***Mesilla Independent*, Saturday, 13 Apr 1878.**

"LINCOLN COUNTY ITEMS

At a Coroner's inquest held on the body of Andrew L. Roberts, who was killed at Blazer's mill on the 4th inst the jury found that the deceased came to his death from gun shot wounds at the hands of Richard Bruer, Charles Bowdry, 'Doc' Scurlock, Waite, Middleton, McKnabbe, John Scroggins, Stephen Stephens, George Coe, Frank Coe and W .H. Antrim, alias 'The Kid'.

Our readers will remember that in our report of the killing of Baker and Morton we stated that Morton, while a prisoner in the hands of Bruer and his party, registered a letter at Roswell, after which he was taken out and killed. The following is a true copy of the letter written on that occasion. It will be observed that Morton anticipated being killed. The letter was directed to H. H. Marshall, a prominent lawyer at Richmond, Virginia, and was received by him March 25th. The letter gives Morton's version of the killing of Tunstall, the act of which precipitated the Lincoln County war."

Depositions of James Longwell and Robert Widenmann probably about 18 Apr 1878.

Territory of New Mexico }
County of Santa Fe } ss

James J. Longwill being duly sworn says that he is the person who was deputized by the late Sheriff Brady of Lincoln County for the purpose of guarding and protecting the goods & chattels attached under and by virtue of a writ of attachment issued out of the 3d District Court in favor of Fritz & Scholand against A A McSween, and which goods were in a house at Lincoln Lincoln County, known as the Tunstall store house, and consisted of a general stock of merchandise and bank property, safe, fixtures &c

I knew J H Tunstall he came into the store while we were making the inventory with a man called Widderman and made threats against the Sheriff telling the Sheriff that he was taking his Tunstall property for McSweens debts, that he would make all of the party suffer for it hereafter and that they had better look out, both Tunstall and Widderman were armed with revolvers, and two of Tunstalls party called "Kid" & "Waite" came up to the door with them and stood there with Win-

chester rifles, and pistols and acted in a threatening manner.

248 I was in possession of the goods from

Deposition of James J. Longwell on the death of John H. Tunstall (Fd Feb 18)

Lincoln County Court Records from T. [illegible] [illegible] the bottom of [illegible] highlighted [illegible] following page

249 the 11th day of February until the 23rd frequently during this time these men with the exception of Tunstall came around the store armed and threatened myself and my assistants with violence, as did quite a number of the other adherants of Tunstall and McSween viz Bowdre, Scurlock, Middleton, George Washington Robertson, Ygnacio Gonzales, Jesus Rodrigues, Kid Antrim & others they would call us d-d sons of bitches & tell us to turn loose, (that is to fire upon them so as to give them a chance to return the fire) that they were ready for the ball to open and tried in every way to provoke a quarrel with deponent and his men.

On one occasion Tunstall told me that I ought to be ashamed to be found in such an outfit, taking his property, I told him that if the property was his that he could take it to the courts and recover, he said d-d the the Court, I then told him that if the Court here did not do him justice that he could appeal it to the Supreme Court or go the the United States Court at Santa Fe he said God-d-n that ring it is the worst G-d-d-d outfit of them all, on one occasion Tunstall

called me a damned thief and at the same time placed his hands on his pistol in a threatening manner, this was the last con

190
p.1 of 3

Deposition of Robert A. Widenmann on the death of Tunstall

fund what the fees would be at this time both Dolan and Morton were armed to the teeth this was the substance of the conversation at that time.

Deponent further says that subsequently Brewer obtained title to the ranch under the Desert Act, the papers being now in deponents possession.

Deponent further says that this is only one of many other instances of L. G. Murphy, Dolan & Rileys attempts to force tithes from the people of this County as deponent is informed and believes and as the general report exists in said County.

Sometime during ~~Augu~~ September 1877 horses and mules of J. H. Tunstall and others, then at the ranch of R. M. Brewer were stolen by Jessie Evans Tom Hill and I think Frank Baker

R. M. Brewer, Charles Bowdre J. G. Scurlock, started after the thieves and at Sheds ranch (also called San Augustine) the party parted, Brewer going to Mesilla while Bowdre & Scurlock remained at Sheds Ranch

p. 2 of 3

Brewer obtained warrants for the
arrest of the thieves sworn out before
I think Justice Rosencrause. In the
meantime the thieves arrived with the
horses at Sheds ranch. Bowdre
& Scurlock asked them to return
the horses and mules especially
those of Brewer he being a poor
man to which they answered that
they would do no such thing, that they
had been to too much trouble to
get the horses to return them again
& the thieves went to Las Cruces
where they arrived with the horses
while Brewer was still there. Brewer
could not induce the Sheriff to arrest
them because he had not the force
to do so. All the above was told me
by Brewer when I met him near Tula Rosa
on his way back he was in company with
Bowdre & Scurlock, I with F. T. Waite
who heard the above facts stated to me
by Brewer. Waite returned with Brewer
& his party while I went on to Mesilla
in company with Lieut Pague.
Subsequently Baker, Evans, Hill
and Davis were arrested by Sheriff
Brady & posse at Seven Rivers. at
191 Beckwiths, and brought to Lincoln

192 and loged in jail from which
p. 3 of 3 they afterwards escaped. Mr Tunstall
took an active part in having them
pursued and arrested, he furnished
funds, horses, saddles and arms
and the thieves knew that he did it.
That subsequently deponent was
appointed Deputy U. S. Marshal and
warrants were placed in his hands
issued out of the U. S. Courts for
the arrest of Evans, Baker, Hill,
Davis, & Nicholas Provencio for
stealing government mules. In
trying to execute those warrants
I tracked them to the Ranch of
L. G. Murphy at the Carrisosa Spring
I was informed by Mr Murphy
personally that they were not at
his ranch and had been there
but once when they sold a
horse to Matthews. Deponent further
says that the horse referred to above
was sold to Matthews prior to their
arrest last above mentioned and
this conversation with said Murphy
was had four months after the

sale of said horse referred to aforesaid
Afterwards and on or about the 13 day of
February 1878 Evans admitted to deponent

And it is further ordered by the court that said cause as to the other defendants, to wit; Dock Scurlock, John Middleton, Wm Bonny, Samuel Smith, Frank Coe, George Coe, Ignacio Gonzales, Jesus Rodrigues, Esequio Sanches, Ramon Borges, Frank McNabb, Wayt and Edwards, be and the same is hereby continued and that warrants issue for each of said defendants returnable to the next term of this Court, And it is further ordered that the Sheriff of Lincoln County be and he is hereby authorized to take bail of each of said defendants in the sum of 500 dollars with two or more good and sufficient sureties to be approved by the sheriff conditioned for the appearance of each of said defendants before this Court on the first day of the next term thereof, and remain in attendance from day to day and from term to term until discharged by authority of law,

Weekly New Mexican, Santa Fe, New Mexico, 20 Apr 1878.

"At a Coroner's inquest held on the body of Andrew L. Roberts, who was killed at Blazer's mill on the 4th inst the jury found that the deceased came to his death from gun shot wounds at the hands of Richard Bruer, Charles Bowdry, 'Doc' Scurlock, Waite, Middleton, McKnabbe, John Scroggins, Stephen Stephens, George Coe, Frank Coe and W .H. Antrim, alias 'The Kid'.

List of names of persons killed and wounded since commencement of the troubles in and about Lincoln county:

Feb. 18th---John Tunstall, killed by Sheriff's posse while serving a writ of attachement.

March 9th---Frank Baker, (outlaw) W. S. Morton and---McCloskey, killed by Bruer's party to revenge the killing of Tunstall.

March 9th---Tom Hill (outlaw) killed, and Jesse Evans (outlaw) wounded in the wrist while attempting to rob a Mr. Wagner's train near Tulerosa.

April 1st---Sheriff Wm. Brady and Geo. Hindman shot down and killed by Bruer's party in the town of Lincoln. W. H. Antrim and Jim French, of Bruer's party, wounded; the first severely, the latter reported fatally. J. B. Wilson was also slightly wounded in the rear of his person by a random shot.

A soldier was shot and killed by mistake while attempting to pass a sentry at Murphy's house.

April 6th---Andrew L. Robert's killed by Bruer's party at Blazer's mills. It is alleged that Robert's was present at the killing of Tunstall. Richard Bruer, leader of the 'regulators' killed by A. L. Roberts, who also wounded---Middleton seriously, Charles Bowdry shot in the side slightly and George Coe shot in the hand. It is reported that others have been killed, but nothing reliable."

Fort Stanton N.M. 2 May 1878

"Lt. Col. N. A. M. Dudley USA
Comdg. Fort Stanton N. M.

Sir,

I have the honor to request that you receive the following named prisoners

R. A. Weideman
Isaac Ellis
Ignacio Gonzales
John Scroggins
W. B. Ellis
J. G. Scurlock
George Wshington

And retain them under guard subject to the order of the Sheriff of Lincoln County N. M. or higher authority.

Very respectfully
your obdt. Servt.

L. Sudey
Dep'y Sheriff of
Lincoln County N. M.

Lincoln N. M. 2 May 1878

"General.

I send you under guard Scurlock, Wideman, Scroggins, Washington, Gonzales Ellis Senior Wm Ellis, Stanley, Sam Corbet is sick I leave him in Town. Sheriff Copeland will be responsible for him.

Scurlock is a bad man the worst in the bunch! (irons would not hurt him.) Lieut. Smith takes half the men and goes to San Patricio across the Mountains. I take the rest and go around the road. We will meet at 12 to-night and without doubt take them all in.

Yours respectfully
M. F. Goodwin
2" Lieut 9" Cav."

Fort Stanton N. M. 4 May 1878

" To General N. A. M. Dudlty
Commanding Officer

Sir,

I have the honor to most respectfully ask you to turn over all Territorial Prisoners now in your charge consisting of the following named persons to wit:

John Hurley	Lewis Paxton
Wm Mathews	Buck Powell
Jack Long	Rob. Ollinger
Robt W. Beckwith	W. A. Johnson
John Beckwith	Reuben Kelly
Joseph Nash	Charles Martin
Wallace Ollinger	A. A. McSween
Isaac Ellis	William Ellis
John Scoggins	Geo. Washington
Ignacio Gonzalos	Saml Corbett
Geo. W. Pepen	Doc Scurlock
John Galocie	Tom Green
Tom Corcoran	Chas Kruling
Sam Perry	R. A. Wideman
Pierce whos first name is	J. Packerson

My object in making this request is that the laws of the Territory are such that I would not be sustained holding prisoners for a long as period than thirty six hours without having them examined according to law.

I am Sir Very Respectfully
Your Obd't Servant
John W. Copeland
Sheriff Lincoln Co. N. M."

Head Quarters Fort Stanton N. M. May 4, 1878

"Lieut. John S. Loud
9" Cavalry
Act. Asst. Adjutant General
District N. M.

Sir:

On May 3 three of the man who surrendered to Lieut Smith swore out an affidavit on which to base a warrant against McSween, Widenmann, Scurlock and 15 or 20 others. Widenmann it is claimed was with the party that killed Brady. Scurlock was at the agency at the killing of Roberts. A lady now a guest of the Officers at the Post saw him and talked with him. The affidavit was sent to Easton, J. P. Precinct No. 3 (by a courier who returned with warrants inside of nineteen hours, eighty miles) which warrants I placed in the hands of the Sheriff and he stated to me, if I would give him the men he would serve it.

His conduct throughout up to this time was of a character to injure him in the opinion of his friends, being of an ex-parte nature all together. Lieuts Goodwin and Smith were ordered to report to the Sheriff as a posse. By 9 P.M. Lieut. Goodwin sent me a note marked "M" with the prisoners of the McSween side of the War named in said paper – all of whom were confined, Scurlock was shackled.

Very Respectfully,
Your Obdt. Servant
N. A. M. Dudley
Lieut Col 9 Cavalry
Comdg. Post"

Fort Stanton New Mexico, 5 May 1878, "C"

"Received of Lieut Col Dudley Comd'g Fort Stanton the person of J. G. Scurlock his Rifle Belt and Pistol, held by him by my request.

John N. Copeland
Sheriff Lincoln County
New Mexico"

Fort Stanton, N. M. 6 May 1878

"The Post Adjutant
Fort Stanton N. M.

Sir:

In compliance with S. O. 17 from the post dated May 2 1878, I accompanied the Sheriff of Lincoln County to Lincoln to assist him in arresting certain citizens charged with riot. The following named persons were arrested by the Sheriff. Scurlock, Ellis, Sen. Wm Ellis, Scroggins, Gonzalos Corbet Weidermann These I sent at the Sheriff's request under guard to Fort Stanton.

We then proceeded to San Patricia 16 miles from the town of Lincoln and there the Sheriff arrested McSween and with him returned to this Post.

Very Respectfully
Your Obdt Servant
M. F. Goodwin
2" Lieut 9" Cavalry"

Fort Stanton N. M., 7 May 1878, "B"

"Lieut Col Dudlty
Cond'g Fort Stanton N. M.

Sir

I have the honor to request that you deliver to me the prisoner J. G. Scurlock, now in your Custody, Subject to my order that he may be disposed of in accordance with law.

Appreciating your efforts to aid the civil authorities

I remain
Very Respectfully
Your Obdt. Servant
John N. Copeland
Sheriff Lincoln County
New Mexico"

Fort Stanton, N. M.. 7 May 1878, "D"

"Commanding Officer
Fort Stanton N. M.

Sir

I have the honor to respectfully request to be furnished with 3 men to escort U. S. prisoner Scurlock to Lincoln N. M.

Very Respectfully,
Your Obdt. Servt
John N. Copeland
Sheriff Lincoln County"

Head Quarters, Fort Stanton, N. M., 11 May 1878

"Act. Asst. Adjutant General
Head Qrs District N. M.
Sant Fe, N. M.

Sir:

In compliance with your letter of instructions of the 23rd and 24th ult. regard to reporting matters relating to civil difficulties in Lincoln County. I have the honor to state that after the closing of my last report the paper marked 'A' was received from Sheriff Copeland. All the prisoners arrested by him with the aid of troops from Stanton were released, except Doc Scurlock, who was retained at the request of Sheriff Copeland, and receipt taken for them.

On the 7th of May the Sheriff made the request for the release of Scurlock, marked 'B' which was granted. Paper marked 'C' covers the delivery of arms of said Scurlock. Paper marked 'D' requests a guard for Scurlock to Lincoln which was given.

Very Respectfully
Your Obdt. Servant
N. A. M. Dudley
Lieut Col 9 Cavalry
Comdg Post"

Seven Rivers, N. M., 19 May 1878

"Gen's N. A. M. Dudley
Cond'g Fort Stanton N. M.

General,

I have the honor to inform you that "Doc Scurlock" claiming to be a Deputy Sheriff with "Kid" "Bowdre" "Coe" Brown Scroggins two others of the Men who murdered Brady with Eleven Mexicans surrounded Camp this morning and stole by forcibly taking about twenty-seven head of horses the property of T. B. Catron of Santa Fe. Owing to the above fact I am entirely unable to handle or drive cattle enough to complete my contracts with the Government and I would respectfully request that what men you in your judgement think necessary be sent here to assist me – in order that I may be able to complete my existing contracts.

This mob have also taken captive an Indian and it is presumed from their previous action that they will murder him. Trusting that you will aid us, and regretting that I am compelled through the acts of those thieves to call on you.

I am General
Very Respectfully
Your Obdt Servant
John H. Riley
Gov't Beef Contractor"

John Riley message to Major Godfroy, 22 May 1878

"Maj Godfrey

We have learned from above that Scurlock and party after stealing our horses killed three employees of ours that Hunter has turned out all his men to aid the Sheriff in arresting: Johnson & party – we leave here for the mountains for protection as we are aware that an arrest means death. That one man an employee was killed in certain that they fired on the others but whether they are killed is only conjecture – that Hunter's party is out is also certain. Please send this to Genl Dudley.

J. H. Riley"

Santa Fe *Weekly New Mexican*, Saturday, 25 May 1878 (excerpt)

"THE TROUBLES IN LINCOLN
Santa Fe, May 16th, 1878

EDITORS NEW MEXICAN:

Gentlemen: - I see by the last issue of the 'Independent' that its editors still continue publishing their malicious lies in regard to the Lincoln Co. troubles . . .

(Brewer) next tried to defraud us, on advice received from Mr. McSween, out of two of our ranches situated on the Rio Ruidosa which we had rented to him on leaving our employ, by entering them under the desert land act, but failed to prove up his right; the circumstances are well known to Mr. Bowman of the land office and another gentleman living in the Mesilla valley and in Lincoln county. Mr. Brewer is owing our firm over two thousand dollars. This is McSween's respected citizen; blessed be his memory.

Bowdre & Scurlock came to us about three years ago for assistance, they had nothing. We being anxious to help them sold them a ranch on the Rio Ruidosa for $1500, which cost the firm of Fritz and Murphy about two thousand dollars, and gave them three years to pay it in; also furnished them farming implements, provisions and paid their employees this we done up to a short time before the trouble commenced, and only stopped their credit after learning tht they had disposed of their crops to McSween and Tunstall for the purpose of defrauding us; they are now owing us for the ranch and over three thousand dollars book account. The Coes complain of our taking contracts too cheap to suit them. McSween wants to keep the ten thousand dollars collected for the Fritz estate, and he knows he can't do it as long as Mr. Riley and myself live; therefore he desires to have us assassinated.

We are in Mr. Chism's way, because our business conflicts. He wants to control contracts in New Mexico as well as in Arizona; in this we have bothered him.

Mr. 'L. S.' or 'thine in the right' is a merchant who lately came to our country, and from what I can learn hasn't left a very clean record behind him; when the trouble commenced he thought he saw a good chance to get rid of a competitor in business, so he linked arms with the so-called regulators, 'Assassasins' would be more appropriate, and has played a very conspicuous part in their foul work from the beginning . . .

I will further state about Mr. Chism a little circumstance which happened between him and Mr. Riley. About a year and a half ago Bowdre and Scurlock came to Mr. Riley and offered to furnish him cattle at very low figures from Mr. Chism's cattle range. Mr. Riley answered stating that he was not doing that kind of business and in a short time afterwards notified Mr. Chism writing of the fact. I believe the letter was confidential. Mr. Chism instead of acting as a gentleman should, sent Mr. Riley's letter to Bowdre and Scurlock, knowing them to be unscrupulous villains; the result was Bowdre and Scurlock denied the charge and swore vengeance against Riley. After such treatment as this I don't think a man would be warranted in breading his neck to look out for the property of such an ungrateful wretch. . . .

James J. Dolan"

Executive Office, Santa Fe, N.M., 30 May 1878

"Col Edward Hatch, U. S. A.

Sir:

I have the honor to enclose for your information a letter from Hon Thos. B. Catron, U. S. District Attorney for New Mexico.

From this letter it appears that three men have been shot recently in Lincoln Co. on the Rio Pecos, by a band of armed men under the command of one Scurlock, who claims to act as Deputy Sheriff and that said Scurlock with some thirty armed men has driven off a large band of horses the property of Mr. Catron and is now preventing by violence Mr. Catron from rounding up and taking care of his cattle, some two thousand in numbers.

To prevent further bloodshed and to enable Mr. Catron to secure his Cattle and have them driven to some safer locality I have respectfully to request that you will order a sufficient number of Troops to remain on the Rio Pecos in the vicinity of Roswell, Lincoln County, to keep the peace and also that you will direct the officer in charge of said Troops to disarm all bands of armed men which he finds in said county of Lincoln, whether claiming to act as Sheriff's Posse or otherwise and to give Receipts to Individuals from whom he takes said arms and to forward said arms to such place as you shall direct for safe keeping, to be restored to their owners whenever in your judgement it shall appear safe to do so. I have reason to believe that there is another party of nearly or quite equal strength with Scurlock's in the same vicinity opposed to Scurlock, and it is my request that you order your Officers to hunt down both of these bands of armed men, and disarm them at all hazards, as I fully believe that peace and order cannot be restored to that County till this is done. By authority of Law I have removed John A. Copeland from the Office of Sheriff of Lincoln County, and have appointed in his stead Geo. W. Peppin, who is now Sheriff.

Respectfully you Obdt. Servt.
S. B. Axtell
Governor N. M."

The United States of America)
Territory of New Mexico) ss
Third Judicial District)

In the United States District Court for said Third Judicial District at the June Term A D 1878.

The Grand Jurors of the United States of America taken from the body of the good and lawful men of the Third Judicial District aforesaid-duly impannelled Sworn and charged at the Term aforesaid to inquiry in and for the body of the Third Judicial District aforesaid up on their oaths do present that Charles Bowdry, Doc Scurlock, Henry Brown, Henry Antrim - alias Kid - John Middleton, Stephen Stevens, John Scroggins, George Coe and Drederick Waite late of the Third Judicial District in the Territory of New Mexico on the fifth day of April in the year of our Lord Eighteen hundred and seventy eight at and within the reservation of the Mescalero Apache Indians in the Said Third Judicial District, Said reservation then and there being a part of the Indian country, with force and arms in and upon one Andrew Roberts, did make an assault, and that the Said Charles Bowdry, Doc Scurlock, Henry Brown, Henry Antrim - alias Kid John Middleton, Stephen Stevens, John Scroggins, George Coe, Frederick Waite certain Guns then and there loaded and charged with gunpowder and divers leaden bullets, which said guns the Said Charles Bowdry, Doc Scurlock, Henry Brown, Henry Antrim (alias Kid) John Middleton Stephen Stevens, John Scroggins George Coe and Frederick Waite in their hands then and there had and held to, against and upon the Said Andrew Roberts then and there and within the Said Reservation feloniously, wilfully, unlawfully of their malice aforethought and from a premeditated design to effect the death of him the Said Andrew Roberts did shoot and discharge, and that the Said Charles Bowdry, Doc Scurlock Hanry Brown, Henry Antrim-alias Kid-John Middleton, Stephen Stevens, John Scroggins George Coe and Frederick Waite, with the leaden Bullets aforesaid, out of the guns aforesaid, then and there by force of the gunpowder, shot discharged and sent forth as aforesaid the Said Andrew Roberts in and upon the right side of the belly of him the Said Andrew Roberts then and there and within the Said Reservation feloniously, wilfully, unlawfully of their malice aforethought and from a premeditated design to effect the death of the Said Andrew Roberts, did strike penetrate and wound, giving to the Said Andrew Roberts then and there and within the Said Reservation with the leaden Bullets aforesaid so as aforesaid, Shot discharged and sent forth out of the guns aforesaid by the Said Andrew Bowdry, Doc Scurlock, Henry Brown, Henry Antrim alias Kid, John Middleton, Stephen Stevens, John Scroggins, George Coe and Frederick Waite in and upon the right side of the belly of him the Said Andrew Roberts one mortal wound of the depth of ten inches and breadth of one half of an inch of which Said mortal wound the Said Andrew Roberts then and there at the Said Reservation instantly died and so the Jury as aforesaid upon their oaths as aforesaid do say that the Said Charley Bowdry, Doc Scurlock, Henry Brown, Henry Antrim-alias Kid-John Middleton, Stephen Stevens, John Scroggins, George Coe, and Frederick Waite the Said Andrew Roberts in manner and form aforesaid feloniously, wilfully, unlawfully of their malice aforethought and from a premeditated design to effect the death of the Said Andrew Roberts, did kill and murder against the form of the Statute in such case made and provided and against the peace and Dignity of the United States.

And the Jurors aforesaid upon their oaths aforesaid do further present that Charles Bowdry late of the Third Judicial District in the Territory of New Mexico on the fifth day of April in the year A. D. Eighteen .. hundred and seventy eight at and within the Reservation of the Mescalero Apache Indians said Reservation being then and there Situate in the Third Judicial District aforesaid and then and there being Indian Country in and upon one Andrew Roberts then and there being in the Said Reservation in the Said District, feloniously, unlawfully, wilfully, of his malice aforethought and from a premeditated design to effect the death of the Said Andrew Roberts did make an assault and that the Said Charles Bowdry a certain gun then and there loaded and charged with gunpowder and one leaden Bullet which gun he the said Charles Bowdry in his right hand then and there had and held to at against and upon the Said Andrew Roberts then and there within the Said Reservation feloniously unlawfully, wilfully of his malice aforethought and from a premeditated design to effect the death of him the Said Andrew Roberts, did shoot and discharge and that the Said Charles Bowdry with the leaden Bullet aforesaid, out of the gun aforesaid then and there by force of the gunpowder aforesaid shot and sent forth as aforesaid the Said Andrew Roberts in and upon the right side of the belly of him the said Andrew Roberts then and there and in the Said Reservation feloniously unlawfully, wilfully, of his malice aforethought and from a premeditated design to affect the death of the Said Andrew Roberts, did strike penetrate and wound, giving to the said Andrew Roberts then and there with the leaden Bullet aforesaid so as aforesaid that discharged and sent forth out of the gun aforesaid by the Said Charles Bowdry in and upon the right side of the belly of the Said Andrew Roberts one mortal wound of the depth of ten inches and of thebreadth of one inch of which Said mortal wound the Said Andrew Roberts then and there at the Said reservation instantly died and the Jurors aforesaid upon their oaths aforesaid do further present that Doc Scurlock, Henry Brown, Henry Antrim-alias Kid-John Middleton Stephen Stevens John Scroggins, George Coe, and Henry Waite late of the Third Judicial District aforesaid on the day and year aforesaid with force and arms at the Said reservation in the Said District aforesaid. feloniously was present aiding abetting and assisting the Charles Bowdry the felony and murder aforesaid to do and commit against the form of the Statute in Such case made and provided and against the peace and dignity of the United States. and the Jurors aforesaid upon their oaths aforesaid do say that the Said Charles Bowdry, Doc Scurlock, Henry Brown, Henry Antrim-alias Kid, John Middleton, Stephen Stevens, John Scroggins, George Coe, and Fredrick Waite in manner and form aforesaid, feloniously, wilfully, unlawfully, of their malice aforethought and from a premeditated design to effect the death of him the said Andrew Roberts, did Kill and murder against the form of the Statute in such case made and provided and against the peace and dignity of the United States.

(signed)

Thomas B. Catron
United States Attorney
for New Mexico

411
The United States vs:
Charles Bowdry
Doc Scurlock
Henry Brown
Henry Antrim alias "Kid"
John Middleton'
Stephne Stevens
John Scroggins
George Coe
Fredrick Waite

***Mesilla Independent*, Saturday, 1 Jun 1878**

"John H. Riley of Lincoln county is in town and will remain with us until after the June term of court.

From him we learn that the Lincoln county 'Regulators' have recently been out on a 'business' trip with the views of straightening out matters, and their success has no doubt been highly satisfactory to the party.

Under the leadership of Scurlock and Bowdre they paid a visit to the cattle ranch of Dolan and Riley on the Pacus with the declared purpose of arresting parties implicated in the killing of McKnab. It does not appear that any arrest were made, but the party (18 in number) succeeded in killing a Navajo Indian who was employed at the ranch as a cook, a hearder named Wair and a boy 15 years of age called Johnny, after which the party drove off 26 head of horses and two mules belonging on the ranch. This way of regulating matters is no doubt highly satisfactory to the 'Regulators' themselves and it will encourage them to persevere in their efforts to bring 'outlaws' to justice."

Santa Fe *Weekly New Mexican*, Saturday, 8 Jun 1878

"FORT STANTON, May 24th 1878

Editors New Mexican:

Reliable information just received reports, that a party of men headed by Doc. Scurlock one of the murderers of Brady, Hindman and Roberts, who in return for his meritorious services, has been rewarded with the appointment of deputy-sheriff, have stolen all the horses formerly belonging to J. J. Dolan & Co., and killed one of their employees. It is rumored that two more have been killed but the report is not substantiated.

EL GATO"

Office of the U. S. Marshal, Territory of New Mexico, Santa Fe, N. M. 14 Jun 1878

"George W. Peppin Esq.
Lincoln N. M.

Sir

You are directed under the within enclosed warrant to arrest and produce before the United States Court at La Mesilla the bodies of the following named persons. Viz. –

Charles Bowdry	Doctor Scurlock
John Middleton	John Scroggins
George Coe	Frank Coe
Henry Brown	-----Waite

Steven Stevens alias Steve Stevens
William Bruner, alias Kid, alias antrim alias 'The Kid'.

John Sherman Jr
U. S. Marshal"

Fort Stanton N. M. 18 Jun 1878, 12 o' clock

"To Col N. A. M. Dudley

Sir:

I have the honor to respectfully submit for your inspection my Commission as Sheriff of the County of Lincoln, N. M. from his excellency Gov. S. B. Axtell Governor of the territory of New Mex. On examination of said Commission you will observe that I have been duly sworn in as Sheriff before the Hon. Warren Bristol Associate Justice – Judge &c. I respectfully submit also warrants issued by the Hon. Judge Bristol for the arrest of Chas. Bowdre, J. G. Scurlock and the others: to arrest said parties and bring them before the United States and territorial Courts, now in session at La Mesilla, N. M. and by instructions from his excellency the Gov. and the Hon. Judge Bristol. I ask of you a military Posse, of not less than one commissioned officer and ten men for the purpose of making these arrest and carrying out my instructions from Judge Bristol and John Sherman Esq. U. S. Marshal for the territory of N. M. Copy of warrants and authority for making these arrests enclosed herewith for your information.

Geo. W. Peppin
Sheriff of Lincoln County
And Actg Deputy U. S. Marshal"

Mesilla News, 29 Jun 1878

MESILLA News, June 29, 1878

COURT PROCEEDINGS

U. S. vs. Chas. Bowdre, Doc Scurlock, Hy. Brown, Hy. Antrim, John Middleton, Stephen Stephens, John Scroggins, George Coe, Fred Wait; murder. Continued.

The territory vs. John Kinney; assault to kill. No 1. pros.

LINCOLN COUNTY

Lincoln Plaza, N.M.)
June 22nd, 1878)

MY DEAR BOND:

Col. John Kinney holds Lincoln. And Lincoln I regret to say presents an appearance as melancholy as an old toper when about to join the Sons of Temperance. While the dozen or so graveyards scattered around town adds a little cheerfulness to the place, nevertheless notwithstanding the late arrival of an $900 piano for Mrs. McSween, and a $500,00 set of Scotch bag pipes for honest Mac; Lincoln is terribly dull--extremely so. It was expected that the election of Juan Bautisto Wilson to be justice of the peace would create a little effervescence in the community and as a consequence make matters lively in town, but it appears that his honor's friends do not care at present to dance to the music of a new Chickering or a set of bagpipes.

Few persons of any means or prominence are to be met with here, most of them I learn being abroad on the green hills taking a little recreation after their arduous duties in this neighborhood. Should they not return before next term of court it will be a matter of impossibility to find 15 good men in this county to make up a grand jury.

Since the arrival of Col. Kinney matters are running smoothly. Everything is quiet, and no person is interfered with in his legitimate business. Ex-Sheriff Copeland, who from what I learn assuredly acted the partisan while in office, was advised to go to his home, attend to his family and honest business, and not be made a cats paw of in the villanies of other people and he would not be molested. Like a good citizen he took the advice, and it is hoped that hereafter he, Copeland, will invariably be found on the side of honesty and law and order in this county. For when bad men combine, the good must associate, else they will fall one by one, as unpitied sacrifice in a contemptible struggle.

I regret to say that Cronin of your place has met with a serious accident. While riding into town alone, he was taken for one of the regulators and ordered to "throw up his hands." His arms went up with such a jerk that its feared there is a dislocation at the sockets which may possibly prove fatal. Considerable sympathy is felt for him by both sides he being an ardent admirer of each. He was taken to brother McSween's house where he is doing as well as circumstances will permit under the spiritual charge of Madame Chaplain. More hereafter.

SCROPE.

Headquarters, Fort Stanton, N. M., 13 Jul 1878

"Act. Asst. Adjutant General
District of N. M.
Santa Fe N. M.

Sir:

Yesterday Mrs. Brady, the widow of the late Sheriff Brady, and the mother of eight little children, presented herself at my quarters weeping, and in apparent great distress, stating to me and others present, that Scurlock one of McSween's party with two other men, fired three shots at her eldest boy in a Canyon only half a mile from his home. This is not the first instance as she stated, of their attempt to kill her children, as the bullet holes in her residence go to prove. It was a sad scene to witness the grief and fears of this poor woman as she told her pitiful story, saying, 'They have murdered my poor husband, and not satisfied with this they now want to kill my boy.'

I offered to receive the boy in the Garrison, and care for him but she said that she could not get along the farm without him, so I sent a guard of one man to remain at the house for a few days, hoping, that, as the two factions are now in full strength, and within a few miles of each other, that one or the other side will be driven out of the country.

Very Respectfully
Your Obdt. Servant
N. A. M. Dudley
Liuet. Col. 9" Cavalry
Comdg Post"

Fort Stanton, N. M., 15 Jul 1878

"Post Adjutant
Fort Stanton N. M.

Sir:

In accordance with your communication of this date I proceeded to Lincoln accompanied by Mr. J. B. Patron and went first to the house of Mr. Baca, where I learned that McSween with a party of nearly sixty men had arrived in town last evening and that he (Mr. Baca) and his family (his wife having been delivered of a baby but three days ago) were very much afraid of being attacked by them. I found six men of the Sheriff's posse occupying the tower adjoining Mr. Baca's house and that threats had been made to dislodge them. On being informed that a part of McSween's party were at Montane's house and others at Ellis's and McSween's, I went to Montane's house and saw that a number of port holes had recently been made through the adobe wall surrounding the roof and I was unable to obtain admittance. I went from there to Ellis's where I saw about twelve men of McSween's party including Bowdrey, Scurlock and Middleton. On inquiring whether they intended to harm Mr. Baca and family, they said no intention of harming anyone who lived in Lincoln, but if fired at by the party in the tower, they would return the fire and then the family would be in danger. They proposed to allow the men to leave the tower and join their friends unmolested and then not to trouble Mr. Baca. Scurlock stated that the reports of his threatening the life of Gen'l Dudley and of his firing at Johnny Brady were false and made an affidavit to that effect, which is here to prefixed and Marked I.

Very Respectfully Your Obdt
Servant D. M. Appel
Asst Surg. U. S. A."

Mesilla *News*, 20 Jul 1878

"LINCOLN COUNTY
Lincoln N. M.
July 14th, 1878

DEAR NEWS;

The war still rages here. A. A. McSween is still in the mountains with twenty five men; they say they defy the law and its officers.

McSween and party are spying on the public highways preparing to waylay the Sheriff and posse. They are also fortifying themselves against officers of the law, who may undertake to serve warrants on them.

McSween has in his party Bowdre, Scurlock, Antrim, (alias the Kid) Henry Brown, John Middleton, Wait, who are said to be part of those who are the hired assassins of Sheriff Brady and deputy Sheriff Geo. Hindman on the public street in the town of Lincoln.

John S. Chisum, it is reported furnishes honest? McSween's boys, with fresh horses to ride after they run a while from the Sheriff until their own horses are jaded. Chisum's house is also opened to them to use as a fort against the officers of the law and Justice. What will come next?

OBSERVER"

Headquarters Fort Stanton, N. M., 9 Aug 1878

"Special Orders
No. 73

I under the Provisions Title XXVIII Section 2150 U. S. R. A. 2" Lieut. M. F. Goodwin 9" Cav. In Command of Detachment now temporarily stationed at the Mescalero Apache Indian Agency will proceed with as little delay as practicable on the trail of 'Scurlock,' alias 'Doc' Antrim alias 'Kid' 'Bowdry' 'Scroggins' 'Dirty Steve' 'Henry Brown' 'Coe' 'Joe Bowers' and others, charged with attacking the Indians on the 5" inst. At Mescalero Apache Indian Agency at South Fork, N. M. killing the Chief Clerk Morris Bernstein and assaulting with intent to kill F. C. Godfroy, U. S. Indian Agent of said Mescalero Apache Indian Agency, and if possible arrest said murders and bring them to this Post to be turned over to the proper authorities, and also recapture the animals stolen by said outlaws from said Agency, using the force under his command for this purpose.

By order of Lieut. Col. Dudley

S. S. Pague
2" Lieut 15" Infty.
Act. Post Adjutant"

Headquarters Fort Stanton, N. M., 31 Aug 1878

"Act Asst Adjutant General
District of New Mexico
Santa Fe N. M.

Sir:

Since my last weekly report of affairs in Lincoln County I have learned nothing of special interest except that there are several parties from Nine to fifteen men each located in different sections of the County, mostly in Canons seemingly recuperating their horses.

Jim French, Scurlock, Bowdry, and that party, come in and out of Lincoln daily without molestation, making threats of what they propose to do as soon as the Sheriff's party have got home, and are off their guard. They openly threaten the lives of myself, Lieut. Goodwin and all others who have assisted the Sheriff to make arrests among their friends. The Sheriff has disbanded his posse, and entirely suspended all official action for the present.

Patron, so I am informed is at the head of twenty five men now reported to be some where near seven rivers.

Very Respectfully
Your Obdt Servant
N. A. M. Dudley
Lieut Col 9" Cavly
Comd'g Post"

Headquarters Fort Stanton, N. M., 7 Sep 1878

"Act'g Asst Adjutant General
District of New Mexico
Santa Fe N. M.

Sir:

I have little to report of interest to the District Commander this week.

Jim French, Kidd, Scroggins, Waite, and three others of the McSween ring hold the town of Lincoln. Stock stealing is being reported as occurring daily, the animals taken being driven towards the Pecos and Seven Rivers.

The Sheriff has no posse now and is making no attempt to arrest anyone. French's Party by threats and acts has forced County Commissioner Baca to leave the town and seek protection for himself and family within the limits of the post.

French makes his Headquarters with McSween. Easton the present business manager of the affairs of J. B. Catron Esq. who only about a week ago reported to me that he was sleeping in the hills, being afraid to sleep in the Murphy building, is now reported on intimate terms with , and a daily visitor of Mrs. McSween has stated that he has no fears now from that party. There is some thirty armed men between old Fort Sumner and Roswell. Scurlock and Middleton is reported to be with this party.

Kinney and his party I am unable to locate just now positively,

Another party of some fifteen men are in the mountains near Tulerosa, the two Coe Brothers are this Band.

I have one non-com-officer and three men at the agency. Their instructions are strictly within the authority given in Par II and III G. O. #28 cs of 1870 Dept of NCo. furnished me for my guidance from District Headquarters. The N. C. O. reports by each mail any information that is of importance.

I enclose copy of his report received last night marked No 1.

Very Respectfully
Your Obdt Servant
N. A. M. Dudley
Lieut Col 9" Cavalry
Comd'g Post"

26 Oct 1878

"The mud squirt, bringing its popgun to bear, informs Governor Wallace that the officers in command at Fort Stanton- -'in any event should not be permitted to exercise authority in Lincoln County.' This is no doubt an honestly expressed inspiration from a retained attorney of bad men in Lincoln county. It is very probable that Col. Dudley and his officers will in due time make it lively for 'Kid' Antrim, 'Doc' Scurlock and others, including the assassins of Sheriff and Deputy U. S. Marshal Brady and Hindman. This organ of murderers and outlaws talks to its clients hopefully: 'We desire to say to our friends in Lincoln County that we are satisfied they will find in Governor Wallace a fair and just official.' It is so seldom we are afforded an opportunity to agree with our contemporary, that when it does come it is worthy of note. We, too, 'are satisfied they will find in Governor Wallace a fair and just official.' But where would 'Kid', Scurlock and the writers for the News & Press be, should justice overtake them? Look well out and soon, for another batch of Springer affidavits."

Fort Stanton N. M., 3 Nov 1878

"To the Commanding Officer
Fort Stanton N. M.

Sir:

I herewith furnish you with a list of persons for whom I have legal warrants, and respectfully request that you will furnish me with sufficient Military force from your command to insure their arrest.

This I believe you are now authorized to do by Orders received yesterday. I will complete a list of Deputies who will be properly warranted to act as such.

These parties will accompany the posses in all instances to serve the warrants named below,

Charles Bowdry	Charge	Murder.
Dock Scurlock	"	"
John Middleton	"	"
John Scroggins	"	"
Stephen Stevens	"	"
Geo Coe	"	"
William Antrim alias 'Kid'	"	"
Waite	"	"
Henry Brown	"	"

All of the above I have U S warrants for issued by Hon Judge Warren Bristol U S District Judge, 3rd Judicial District. Also

Chas Morsner alias Oriss	Charge	Larceny
Frank Rivers	"	Murder
Ensegnia Sanchez	"	Larceny
Fernando Herrera	"	"
Jasper Coe	"	"
Ignacio Gonzales	"	"

These latter named parties I have Warrants for issued by Hon Judge Warren Bristol Territorial Judge 3rd Judicial District, which I present you herewith.

Respectfully
Your Obt Servant
Geo W. Peppin
Sheriff Lincoln Co. N. M."

Headquarters Fort Stanton, N. M., 30 Nov 1878

"To the
Act. Asst. Adj't General.
District of N. M.
Santa Fe N. M.

Sir:

I have the honor to report that nothing of importance has occurred, that has come to my notice since my last report, in this section, relating to the civil affairs of Lincoln Co.

The proclamation of his Excellency the Governor has had the effect of bringing back into the Country, or from their hiding places within the County, on to the public highways some of the noted outlaws, among the number Jim French and Scurlock. The former was at Mrs. McSweens, and Patron's house yesterday, and the day before, so reported to me by parties who saw him.

Very Respectfully
Your Obdt. Servant
N. A. M. Dudley
Lieut. Col 9" Cavalry
Commanding Post"

***Mesilla News*, 30 Nov 1878**

"Peace was dawning in Lincoln Co. when Gov. Wallace extended a pardon to absent thieves, cutthroats and murderers and virtually invited them to come back and take fresh start (in their 'usual occupations.')

The Governor has pardoned Scurlock, Bowdre, Bonny alias the 'Kid', Wait and all the murdering gauge of Lincoln County. That's one way of restoring 'law and order.'"

Headquarters Ft. Stanton, N. M., 1 Feb 1879

"Gov Lew Wallace

Lincoln

Dr Sir

Mathews has just been sent in.

The men Scurlock & Bonney at Sumner or reported there are all probably north of that point at least 175 miles from here will require more than ordinary preparation for. Should prefer sending troops from Union. They would be much more likely to succeed than if sent from here.

Yours Truly
Edward Hatch

Mr. Watts sends box of cigars & note

E. H."

Lincoln, N. M., 3 Mar 1879

"Captain Juan Patron.

Sir:

Please select ten of your Rangers, make the necessary preparation and set out quickly as possible to arrest Scurlock and Bowdre, who are thought to be at a ranch 10 or 12 miles east of old Fort Sumner. Use your best endeavor to accomplish the purpose.

Take the old dry trail north of this plaza, travel in the night time, lying over in cover during the day. Avoid persons and houses on the way. Strike the Pecos at some point north of Sumner and approach the rancho from that direction.

Respectfully,
Your friend,
Lew Wallace
Gov. New Mexico"

Lincoln, N. M., 6 Mar 1879

"Gen. Edward Hatch,
Com'g Dist. New Mexico

Sir:

I have reliable information that J. G. Scurlock and Charles Bowdre are now at a ranch called Taiban, about twelve miles east of Fort Sumner. They are parties included in the writ issued by Judge Bristol out of the U. S. Court upon indictment for the murder of Andrew L. Roberts in April 1876. Up to this time it has seemed impossible to secure their arrest. But Sheriff Kimbrall having been appointed Deputy U. S. Marshal, and qualified as such, and being new in possession of the writ, and, willing to attempt the arrest, I have to request you will send me a detachment (under an energetic officer) to accompany him or his deputy in the effort to secure these men. I would suggest that you enlist a good trailer – an Indian, if possible – and provide the detachment suitably for a long chase. If the officer can come over with his man tonight, I will bring him in communication with a party here who knows the best route to the point indicated.

I have the honor to be,
Very respectfully
Your friend and servant,
Lew Wallace
Gov. New Mexico"

Las Cruces *Thirty-Four*, Wednesday, 23 Apr 1879

"MILITARY ITEMS

Dr. W. B. Lyon has left the army and will locate in Mesilla.

Lt. S. S. Prague, 15th Inf., is on duty at Marcy.

SCRAPS

Doc Scurlock is in jail in Lincoln County

LOCALS

Fountain has been appointed counsel for 'Kid' Antrim and a change of venue will probably be taken to this county.

LINCOLN COUNTY

From gentlemen just arrived from Lincoln we learn the following facts:

Gov. Wallace left for Santa Fe on Friday, Gen. Dudley has arrived in Stanton. Col. Purington is still in command and Maj. Morrow will not assume command. The Grand Jury was convened on Thursday. It is a good body and Isaac Ellis is Foreman. No jury trials had yet been had, as the county had to be scoured to secure jurors. In Riley's case a change of venue was taken to Grant county. Some twenty of the Dolan party have been arrested and are in irons at the post, while only three of the other party have been arrested and are held at Lincoln but allowed to walk around town with their arms and accompanied by a guard. The Dolan party claim that the Governor has shown great partiality and think there will be more trouble after court has adjourned. Our information comes through Dolan channels."

Headquarters Fort Stanton, N. M., 3 May 1879, letter from Capt. George Purington to Governor Lew Wallace

"'Doc' Scurlock and the 'Kid', the two most notorious murderers of the county, have been in custody of the sheriff, (who is also a U.S. Deputy Marshal) released them, although he knew there were indictments against them for murder in the U.S. Court, and the warrants for their arrest are said to be in his hands."

Headquarters Fort Stanton, N. M., 3 May 1879

"To the
A. A. A. General
Dist N. M.

Sir:

The District Court adjourned on Thursday the 1st inst. The Grand jury returned nearly two-hundred indictments against one of the factions, and none against the other. Lt. Col. N. A. M. Dudley, U. S. A., was indicted for Arson. He appeared in Court and took a change of venue to Dona Ana County, to appear on the 16th of June. He was held on his own recognizance, in two thousand dollars ($2000.00) to so appear. Most of the Citizen prisoners who were indicted by this grand Jury were arraigned and pleaded the Governor's amnesty, for all offences coming within its provisions. The prisoners were discharged. Doc Scurlock, and the 'Kid' the two most notorious murderers of the County, have been in custody of the Sheriff at Lincoln. The Grand Jury did not indict them. The Sheriff who is deputy U. S. Marshal released them, although he knew that there were indictments against them, for murder in the U. S. Court, and the warrants for their arrest said to be in his hands. Mr. Dolan, and Ex-Sheriff Peppen did not avail themselves of the Governor's proclamation. They changed their venue to Socorro County. Mr. Dolan is still in Confinement at the Post. Mr. Peppin is under bonds. The Hudgens and Henry were taken to Lincoln for a hearing before the Court, but were allowed to escape. On the 2nd inst. the sheriff sent for the horses alleged to have been stolen by them, and they were turned over to the 'Kid' and Deputy Sheriff McPheron.

There was but one trial on the indictment presented to this Court and he was acquitted.

I am, Sir
Very respectfully
Your obedient Servant
Geo. A. Purington
Capt. 9th Cavalry
Comd'g"

Santa Fe *Weekly New Mexican*, Saturday, 17 May 1879

"A correspondent of the News, under date of May 1st, writes as follows: - "Court still in session. The grand jury adjourned yesterday after finding nearly 200 indictments; over 100 being for murder. Col. Dudley and Geo. Peppin were indicted for burning McSween's house last summer; they were indicted on the evidence of a colored man in Mrs. McSeeen's employ and Mrs. McSween. The cause has been changed to Socorro county as to Peppin and to Dona Ana as to Col. Dudley. The action of the grand jury was extremely partisan as there was no disposition to indict except persons of the anti-McSeeen, anti-'Kid' and anti-Scurlock party. Court will probably adjourn today or tomorrow. Three prisoners held as horse thieves escaped from the sheriff yesterday and are at large, viz: John Hudgens, Tobe Hudgens and Robert Henry. The 'Kid' and Scurlock are expected to walk off any time as but little restraint is placed upon these favorites of the governor. Last week one of the militia of His Excellency, here known as 'heelflies,' accidentally shot himself and died; his name is Eli Gray. Lucas Gallegos an old offender was tried for murder, found guilty in the 4th degree and given a year in jail. Dan Deetrich was tried for assault to murder and acquitted. It is thought that troubles will be worse than ever here as soon as court adjourns."

Cimarron *News and Press*, 22 May 1879

"The *Mesilla News* states that the Kid, Scurlock, and other warriors of the McSween party have been arrested and that the Governor made the request of Prosecuting Attorney Rynerson that the Kid be allowed to turn state's evidence, and that Colonel Rynerson indignantly refused the request.

The *News* by this little story – which doubtless entirely originated with the editor – endeavors to show partisanship and reflect ridicule on the Governor.

Now the facts are these. The Kid was a very conspicuous actor in Lincoln County War drama, but has not committed any overt act since the issue of the Governor's amnesty proclamation – at least no such act has been chronicled in the local papers and we have heard of none. Therefore he could properly plead the Governor's pardon. He was, however, an eyewitness of the dastardly murder of poor Chapman, which was committed after the amnesty proclamation, and for which Dolan, Evans, and Campbell have been indicted. And the fact of his being an important witness against the favorites of the *News* fully accounts for the milk in the cocoa-nut."

Los Lunas, N. M., 30 May 1879

"Charles Devins Atty Genl
Of the United States

Sir

On 21st day of June 1878, an Indictment was found by the Grand Jury of the United States in the 3rd Judicial District Territory of New Mexico against (9) persons to wit Charles Bowdry, Doc Scurlock, Henry Brown, Henry Antrim (alias) Kidd, John Middleton, Stephen Stevens, John Scroggins, George Coe & Frederick Waite charging them with murdering Andrew Roberts in April 1878, on the Mescalero Apache Indian Reservation New Mexico. Three of the Defendants Coe, Antrim & Scurlock are confined at Fort Stanton. I hope others will be arrested by 9th June day of Commencement of Court at Mesilla 3rd District. Those arrested are reported to be terrible offenders. I am anxious to bring them to a speedy trial I forward you herewith a copy of the Indictment & Marshall Sherman Dispatch.

The Defendants will be represented by able lawyers – I believe the ends of Justice require me to submit the case to you and ask you to clothe me with discretion & power to secure the aid of an additional Attorney in the event I come to the conclusion when I get to Mesilla & investigate the case fully that I need help. I do not desire to incur expense unnecessarily. T. B. Catron former Atty offers to aid me if requested by you. I am not certain that I desire his services – wish the privilege to determine for myself.

If you conclude to obtain help advise me at once by Telegraph at Mesilla. Communication by Mail will not reach me in time. I send newspaper also.

Respectfully
Sidney M Barnes, United
States Atty New Mexico

1 Newspaper – The News and Press
Cimarron, N. M., May 22, 1879."

***The Mesilla News*, 21 Jun 1879**

"A private letter from Mr. Ellis from the town of Lincoln, N. M. dated June 18, 1879, sys: That on the night of the 17th inst. 'The Kid' very suddenly disappeared: Mr. Ellis thinks it unnecessary to be at the trouble and expense of attending the court in Mesilla. We suppose 'The Kid' had the same feeling, or perhaps he was anxious to save the county and territory the heavy costs of a trial.

Mr. Ellis says however that if the sheriff should recapture 'The Kid' in time to be present at this court he (Ellis) may attend also.

Doc Scurlock also thought there was very little use in his appearing at court in Dona Ana Co, to answer to indictments or other charges, so he skipped with 'The Kid.'"

Las Cruces *Thirty-Four*, Wednesday, 25 Jun 1879

"The Dudley court of inquiry has summoned ex-Gov. Axtell as a witness.

Porter Stockton, the murderer of Withers, at Otero has not been arrested.

Scurlock and 'Kid' have escaped from the Lincoln County authorities.

Ed. Withers was murdered at Otero last week. Porter Stockton is said to be the murderer.

Quite a number of Lincoln county men are in town as witnesses on Dolan's habeas corpus case.

Deputy Sheriff Redman, of Lincoln County, is in town with an escort of six soldiers. They come from Stanton as a guard to J. J. Dolan.

The trial of Alex. Bull for the murder of A. Lee Campbell is still progressing this, Tuesday, P. M. We should be glad to give a full account of it, but must wait until its conclusion. The general impression is that Bull will be cleared, because it is considered impossible to convict him in this county. At the same time the opinion is universal that he is guilty and should be punished in the full extent of the law. We have talked to no one, except his lawyers, who expresses any other opinion. Next week we shall have more to say on the subject."

Request from Juan Patron for compensation for rent and expenses of keeping prisoners dated 12 Nov 1880.

Lincoln N. Mex
November 12th 1880

Lincoln County
In a/c with
Juan B. Patron Dr.

Rent of House for Keeping Prisoners from March 21st/79 to June 17th/79 @ $5.00 per month	$14.33
To Board of Wm Bonny 27 days	27.00
" " " Lucas Gallegos 27 days	27.00
" " " Dock Scurlock 27 days	27.00
" " " Thomas O'Folliard 10 days	10.00
" " " Dan Dedrick 4 days	4.00
Total	$109.33

Territory of New Mexico }
County of Lincoln }

Juan B. Patron, being duly sworn deposes and says; that the forgoing account is just and correct, and that the County of Lincoln is justly indebted to deponent in the above a/c.

Juan B. Patron

Sworn to and subscribed this 13th day of November A.D. 1880.

Ben N. Ellis
Probate Clerk
By S. R. Corbet
Depty

Mabank *Manner* Newspaper, 11 May 1916. Advertisement for Doc teaching Spanish.

WILL TEACH SPANISH.

J. G. Scurlock informs us that he will open a Spanish class in Mabank in the near future. Mr. Scurlock has had unusual advantages in his long residence in Mexico, where he was for a long time employed in the translation of official records.

His English education has been no less proficient, thereby better fitting him for the work in hand. Owing to the great number of Spanish speaking people our state, and the near relation between our state and that of Mexico, it is very wise for anyone who has the time and means to avail themselves of this unusual opportunity.

Mr. Scurlock has appeared before the teacher of Spanish in the Dallas public schools and satisfied him of his ability to teach the language.

CRIPPLED BY TRAIN.

J. T. Luther informed us that his oldest son, J. C. Luther, Freight Agent for the Rock

1922 Eastland, Texas Phone Directory. Doc listed as working for Highway Dept.

SCRIPTURE E A LUMBER CO, Calvin Brown mgr, rigs and lumber, 200 E White, phone 64 (see left bottom lines)
Scroggins Roy L (Edith) r 215 S Ammerman av
Scurlock John J (Amy E) contr r 106 N Ammerman av
Scurlock J G checker Eastland County Highway Dept rms 320 N Lamar
SEABERRY VIRGIL T (Cleo) (Turner & Seaberry) attorney-at-law, Frost bldg, phone 56, r 145 W Burkett blvd, phone 483
Seale Bros & McElreath (John D and Henry Seale, A R McElreath) real est 208 First State Bank bldg
Seale Henry (Axcie C) (Seale Bros & McElreath) r 727 S Daugherty av
Seale John D (Bertha M) (Seale Bros & McElreath) r 505 S Seaman
SEALE JOHN D JR, v-pres Eastland Motor Co, h 505 S Seaman
Seastrunk J W h 615 S Seaman
Seastrunk Simon P (Lura) transfer r 615 S Seaman
Seastrunk William W mech Elliott & Wright rms 115 N Dixie
Security State Bank Building 100-2 N Lamar
Security State Bank & Trust Co in charge J R Burnet spcl agt State Dept of Ins & Banking 100-2 N Lamar
Sees Bert driller rms 407 W Patterson
SELF CHARLES F, chf clk Empire Gas & Fuel Co, r same, phone 34
Self Dere Miss h 405 S Walnut av
Self Ina May Miss h 405 S Walnut av
Self Lewis H (Effie) lino opr Oil Belt Publishing Co r W Sadosa nw cor Green
Self William T (Ola) (Paris Tailoring Co) r 405 S Walnut av
Sells John H (Lee) lab r ss Lackland 1 e Simmons
Selman Grace (c) dom 702 S Seaman h rear same
Selman John (c) (Grace) r rear 702 S Seaman
Semple Robert W (Helen) draftsman Prairie Pipe Line Co r C 400 N Lamar
SENATE CAFE, Louis Rosse prop, strictly American, newest and most up-to-date cafe in the city, 103 W Main
Serano Guadalupe h Mrs Celsa Gonzalez
Serano Guadalupe (Elvira B) rest N Bassett sw cor Moss r same
SERVICE GASOLINE CO (A L Bean, O A Kelly) gasoline and auto accessories, 115 N Lamar, phone 110
Seth John A (Glenna) eng engr Arab Gasoline Corp r 1201 S Seaman

1926 Eastland, Texas Phone Directory. Listed in his son-in-law Columbus Buckbee's house.

Satterwhite H Oscar (Martha) clk Satterwhite Hardware Co r 508 S Seaman

Sawyer A John r ss W Valley 1 w Dixie av

Sawyer Jewett Miss opr Southwestern Bell Tel Co h A J Sawyer

SAYLES JOHN (Sayles & Sayles) attorney, 316-20 Texas State Bank bldg, phone 135, rms 305 N Daugherty

SAYLES PERRY (Juanita) (Sayles & Sayles) attorney 316-20 Texas State Bank bldg, phone 135, r 604 S Bassett, phone 489

SAYLES & SAYLES (John and Perry Sayles) attorneys, 316-320 Texas State Bank bldg, phone 135 (see page 5)

Scarborough Oliver C (Rossie B) delman r 203 W Sadosa

Schmich James K rms 309 S Lamar

Scott C C opr Arab Gasoline Corp r Hand booster sta

SCOTT DALLAS K (Scott, Brelsford, McCarty & Brelsford) r Cisco, Texas

SCOTT, BRELSFORD, McCARTHY & BRELSFORD (D K Scott, H P Brelsford, Milburn McCarty, Harry Brelsford) attorneys-at-law, 300-14 Texas State Bank bldg, phone 176 (see page 5)

Scott Robert E h C G Pena

Scott Thomas rms 109 N Daugherty

Scott William V (Veo) trav slsmn rms 314 S Seaman

Scoville U R rms Charlotte Hotel

Scurlock J Gordon h C E Buckbee

Scurlock John J (Amy) contr r 316 N Green

Seaberry Reva Miss tchr South Ward School h 206 W Burkett blvd

Seaberry Virgil T (Turner Seaberry & Springer) r 206 W Burket blvd

Seale John D (Bertha) real est r 308 (209) N Connellee

Seale Walter A (Fannie L) mgr Western Union Telegraph Co r 107 E Valley

Seale Wortham H (Beatrice) clk Gulf Refining Co r 16 Gulf Co lease

1928 Eastland, Texas Phone Directory. Listed in his son-in-law Columbus Buckbee's house.

Ross Jacob A (Bertha) barber West Side Barber Shop r 608 W Commerce
Rotary Club meets Monday 12:15 P M at Connellee Hotel J M Weaver pres Earl Bender v-pres Tom McManus sec
Rotramel Jane Miss student h 217 E Sadosa
Rotramel Joseph H (Allie) slsmn r 217 E Sadosa
Rotramel Roscoe tool dresser h 217 E Sadosa
Rotramel Walter J (Nancy) h 217 E Sadosa
Rowan S Maria Mrs r es N Bassett av 4 N Moss
Rowe Montie drvr h 112½ N Seaman
Rowe Robert L (Earl) (Rowe Rooms) shoemkr 112 N Seaman r 112½ same
Rowe Rooms (R L Rowe) 112½ N Seaman
Rowell Herman (Donna) driller r 909 S Seaman
Roy Frank (Johnnie) formn Eastland Lndry Co rms 302 W White
Rumph Mary Sue Miss tchr West Ward School h 1206 S Seaman
Rumph Sterling P (Maud G) r 1206 S Seaman
Russell A William (Mable) slsmn r 409 E Sadosa
Russell F E rodmn Prairie Oil & Gas Co h 519 S Daugherty
Russell John A (Mandie) claim agt r 208 W Sadosa
Russell Philip G (Ethel) r 519 S Daugherty
Rust Building 117½ S Lamar
Rust Robert L (Olive I) atty 117½ S Lamar r same
Ruthenborg M P firemn Leon plant Texas Elec Sevice Co r same

S

Saavedra Arnulfo (Elena B) peddler r 315 (210) N Seaman
St Francis Xavier Catholic Church S Hal Bryan se cor Foch
Saffen James M (Leona) caser r 608 S Daugherty
St John's Episcopal Church es S Lamar 1 s Valley
Samford James E (Evelyn) contr r ws S High av 2 s W Plummer
Sample Harry M (Roberta) land dept Vacuum Oil Co r 715 Hal Bryan
Samuels Dominick (Geneva) barber Rose Beauty Shop r 1206 (1006) W Main
Sanderford Ghent (Lois) atty 100½ W Commerce r 902 S Bassett av

SANDERS DEE (Dee Sanders Motor Co) rms Alhambra Hotel, 306 S Seaman
SANDERS DEE MOTOR CO (Dee Sanders, E H Johnson) Dodge Brothers Motor Cars and Graham Brothers Trucks, sales and service, Eastland, 405 S Seaman, phone 620, Ranger, 320-24 Pine, phone 23 (see left bottom and left side lines)
Sanders Willie E (wid W E) h 1212 (1012) W Main
Sanitary Barber Shop (M W Hague) 108 W Commerce
Sanitary Towel Supply (V E Griffith) 414 N Lamar
Sankey Paul K asst geologist Vacuum Oil Co rms 112½ N Lamar
Sargent Norman E (Flossie) servicemn Eastland Nash Co rms 109 N Dixie av
Satterwhite E Collen (Lina) (Satterwhite Hardware Co) r 509 S Seaman
SATTERWHITE HARDWARE CO (E C Satterwhite) shelf and heavy hardware, sporting goods, 110 S Seaman, phone 386
Satterwhite Henry O (Martha M) clk Satterwhite Hdw Co r 508 S Seaman
Saurez Wallace mess W U Tel Co
Sawyer A John h Mis Jewett Sawyer
Sawyer Jewett Miss opr S W Bell Tel Co r ws Slay 2 s Lackland
Sawyer J D mach Leon plant Texas Elec Service Co r same
SAYLES JOHN (Sayles & Sayles) r Abilene, Texas
SAYLES PERRY (Juanita) (Sayles & Sayles) r 604 S Bassett
SAYLES & SAYLES (John and Perry Sayles) attorneys, 316-324 Texas State Bank bldg, phone 135
Schenck F Roland (Ina Mae) levelmn Prairie Oil & Gas Co r L 400 N Lamar
Schmick James K r 309 S Lamar
Schurbell Arthur M driller rms 112½ N Lamar
Scott Bailey (Meta) batteries 300 W Commerce r 410 S Lamar
SCOTT, BRELSFORD, McCARTY & BRELSFORD (D K Scott, H P Brelsford, Milburn McCarty, Harry Brelsford) attorneys-at-law, 300-14 Texas State Bank bldg, phone 176 (see page 4)
Scott C C plant opr Arab Gasoline Corp
SCOTT DALLAS K (Scott, Brelsford, McCarty & Brelsford) r Cisco, Texas
Scurlock Josiah G h 114 N Ostrom av
Seaberry Reva Miss tchr South Ward School h 206 W Burkett blvd

PART V – DOCUMENTS IN DOC'S OWN HAND

Record of Scurlock family Bible, date unknown, as recorded by Doc in Spanish, 5 Pages

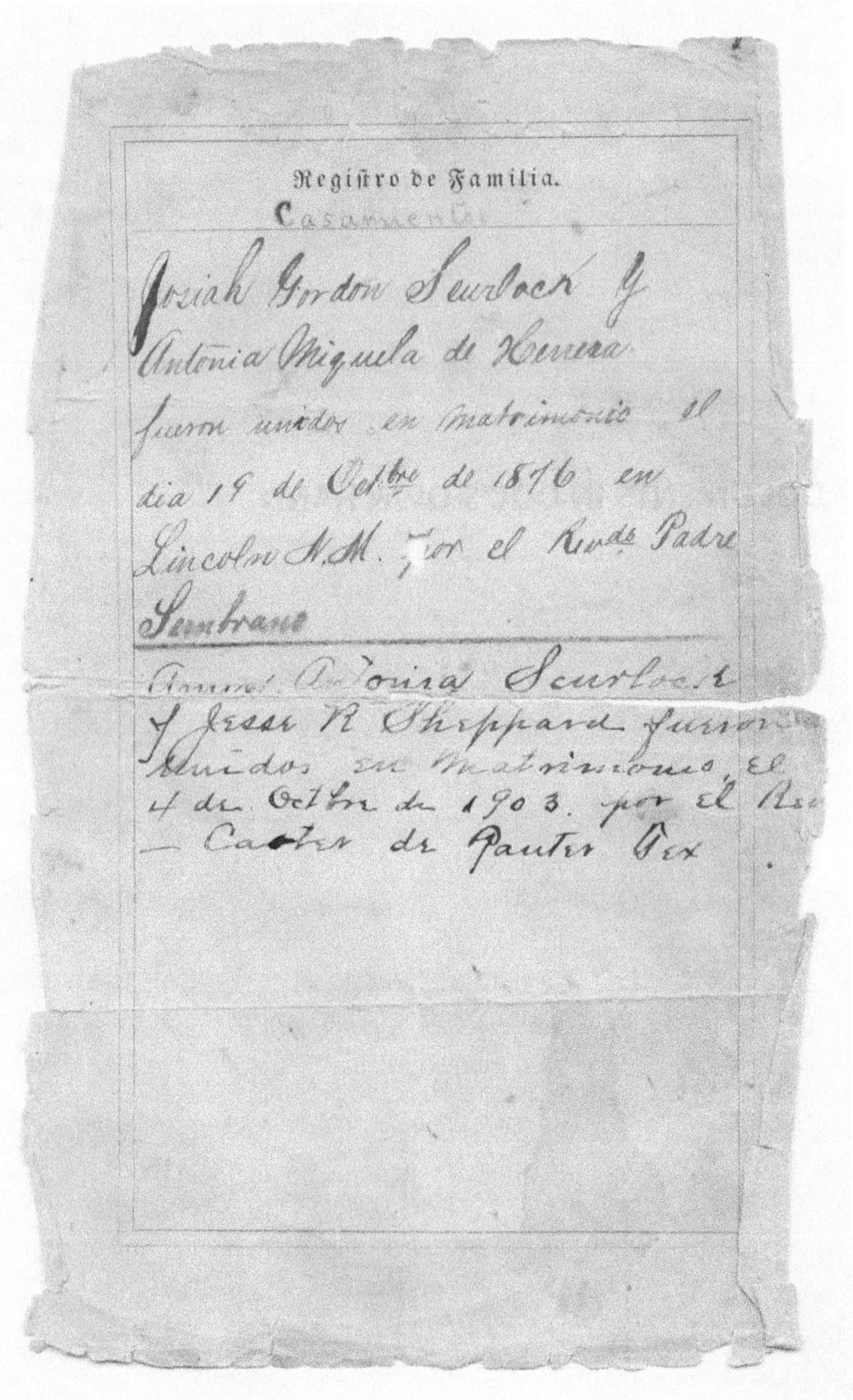

Registro de Familia.

Casamientos

Josiah Gordon Scurlock y
Antonia Miguela de Herrera
fueron unidos en matrimonio el
dia 19 de Octbre de 1876 en
Lincoln N.M. por el Revdo Padre
Sembrano

Amme Antonia Scurlock
y Jesse R Sheppard fueron
unidos en matrimonio, el
4 de Octbre de 1903. por el Rev
— Carter de Panter Tex

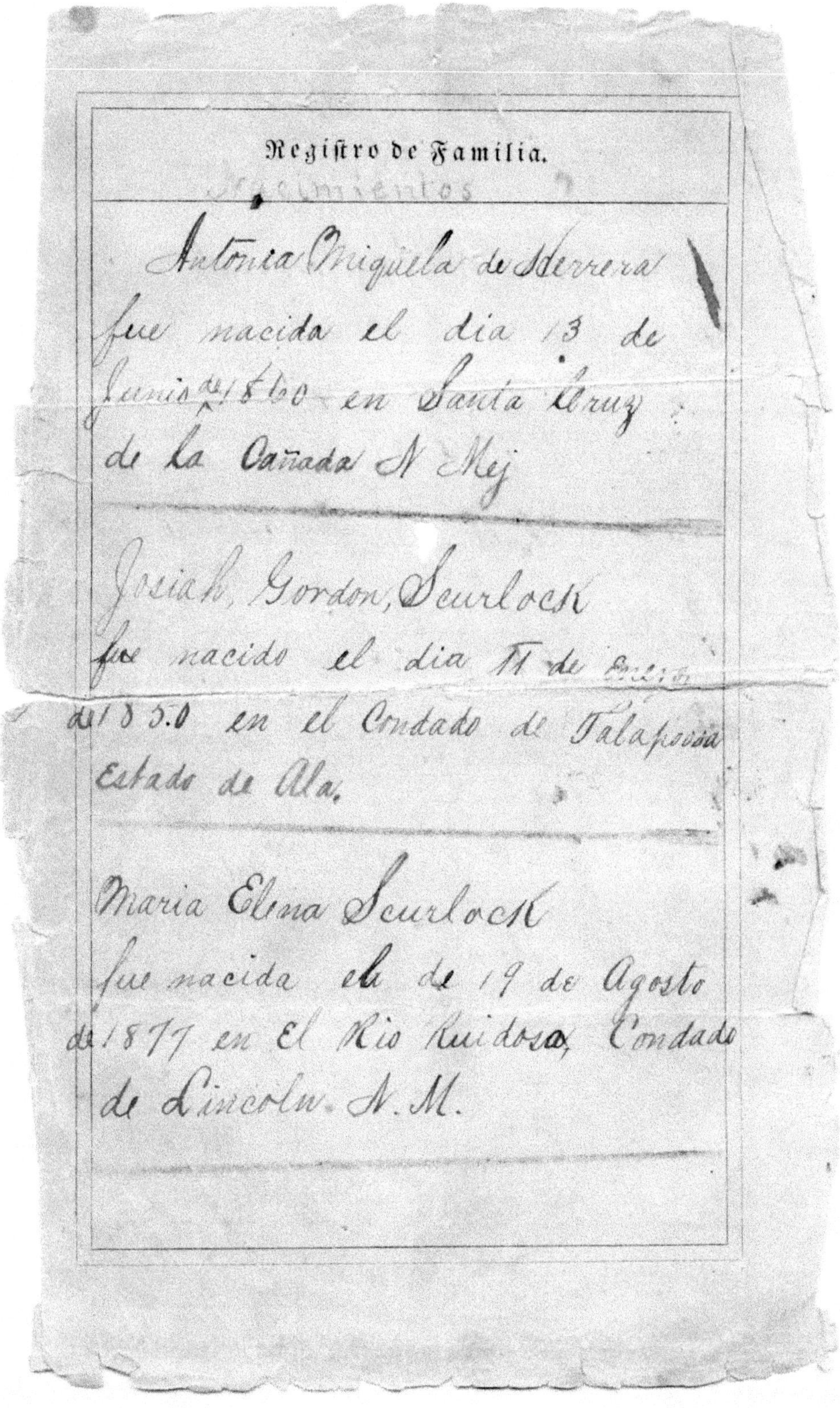

Registro de Familia.

Nacimientos

Antonia Miquela de Herrera
fue nacida el dia 13 de
Junio de 1860 en Santa Cruz
de la Cañada N Mej

Josiah, Gordon, Scurlock
fue nacido el dia 11 de enero
de 1850 en el Condado de Talaposa
Estado de Ala.

Maria Elina Scurlock
fue nacida el de 19 de Agosto
de 1877 en El Rio Ruidoso, Condado
de Lincoln. N.M.

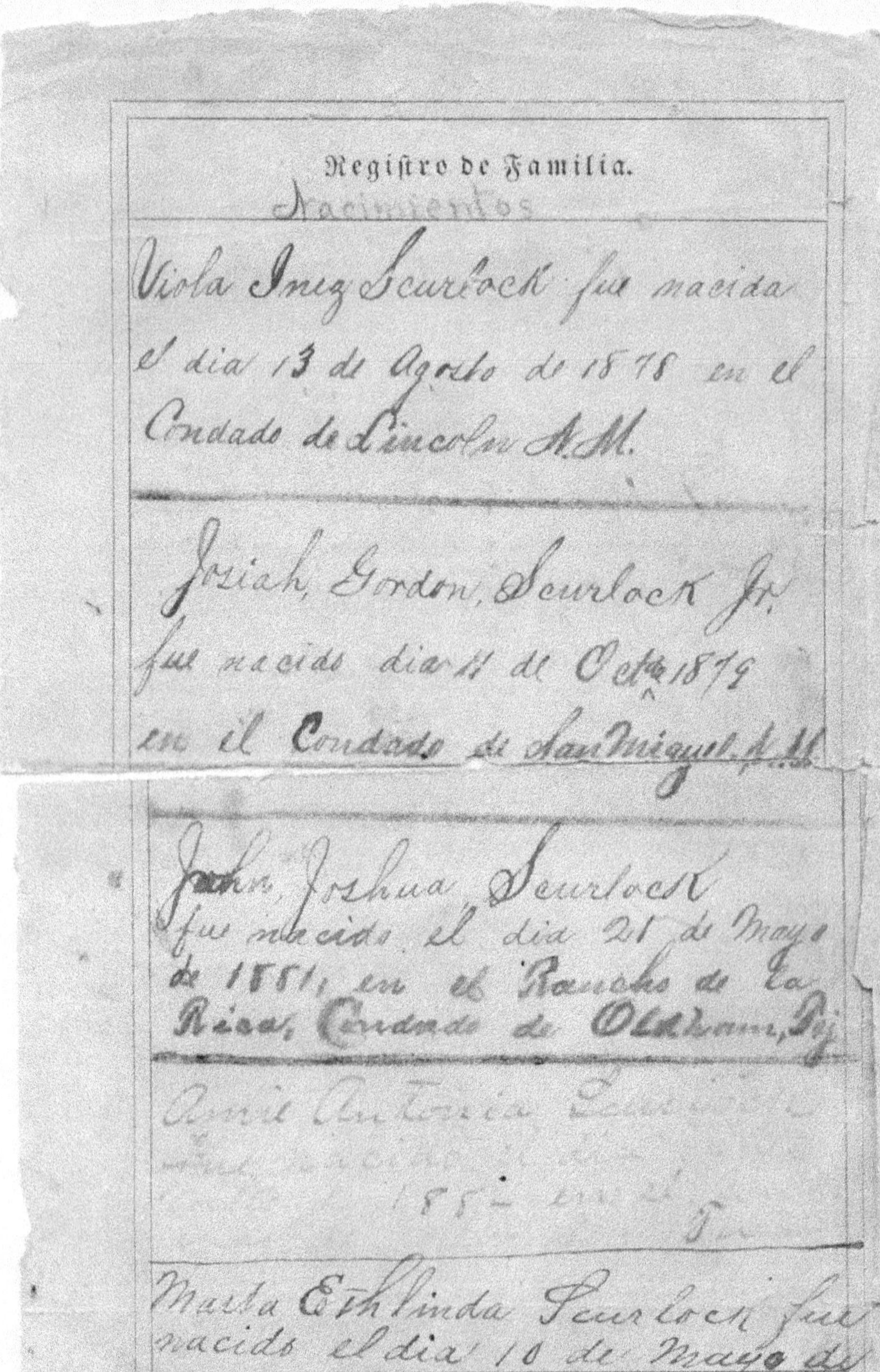
Registro de Familia.
Nacimientos

Viola Inez Scurlock fue nacida el dia 13 de Agosto de 1878 en el Condado de Lincoln N.M.

Josiah, Gordon, Scurlock Jr. fue nacido dia 11 de Octe 1879 en el Condado de San Miguel N.M.

John, Joshua Scurlock fue nacido el dia 21 de Mayo de 1881, en el Rancho de la Rica, Condado de Oldham, Tej

Annie Antonia Scurlock [illegible] 1882 en el [illegible]

Maria Ethlinda Scurlock fue nacido el dia 10 de Mayo de 1886 en el Condado de Wilbarger Estado de Texas

Registro de Familia.

Fallecimientos

Maria Elena Scurlock fallecio el dia 14 de Agosto de 1879 de 1 año 11 meses y 28 dias de edad

Viola Inez Scurlock fallecio el dia 7 de Junio de 1894. a la edad de 15 años 9 meses y 24 dias

Mother died Nov. 27, 1912

Father died July 25 1929.

Prestley Fernando Scurlock
fue nacido el dia 27 de Agosto
de 1888; en el Condado de
Wilbarger, Estado de Texas

Dolores Scurlock fue nacid[illegible]
[illegible]ia 10 de Marzo de 1891 en
[illegible]dado de Wilbarger Estado de Tex.

[illegible] Scurlock
fue nacido el dia 14 de Abril
de 1893 en el condado de Wilbarger
Estado de Texas

Josephine, [illegible], Scurlock
fue nacido el dia 2 de Agosto
de 1895, en el condado de Johnson
estado de Tex

This promissory note date 25 Jun 1877 between Alexander McSween and Doc sold at auction in 2019 along with various other items for $1,400. Another Wild West item in the Robert McCubbin collection

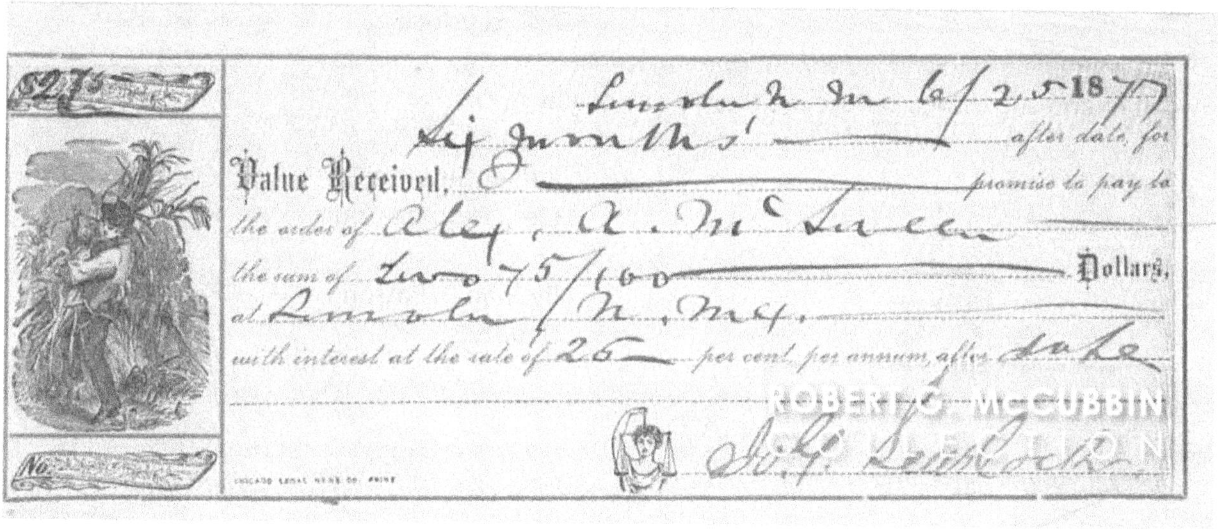
$2.75

Lincoln N. M. 6/25 1877

Six months after date, for

Value Received, I promise to pay to

the order of Alex. A. McSween

the sum of two 75/100 Dollars,

at Lincoln, N. Mex.

with interest at the rate of 26 per cent. per annum, after date

No.

CHICAGO LEGAL NEWS CO. PRINT

Jo. G. Scurlock

Lincoln, N. M., 15 Jul 1878

"I having been accused of attempting to kill Mrs. Brady's boy and also with threatening the life of Gen. Dudley, most positively deny both accusations, and there is no real foundation for either.

J. G. Scurlock

Sworn to and subscribed before me this 15 day of July A. D.

Rafael Gutierres
Clerk Probate Court

By Juan B. Patron
Deputy"

Lincoln N.M. July 15 1878

I having been accused of attempting to take Mrs Brady's life and also threatening the life of Gen Dudley must positively deny both accusations and there is no real foundation for such

(sd) J.G. Scurlock

Sworn to and subscribed before me this 15 day of July AD 1878

(sd) Rafael Gutierrez

Clerk Probate Court

By Juan B Patron

Dept

A true copy

Henry H. Humphreys

Capt 15 Infantry

Recd Cour Inqry

These are the two complete poems in Doc's hand he wrote 14 May 1893: *The Ship* and *Pulling Hard Against the Stream*.

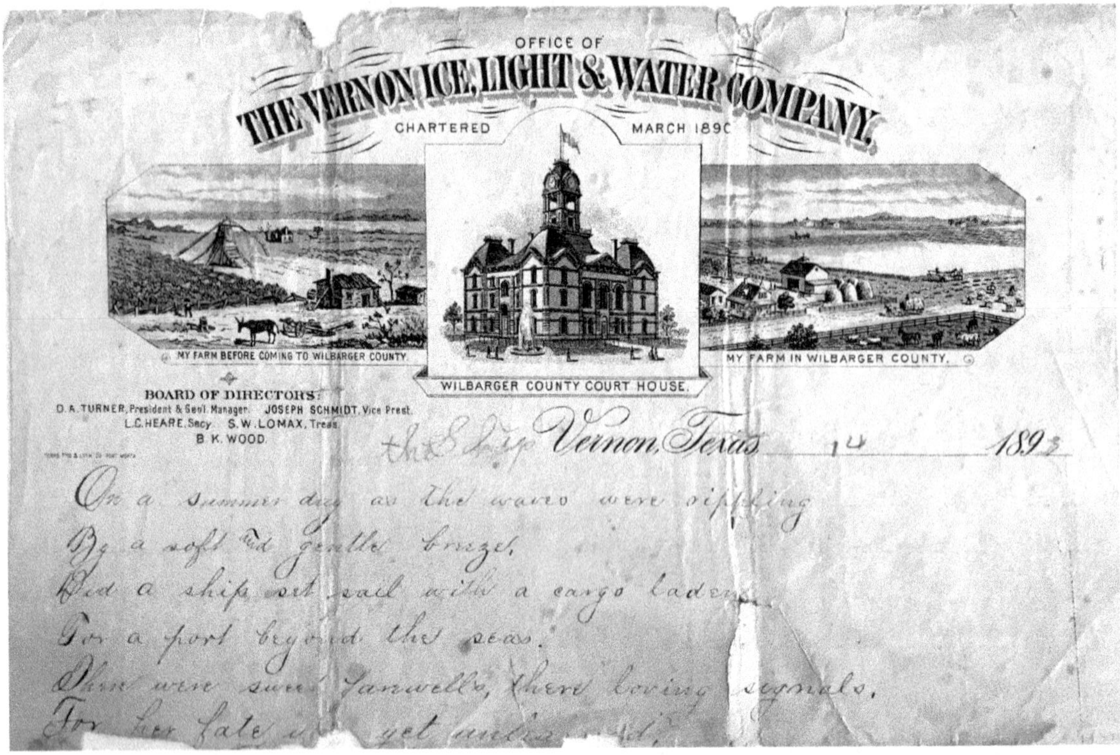

OFFICE OF

THE VERNON ICE, LIGHT & WATER COMPANY.

CHARTERED MARCH 1890

BOARD OF DIRECTORS:
D. A. TURNER, President & Genl. Manager. JOSEPH SCHMIDT, Vice Prest.
L.C. HEARE, Secy. S.W. LOMAX, Treas.
B. K. WOOD.

the Ship Vernon, Texas 14 1893

On a summer day as the waves were rippling
By a soft and gentle breeze,
Did a ship set sail with a cargo laden
For a port beyond the seas.
There were sweet farewells, there loving signals,
For her fate is yet unlearned,

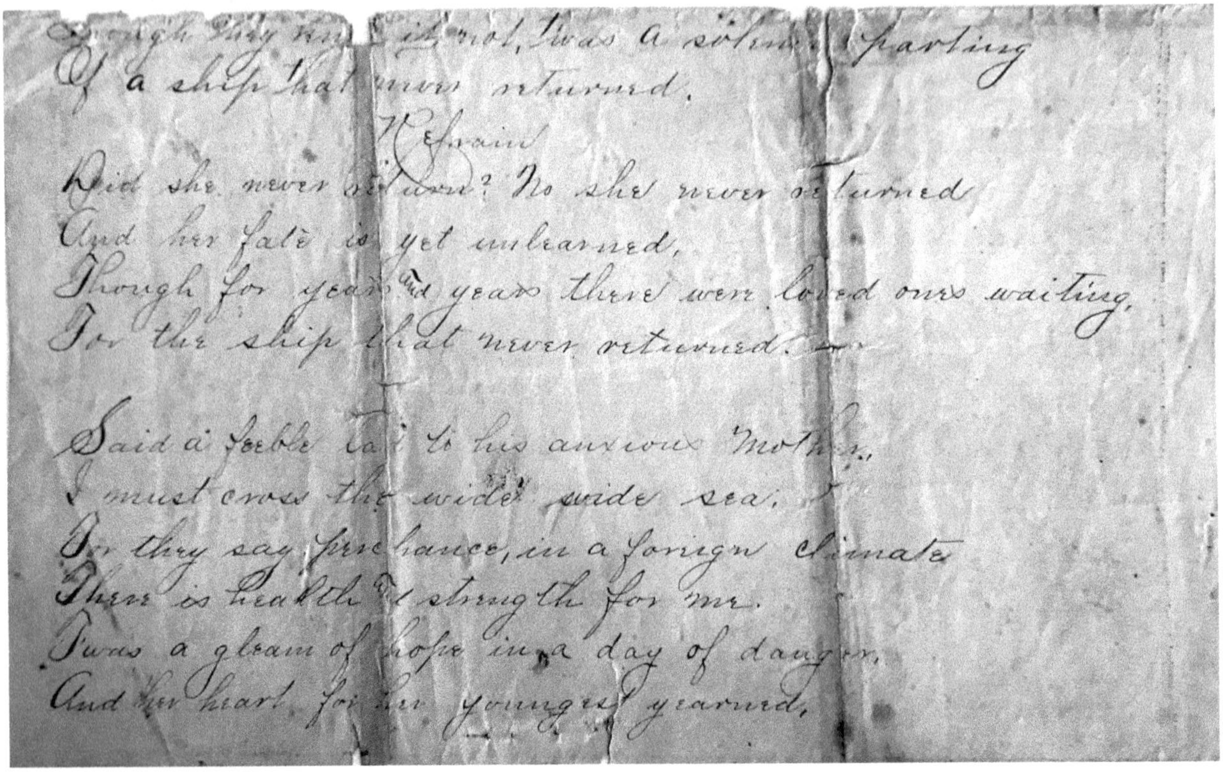

Though they knew it not, 'twas a solemn parting
Of a ship that never returned.

Refrain

Did she never return? No she never returned
And her fate is yet unlearned,
Though for years and years there were loved ones waiting,
For the ship that never returned.

Said a feeble lad to his anxious Mother,
I must cross the wide wide sea,
For they say perchance, in a foreign climate
There is health and strength for me.
'Twas a gleam of hope in a day of danger,
And her heart for her youngest yearned,

AVERY® POLY-VU

"1 of 3"

OFFICE OF
THE VERNON ICE, LIGHT & WATER COMPANY.
CHARTERED MARCH 1890

BOARD OF DIRECTORS:
D. A. TURNER, President & Gen'l. Manager. JOSEPH SCHMIDT, Vice Presd.
L. C. HEAPE, Secy. S. W. LOMAX, Treas.
B. K. WOOD.

The Ship Vernon, Texas 1st 189

On a summer day as the waves were rippling
By a soft and gentle breeze,
Did a ship set sail with a cargo laden
For a port beyond the seas.
There were sweet farewells, there loving signals,
For her fate [illegible] yet [illegible]

This original had been folded for a long period of time and is now in 3 pieces where it fell apart along major fold lines.

"2 of 3"

[illegible] Twas a solemn parting
Of a ship that never returned,

Refrain

Did she never return? No she never returned.
And her fate is yet unlearned,
Though for years and years there were loved ones waiting,
For the ship that never returned.

Said a feeble lad to the anxious mother,
I must cross the wide wide sea,
For they say perchance, in a foreign climate
There is health and strength for me.
Twas a gleam of hope in a day of danger,
And her heart for her youngest yearned,

[illegible] a smile [illegible]
On a ship that never returned.

Refrain

Did she ever return &c.

Only one more trip said a gallant seaman,
As he kissed his weeping wife,
Only one more bag of golden treasure
And 'twill last us all through life.
Then we'll spend our days in our cozy cottage,
And enjoy the rest we've earned,
But alas poor man who sailed commander
On a ship that never returned.

Refrain

Did she [illegible] &c

OFFICE OF

THE VERNON ICE, LIGHT & WATER COMPANY.

CHARTERED MARCH 1890.

MY FARM BEFORE COMING TO WILBARGER COUNTY

WILBARGER COUNTY COURT HOUSE

MY FARM IN WILBARGER COUNTY.

BOARD OF DIRECTORS:
D. A. TURNER, President & Genl. Manager JOSEPH SCHMIDT, Vice Presl
L. C. HEARE, Secy. S. W. LOMAX, Treas
B. K. WOOD

Vernon, Texas May 14 189

(Pulling hard against the Stream)

1 Its in this world I've gained my knowledge
And for it I've had to pay
Although I've never been to College
Yet I've heard the Poets say
This is like [illegible] waves
Rolling me from [illegible]
And we as ships are launched upon
Some get wrecked and cast away

Refrain

Then do your best for one another
Make this life a pleasant dream
Help a weary worn brother
Pulling hard against the stream.

OFFICE OF

THE VERNON ICE, LIGHT & WATER COMPANY.

CHARTERED MARCH 1890.

BOARD OF DIRECTORS:
S. A. TURNER, President & Gen'l Manager   JOSEPH SCHMIDT, Vice Prest.
L. C. HEARE, Secy.   S. W. LOMAX, Treas.
B. K. WOOD.

(Pulling hard against the stream)   Vernon, Texas May 14 18

Its in this world I've gained my knowledge
And for it I've had to pay
Although I've never been to College
[illegible] I've heard the Poets say
[illegible]
[illegible]
[illegible] we as ships are launched upon [illegible]
Some get wrecked & cast away
Refrain
Then do your best for one another
Make this life a pleasant dream
Help a weary [illegible] brother
Pulling hard against the stream.

Original for Abstract #3, p. 1 of 2

OFFICE OF

THE VERNON ICE, LIGHT & WATER COMPANY.

CHARTERED MARCH 1890.

MY FARM BEFORE COMING TO WILBARGER COUNTY.

WILBARGER COUNTY COURT HOUSE.

MY FARM IN WILBARGER COUNTY.

BOARD OF DIRECTORS:
D. A. TURNER, President & Gen'l Manager. JOSEPH SCHMIDT, Vice Pres.
L. C. HEARE, Sec'y. S. W. LOMAX, Treas.
B. K. WOOD.

Vernon, Texas.

2 There's many a bright good hearted fellow
Many a noble minded man
Who find themselves in waters shallow
Then assist him if you can
Some succeed at any turning
Fortune favors every scheme
While others far [illegible] the more deserving
Have to pull against the stream.

Refrain

Then do your best &c

3 As in this life we journey onward
Striving hard for wealth or fame
As favored ones, we're never thinking
Of those struggling in the stream
But the darkest night must have an ending
Though the way [illegible]

Original for Abstract #3, p 2 of 2

Note from Doc to children about health of his son, 20 Mar 1909. Willie is Doc's son William who would've been about 16 years old. Jess and Amy refers to Amy Antonia, his daughter, and her husband Robert Jessie Sheppard. Johny is Doc's son John Joshua.

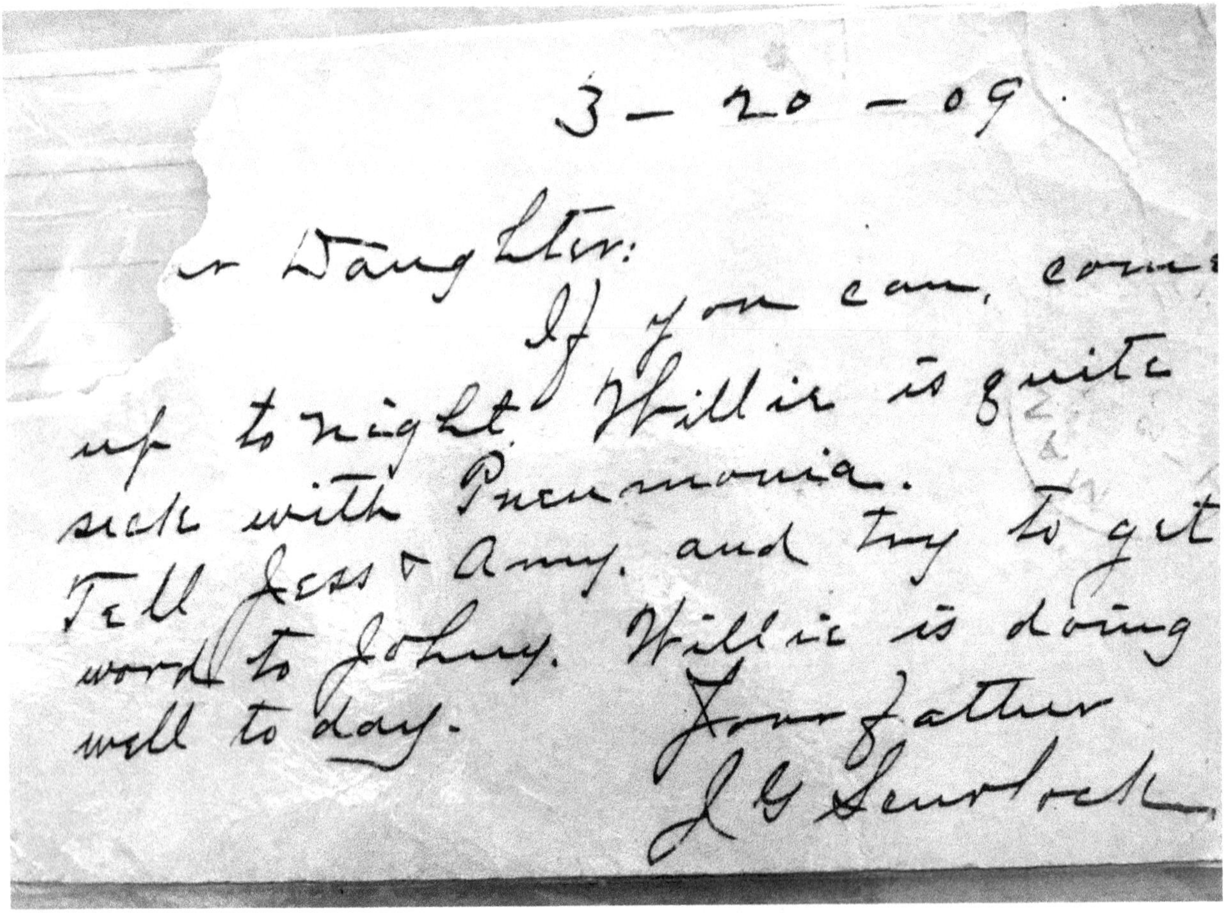

3-20-09.

...r Daughter:

If you can, come up tonight. Willie is quite sick with Pneumonia. Tell Jess & Amy, and try to get word to Johny. Willie is doing well to day.

Your father
J G Scurlock

Letter dated 3 Sep 1909.

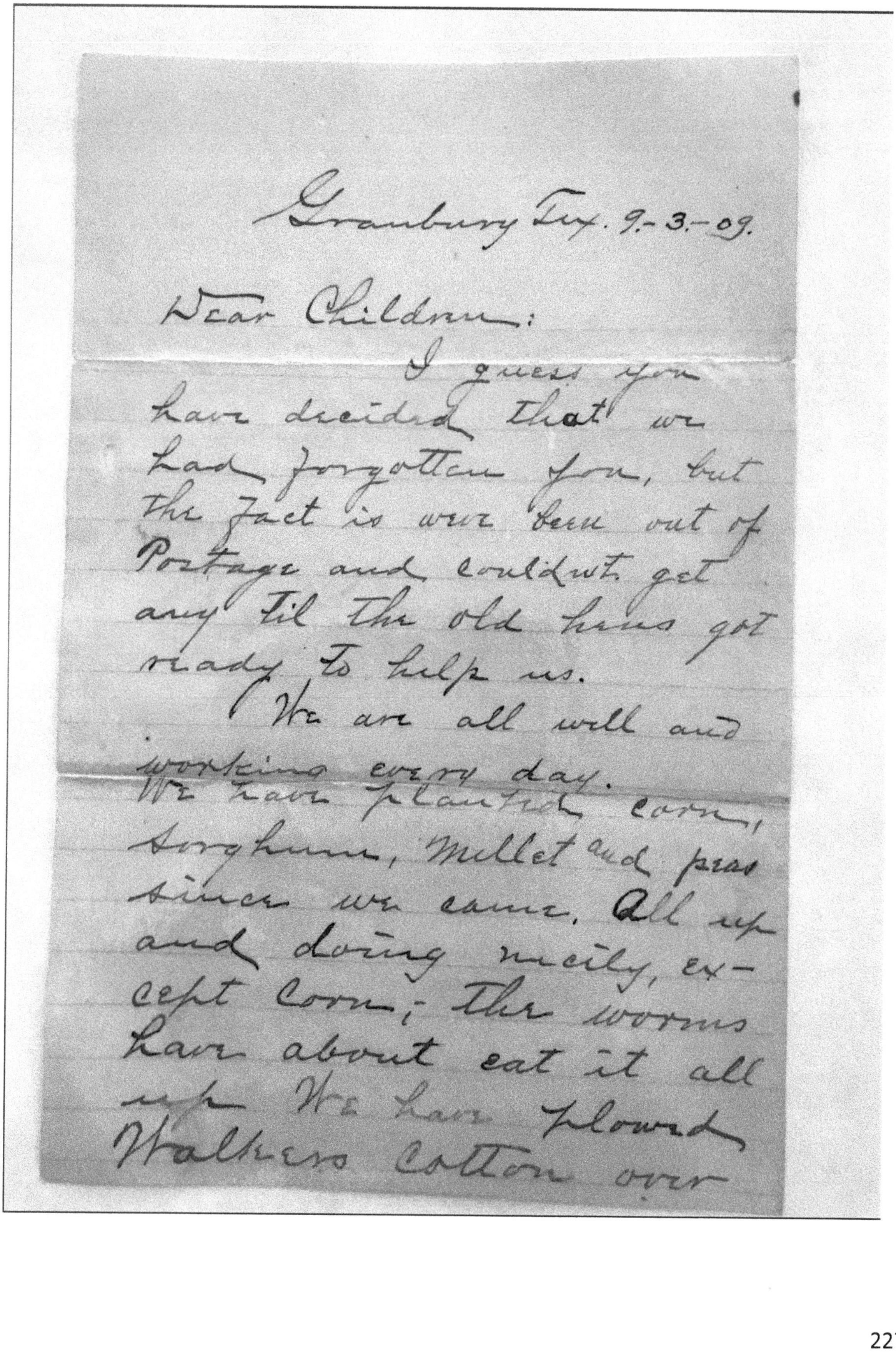

Granbury Tex. 9-3-09.

Dear Children:

I guess you have decided that we had forgotten you, but the fact is we've been out of Postage and couldnt get any til the old hens got ready to help us.

We are all well and working every day. We have planted corn, sorghum, Millet and peas since we came. All up and doing nicely, except corn; the worms have about eat it all up. We have plowed Walkers cotton over

again since the the
first big rain.
Since you were here
we've had three good
rains. First the night
I staid at your house,
next two weeks ago today,
and again Tuesday of
this week, consequently
everything is looking
all right. The worms
are eating the grass
and corn and I'm
afraid they will work
on the sorghum and
Millet. If they don't
we'll make plenty of
hay to do us

Have no news to speak of
that would be of interest
to you. I want you
to come to see us if
you can.

Lola wants to write
some so I'll quit.
Write soon
Address Granbury
R.F.D. No 2.

Your father
J. F. Scurlock.

Letter dated 26 Sep 1909.

Granbury Tex 9-26-09.

Dear Daughter:

Your letter came to us all right and I should have answered sooner but have been so busy that I could find no time to write except at night, and then I'm too tired.

We coulnt come down there yesterday, but will try to get off next Saturday if we can, but of course cannot tell surely that far ahead. We are all busily engaged some picking cotton, some cutting

2

sprouts and first one thing
and then another.
We've just finished cutting
and stacking our Colorado
grass, and it is fine. Think
we will have a hundred
or a hundred and fifty bales
between us and Tidwell.
If we can get a baler, we
want to bale it as soon
as we can.
Its getting very dry again.
Our late sorghum and
millet is needing rain badly.
How are things getting
along with you? How
much cotton does Ed.
Think he'll make now.

Letter dates 21 Apr 1910.

Granbury Tex 4-21-10

Dear Children;

Your letter came to us yesterday and we were glad to hear from you. We are so busy that we will not be able to come down this week. Are just finishing planting our old land Cotton and have Twenty acres of New ground to cross break before planting so at the best we can do, it will be well into May before we can finish, as you see we can't lose

2

even one day. But just
wait patientlly we'll get
them bye and bye.
Sorry we couldn't get
the cotton seed.
Guess Ed and I will have
to rustle some mortgage
builder seed.
Mama has had hatched
about one hundred and
twenty five little chicks
and has three more hens
setting; but has lost a
few of the chicks; I
don't know just how
many

Note dated 12 Oct 1916 of Doc relaying the deteriorating health of his daughter Lola. She passed away fifteen days later due to complications from the operation.

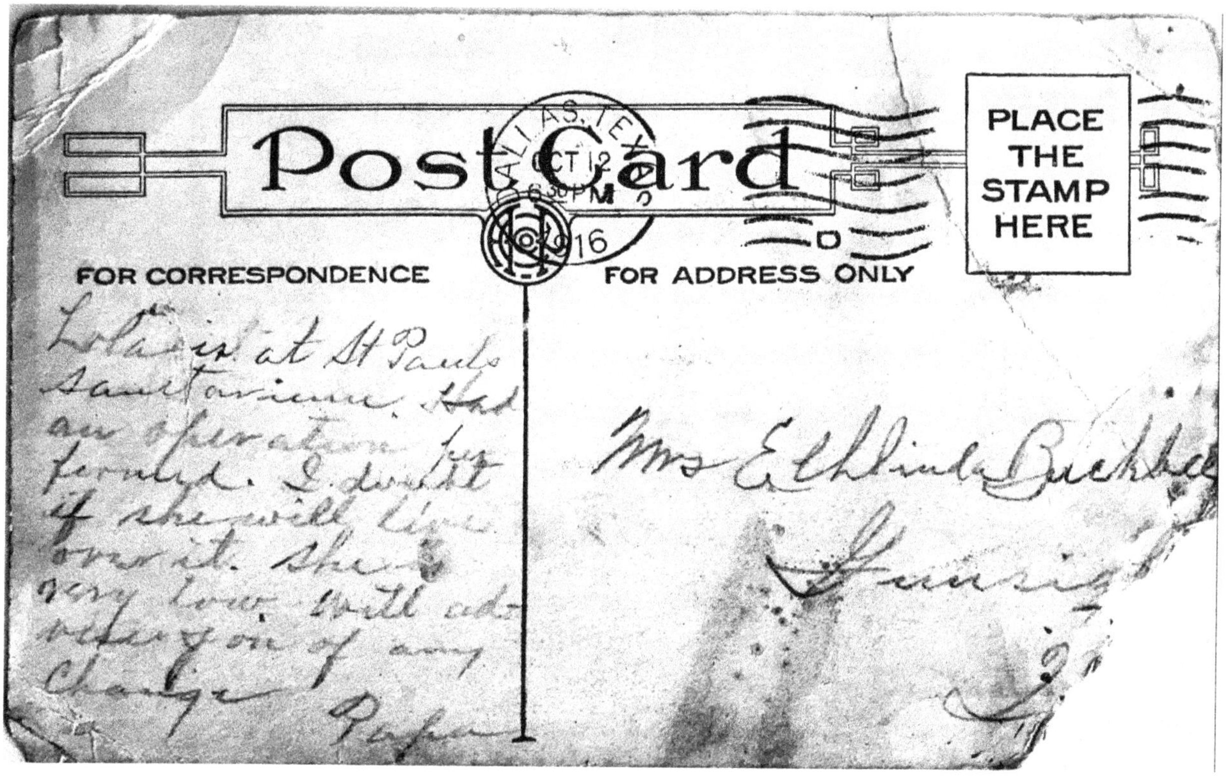

Post Card

PLACE THE STAMP HERE

ALLAS, TEX. OCT 12 6:30 PM 1916

FOR CORRESPONDENCE

Lola is at St Pauls Sanitarium. Had an operation performed. I doubt if she will live over it. She is very low. Will advise you of any change

Papa

FOR ADDRESS ONLY

Mrs Ethlinda Buckbee
Gunsight
Tex

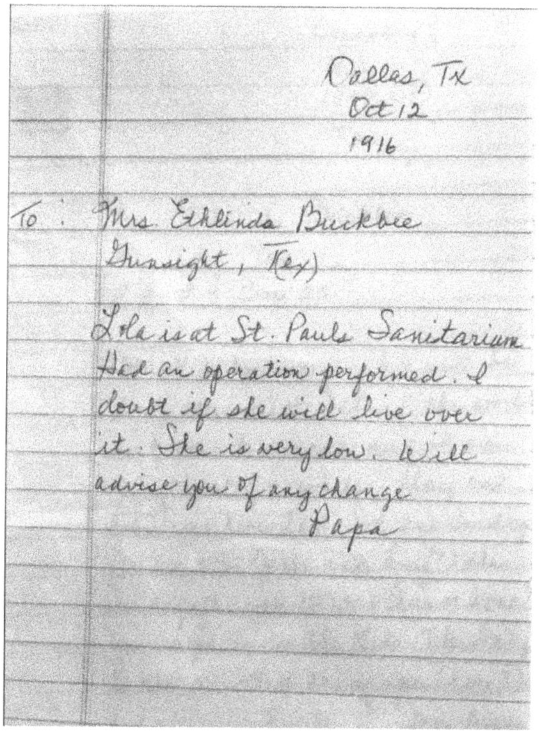

Dallas, Tx
Oct 12
1916

To: Mrs. Ethlinda Buckbee
Gunsight, Tex)

Lola is at St. Pauls Sanitarium. Had an operation performed. I doubt if she will live over it. She is very low. Will advise you of any change

Papa

Lola's death certificate 27 Oct 1916.

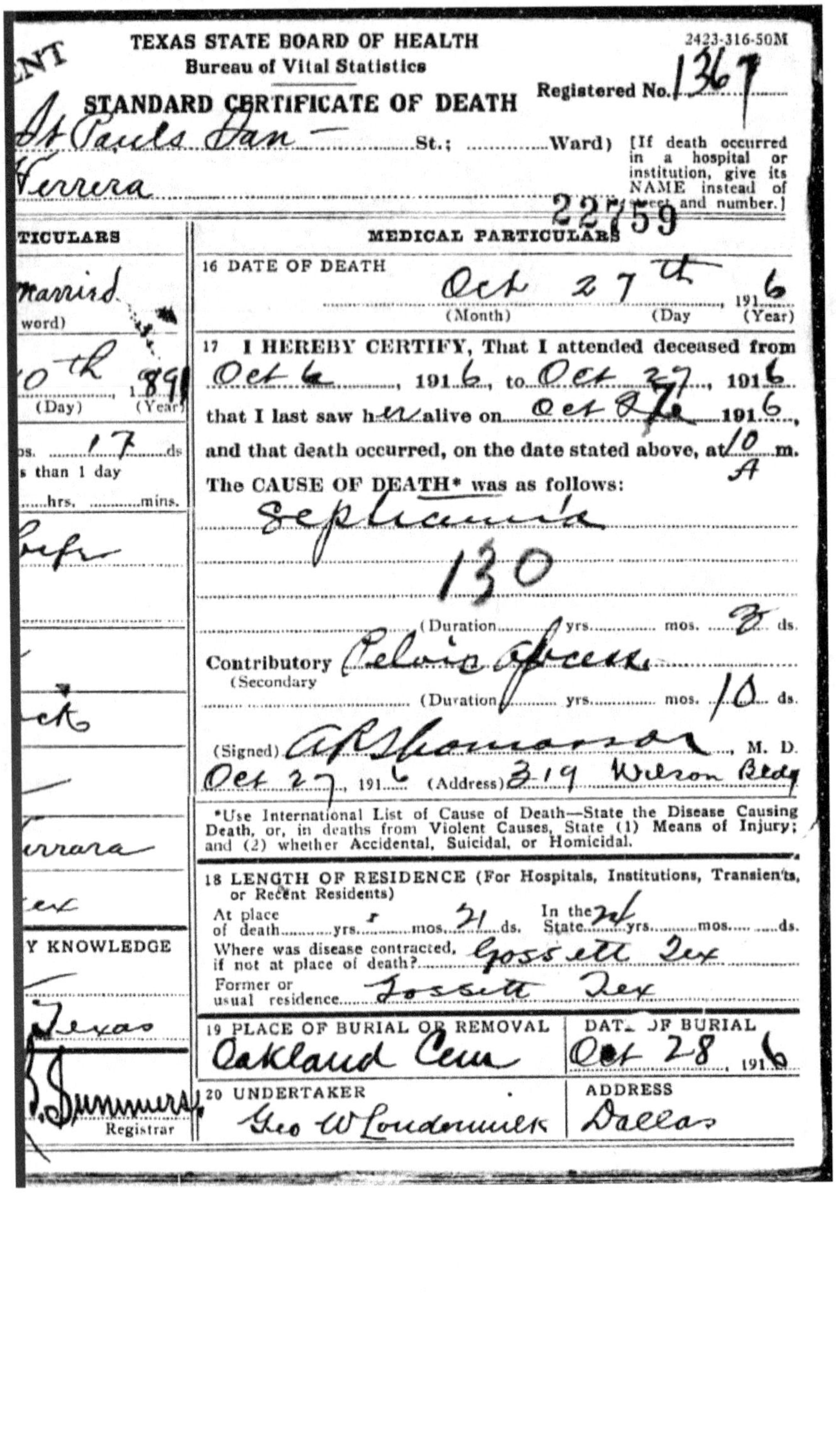

TEXAS STATE BOARD OF HEALTH
Bureau of Vital Statistics

2423-316-50M

STANDARD CERTIFICATE OF DEATH

Registered No. 1367

St Pauls San- ..... St.; ..... Ward) [If death occurred in a hospital or institution, give its NAME instead of street and number.]

Verrera

22759

...TICULARS

MEDICAL PARTICULARS

married
...word)

16 DATE OF DEATH Oct 27th (Month) (Day) 1916 (Year)

...0th (Day) 1891 (Year)

17 I HEREBY CERTIFY, That I attended deceased from Oct 6, 1916, to Oct 27, 1916 that I last saw her alive on Oct 27, 1916, and that death occurred, on the date stated above, at 10 A m.

...os. 17 ds
...s than 1 day
...hrs. ..... mins.

The CAUSE OF DEATH* was as follows:

Septicaemia

130

(Duration ..... yrs. ..... mos. 3 ds.

Contributory Pelvic Abscess
(Secondary)

(Duration ..... yrs. ..... mos. 10 ds.

(Signed) A R Thomasson, M. D.

Oct 27, 1916 (Address) 319 Wilson Bldg

*Use International List of Cause of Death—State the Disease Causing Death, or, in deaths from Violent Causes, State (1) Means of Injury; and (2) whether Accidental, Suicidal, or Homicidal.

...errara

18 LENGTH OF RESIDENCE (For Hospitals, Institutions, Transients, or Recent Residents)

At place of death ..... yrs. ..... mos. 21 ds. In the State 24 yrs. ..... mos. ..... ds.

Where was disease contracted, if not at place of death? Gossett Tex

...Y KNOWLEDGE

Former or usual residence Gossett Tex

Texas

19 PLACE OF BURIAL OR REMOVAL Oakland Cem

DATE OF BURIAL Oct 28, 1916

20 UNDERTAKER Geo W Loudermilk

ADDRESS Dallas

...S. Summers
Registrar

Letter from Doc to son-in-law Ed Buckbee and daughter Linda relating a shooting he saw 9 Mar 1913.

"Mabank, Tex 3-9-13

Ed & Linda
Dear Children

We are just back from a wild goose chase.

Last Tuesday we (the boys and I) left Cedar for Dallas to see if we could find some employment more to our liking than our job here.

We spent the balance of the week and about thirty dollars chasing the 'Jack O Lantern' then give up the chase and returned to Cedar, to take up our old job. It's pretty hard work, but it's $1.50 apiece every day we work. The only objection I have to the work is so mud and slush.

It rained half the night last night and nearly all day today, so this work will be all mud but we seem to stand it all right.

We are well. Lola only weighs 168#. The boys are hearty bucks and I weigh more than I've weighed in twenty five years, so it appears that we ought to satisfied.

Oh! I liked to have forgot to say, I saw a man shot the other night. First man I've seen shot in a long time. Two Mexicans quarreled and one of them shot the other three times, once through the breast once through the stomach and once through the thigh. If he had any common sense he would have died in two or three hours, but it has been seven days now, and today he got up and walked about the tent, so guess he has decided to live so he can hunt the other fellow up.

He (the shooter) disappeared in the darkness immediately after the shooting and has not been heard of since. I forgot to mention the affair in my letter to Brony & Gladys. I think they know the man who did the shooting. His name is Juan Lara. The man shot was Francisco Nino.

With love to all and kisses for the babies I'll close. Write soon and often to

Your Affectionate
Papa"

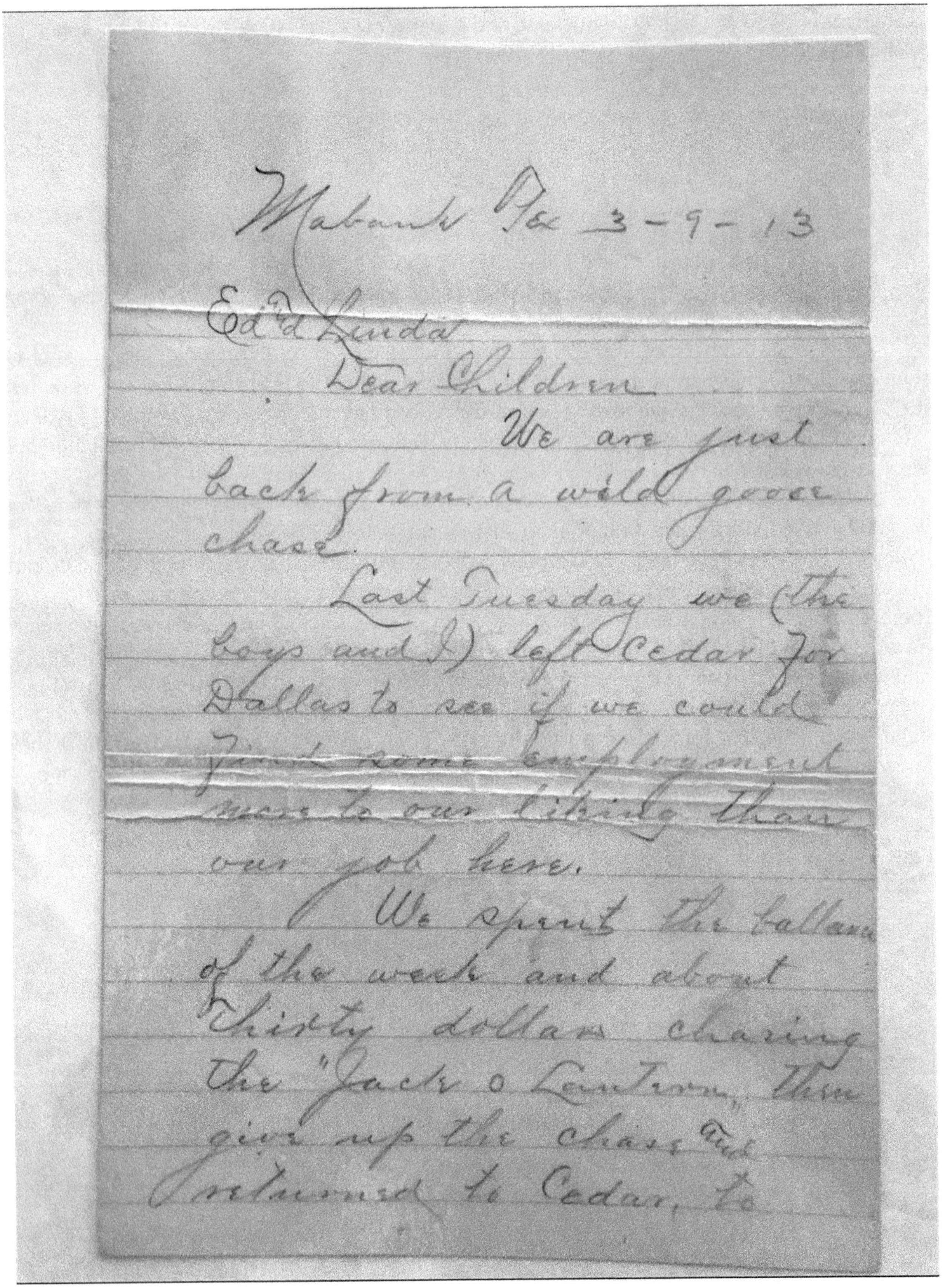

Mabank Tex 3-9-13

Ed & Linda

Dear Children

We are just back from a wild goose chase.

Last Tuesday we (the boys and I) left Cedar for Dallas to see if we could find some employment more to our liking than our job here.

We spent the ballance of the week and about thirty dollars chasing the "Jack o Lantern" then give up the chase and returned to Cedar, to

2

take up our old job.
It's pretty hard work, but
its $1.50 apiece every day
we work. The only objec-
tion I have to the work, is
so mud and slush.

It rained half
the night last night and
nearly all day today, so
this week will be all mud. but
we seem to stand it all
right

We are all well.
Lola only weighs 168#.
The boys are hearty as
bucks and I weigh more
than I've weighed in

3

twenty five years, so it appears that we ought to satisfied.

Oh! I liked to have forgot to say, I saw a man shot the other night First man I've seen shot in a long time, Two Mexicans quarreled and on of them shot the other three times, once through the breast once through the stomach and once through the thigh.

If he had [had] any common sense he would have died in two or three

4

hours, but it has been seven days now, and today he got up and walked about the tent, so I guess he has decided to live so he can hunt the other fellow up.

He (the shooter) disappeared in the darkness immediately after the shooting and has not been heared of since. I forgot to mention the affair in my letter to Brony & Gladys. I think they know the man who did the shooting.

Letter from Doc to children relating the death of his grandson dated 20 Apr 1920.

"Eastland, Tex 4/20/20
Ed, Linda & children

Dear Children:

I just received a letter from Amy this morning bringing the news of little Wilbur's death. It was a great shock to me, and I fain would say something that would in some measure console you for your great loss, but we all know that words of consolation and sympathy sound very meaningless in a case of this kind. About all we can say is that it is a trial that we ought to be prepared to meet, for it is the one thing that we <u>must</u> all meet sooner or later. It comes to us all Young or Old, High or Low. When our child is born, we know but one thing as to its future and that is <u>it must die</u>. Now I can but believe that whatever is, is best. We can't understand always, but time shows us that all is for the best. What the final outcome of it all is to be, no one knows. There are and yet will be many guesses, but no one knows. But whatever it may be you may be assured it will be <u>best</u>, for the Supreme Intelligence that governs the universe makes no mistakes.

If I was in shape so I could I would come and spend a few days with you but don't see how I can just now. I have just finished taking a course of treatment for my kidney trouble and rheumatism and am much impaired in health, but my bank account is at low ebb, so I must go to work again.

Let me hear from you soon. I will come to see you just as soon as I can get off. Be brave and bear your sorrow with fortitude is all that I can advise.

Your Affectionate Papa"

Eastland Tex 11/20/20

Ed Linda & Children

Dear Children:

I just recieved a letter from Amy this morning bringing the news of little Wilburs death. It was a great shock to me, and I fain would say something that would in some measure console you for you for your great loss, but we all know that words of consolation and sympathy sound very meaningless in a case of this Kind. About all we can say is that it is a trial that we ought to be prepared to meet, for it is the one thing

2

that we *must* all meet sooner
or later. It comes to us all.
Young or Old High or low.
When our child is born, we
know but one thing as to its
future and that is, it *must*
die. Now I can but believe
that whatever is, is best. We cant
understand allways, but Time
shows us that all is for the best.
What the final outcome of it all
is to be, no one knows. There
are and yet will be many guesses, but no one knows. But whatever
it may be you may be assured
it will be *best*, for the Supreme
Intelligence that governs the universe makes no mistakes

3

If I was in shape so I could I would come and spend a few days with you but don't see how I can just now.

I have just finished taking a course of treatment for my kidney trouble and rheumatism and am much improved in health, but my Bank account is at low ebb, so I must go to work again.

Let me hear from you soon. I will come to see you just as soon as I can get off.

Be brave and bear your sorrow with fortitude is all that I can advise.

Your Affectionate
Papa

PART VI – AFTER DOC'S PASSING

Doc's death certificate dated 25 Jul 1929. There are several issues with the document. First, if Doc was born 11 Jan 1849 and died on 25 Jul 1929, he would be 80 years, 6 month and 14 days – not 79 years, 4 months and 16 days. Because of these discrepancies, it's believed his son William just gave the wrong information. Doc was born 11 Jan 50 and died 79 years 6 months and 14 days later.

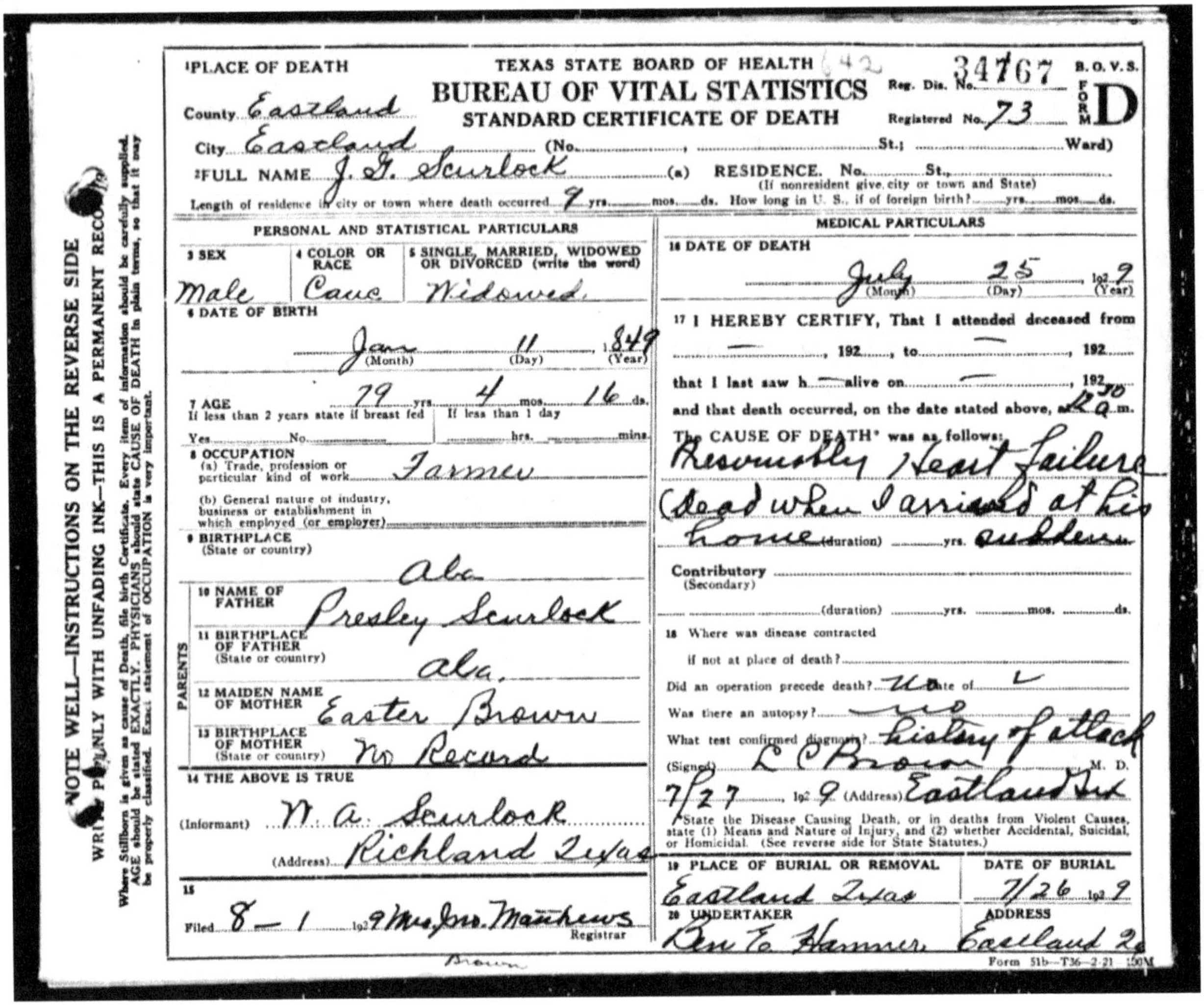

1 PLACE OF DEATH — TEXAS STATE BOARD OF HEALTH — BUREAU OF VITAL STATISTICS — STANDARD CERTIFICATE OF DEATH — B. O. V. S. FORM D

Reg. Dis. No. 34767 — Registered No. 73

County Eastland

City Eastland (No. St.; Ward)

2 FULL NAME J. G. Scurlock — (a) RESIDENCE. No. St. (If nonresident give city or town and State)

Length of residence in city or town where death occurred 9 yrs. mos. ds. How long in U. S., if of foreign birth? yrs. mos. ds.

PERSONAL AND STATISTICAL PARTICULARS

3 SEX: Male — 4 COLOR OR RACE: Cauc — 5 SINGLE, MARRIED, WIDOWED OR DIVORCED (write the word): Widowed

6 DATE OF BIRTH: Jan (Month) 11 (Day), 1849 (Year)

7 AGE 79 yrs. 4 mos. 16 ds. If less than 2 years state if breast fed — If less than 1 day — Yes No hrs. mins.

8 OCCUPATION (a) Trade, profession or particular kind of work: Farmer

(b) General nature of industry, business or establishment in which employed (or employer)

9 BIRTHPLACE (State or country): Ala

PARENTS

10 NAME OF FATHER: Presley Scurlock

11 BIRTHPLACE OF FATHER (State or country): Ala.

12 MAIDEN NAME OF MOTHER: Easter Brown

13 BIRTHPLACE OF MOTHER (State or country): No Record

14 THE ABOVE IS TRUE

(Informant) W. A. Scurlock

(Address) Richland Texas

15 Filed 8–1 1929 Mrs. Jno. Mathews, Registrar

MEDICAL PARTICULARS

16 DATE OF DEATH: July (Month) 25 (Day), 1929 (Year)

17 I HEREBY CERTIFY, That I attended deceased from — 192 , to — 192

that I last saw h — alive on — 192

and that death occurred, on the date stated above, at 2 30 a.m.

The CAUSE OF DEATH* was as follows: Presumably Heart failure. Dead when I arrived at his home (duration) yrs. sudden

Contributory (Secondary) (duration) yrs. mos. ds.

18 Where was disease contracted if not at place of death?

Did an operation precede death? No Date of —

Was there an autopsy? no

What test confirmed diagnosis? history of attack

(Signed) L C Brown M. D.

7/27 1929 (Address) Eastland Tex

*State the Disease Causing Death, or in deaths from Violent Causes, state (1) Means and Nature of Injury, and (2) whether Accidental, Suicidal, or Homicidal. (See reverse side for State Statutes.)

19 PLACE OF BURIAL OR REMOVAL: Eastland Texas — DATE OF BURIAL: 7/26 1929

20 UNDERTAKER: Ben E. Hamner — ADDRESS: Eastland Tx

Form 51b–T36–2-21 150M

N.B.—WRITE PLAINLY WITH UNFADING INK—THIS IS A PERMANENT RECORD. NOTE WELL—INSTRUCTIONS ON THE REVERSE SIDE

Where Stillborn is given as cause of Death, file birth Certificate. Every item of information should be carefully supplied. AGE should be stated EXACTLY. PHYSICIANS should state CAUSE OF DEATH in plain terms, so that it may be properly classified. Exact statement of OCCUPATION is very important.

Doc's Obituary 26 Jul 1929.

Eastland Woman's Relative Is Dead

Funeral services for Mr. Scurlock, 79, an uncle of Mrs. J. C. Buckbee, and who died Thursday, are to be conducted from the Buckbee home this afternoon at 4:00 o'clock by Rev. W. T. Turner, pastor of the First Baptist church.

Peruvion Plot Discovered

LIMA, Peru, July 26 — The newspaper La Prena published an article today saying the police had uncovered a plot against the government and had arrested a Senator ,a deputy, and four other principals, and seized incriminating documents. Other arrests were expected.

Eastland Telegram
Fri July 26 1929

Doc's Headstone located in Eastland, Texas.

After Doc passed away many of his personal effects were inherited by various descendants. In 2009 the Scurlock family, in conjunction with the Eastland County Museum held a Scurlock family reunion that included a Doc Scurlock display of many of these items. Thanks goes to cousin Mica for ensuring these items were brought together again.

Doc's glasses

Medicine Bottle (Cherry Bark Cough Syrup) & Cigarette Holder

COMPOUND
CHERRY BARK
COUGH SYRUP
Each fluid ounce contains
grains of Codeine Sulphate
(Opium Derivative)

Personalized Key Ring.

Doc's books

EVOLUTION

POPULAR LECTURES AND DISCUSSIONS
BEFORE THE
BROOKLYN ETHICAL ASSOCIATION.

BOSTON:
JAMES H. WEST, PUBLISHER
1894

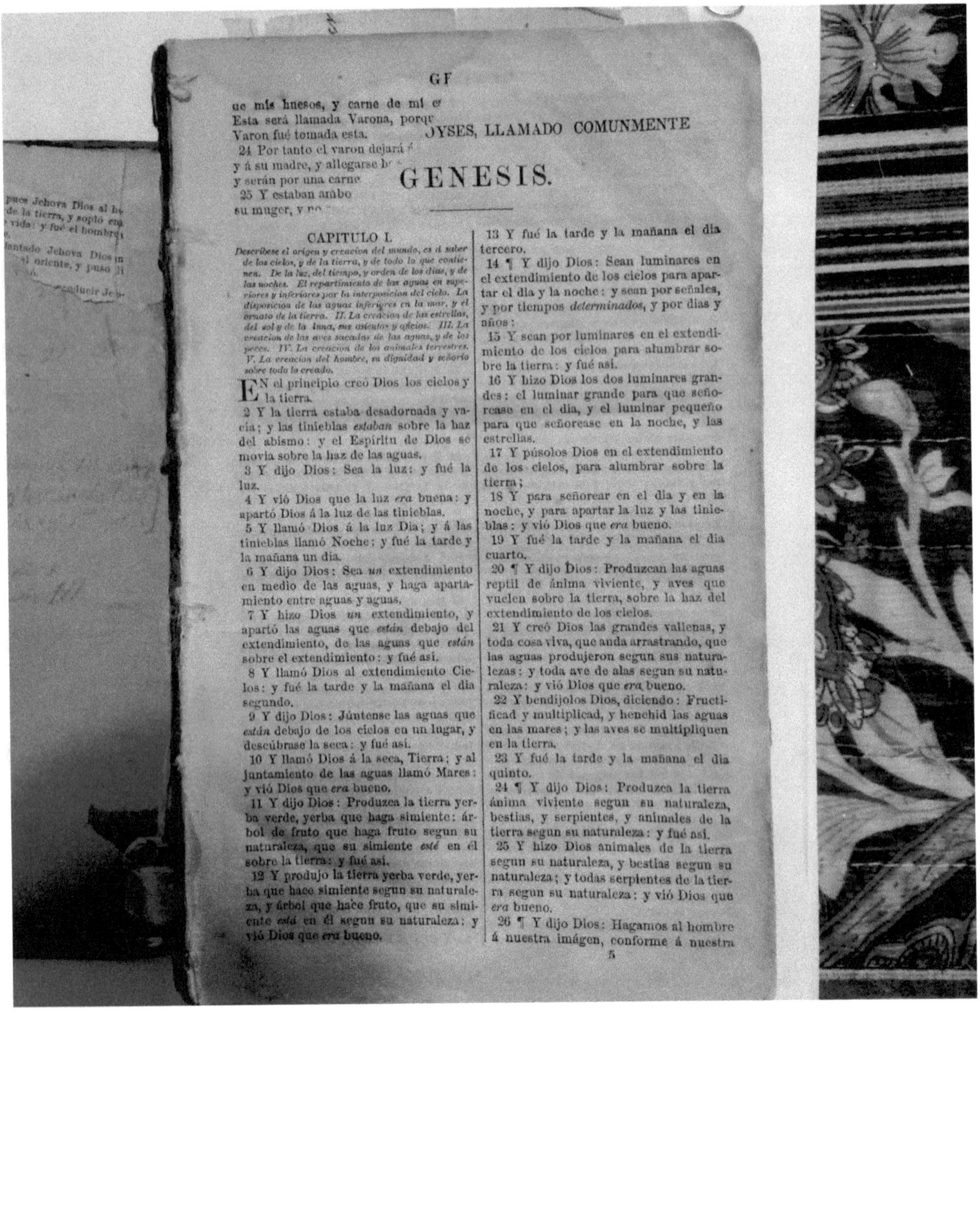

GF

ue mis huesos, y carne de mi c· Esta será llamada Varona, porq Varon fué tomada esta.
24 Por tanto el varon dejará y á su madre, y allegarse b y serán por una carne
25 Y estaban ambo su muger, y no

OYSES, LLAMADO COMUNMENTE

GENESIS.

CAPITULO I.

Descríbese el orígen y creacion del mundo, es á saber de los cielos, y de la tierra, y de todo lo que contienen. De la luz, del tiempo, y orden de los dias, y de las noches. El repartimiento de las aguas en superiores y inferiores por la interposicion del cielo. La disposicion de las aguas inferiores en la mar, y el ornato de la tierra. II. La creacion de las estrellas, del sol y de la luna, sus asientos y oficios. III. La creacion de las aves sacadas de las aguas, y de los peces. IV. La creacion de los animales terrestres. V. La creacion del hombre, su dignidad y señorío sobre todo lo creado.

EN el principio creó Dios los cielos y
la tierra.
2 Y la tierra estaba desadornada y va-
cía; y las tinieblas *estaban* sobre la haz
del abismo: y el Espíritu de Dios se
movia sobre la haz de las aguas.
3 Y dijo Dios: Sea la luz: y fué la
luz.
4 Y vió Dios que la luz *era* buena: y
apartó Dios á la luz de las tinieblas.
5 Y llamó Dios á la luz Dia; y á las
tinieblas llamó Noche: y fué la tarde y
la mañana un dia.
6 Y dijo Dios: Sea *un* extendimiento
en medio de las aguas, y haga aparta-
miento entre aguas y aguas.
7 Y hizo Dios *un* extendimiento, y
apartó las aguas que *están* debajo del
extendimiento, de las aguas que *están*
sobre el extendimiento: y fué así.
8 Y llamó Dios al extendimiento Cielos: y fué la tarde y la mañana el dia
segundo.
9 Y dijo Dios: Júntense las aguas que
están debajo de los cielos en un lugar, y
descúbrase la seca: y fué así.
10 Y llamó Dios á la seca, Tierra; y al
juntamiento de las aguas llamó Mares:
y vió Dios que *era* bueno.
11 Y dijo Dios: Produzca la tierra yerba verde, yerba que haga simiente: árbol de fruto que haga fruto segun su
naturaleza, que su simiente *esté* en él
sobre la tierra: y fué así.
12 Y produjo la tierra yerba verde, yerba que hace simiente segun su naturaleza, y árbol que hace fruto, que su simiente *está* en él segun su naturaleza: y
vió Dios que *era* bueno.
13 Y fué la tarde y la mañana el dia
tercero.
14 ¶ Y dijo Dios: Sean luminares en
el extendimiento de los cielos para apartar el dia y la noche: y sean por señales,
y por tiempos *determinados*, y por dias y
años:
15 Y sean por luminares en el extendimiento de los cielos para alumbrar sobre la tierra: y fué así.
16 Y hizo Dios los dos luminares grandes: el luminar grande para que señorease en el dia, y el luminar pequeño
para que señorease en la noche, y las
estrellas.
17 Y púsolos Dios en el extendimiento
de los cielos, para alumbrar sobre la
tierra;
18 Y para señorear en el dia y en la
noche, y para apartar la luz y las tinieblas: y vió Dios que *era* bueno.
19 Y fué la tarde y la mañana el dia
cuarto.
20 ¶ Y dijo Dios: Produzcan las aguas
reptil de ánima viviente, y aves que
vuelen sobre la tierra, sobre la haz del
extendimiento de los cielos.
21 Y creó Dios las grandes vallenas, y
toda cosa viva, que anda arrastrando, que
las aguas produjeron segun sus natura-
lezas: y toda ave de alas segun su naturaleza: y vió Dios que *era* bueno.
22 Y bendíjolos Dios, diciendo: Fructi-
ficad y multiplicad, y henchid las aguas
en las mares; y las aves se multipliquen
en la tierra.
23 Y fué la tarde y la mañana el dia
quinto.
24 ¶ Y dijo Dios: Produzca la tierra
ánima viviente segun su naturaleza,
bestias, y serpientes, y animales de la
tierra segun su naturaleza: y fué así.
25 Y hizo Dios animales de la tierra
segun su naturaleza, y bestias segun su
naturaleza; y todas serpientes de la tierra segun su naturaleza: y vió Dios que
era bueno.
26 ¶ Y dijo Dios: Hagamos al hombre
á nuestra imágen, conforme á nuestra

5

Inscription bearing C. B. Vivian and J. G. Scurlock.

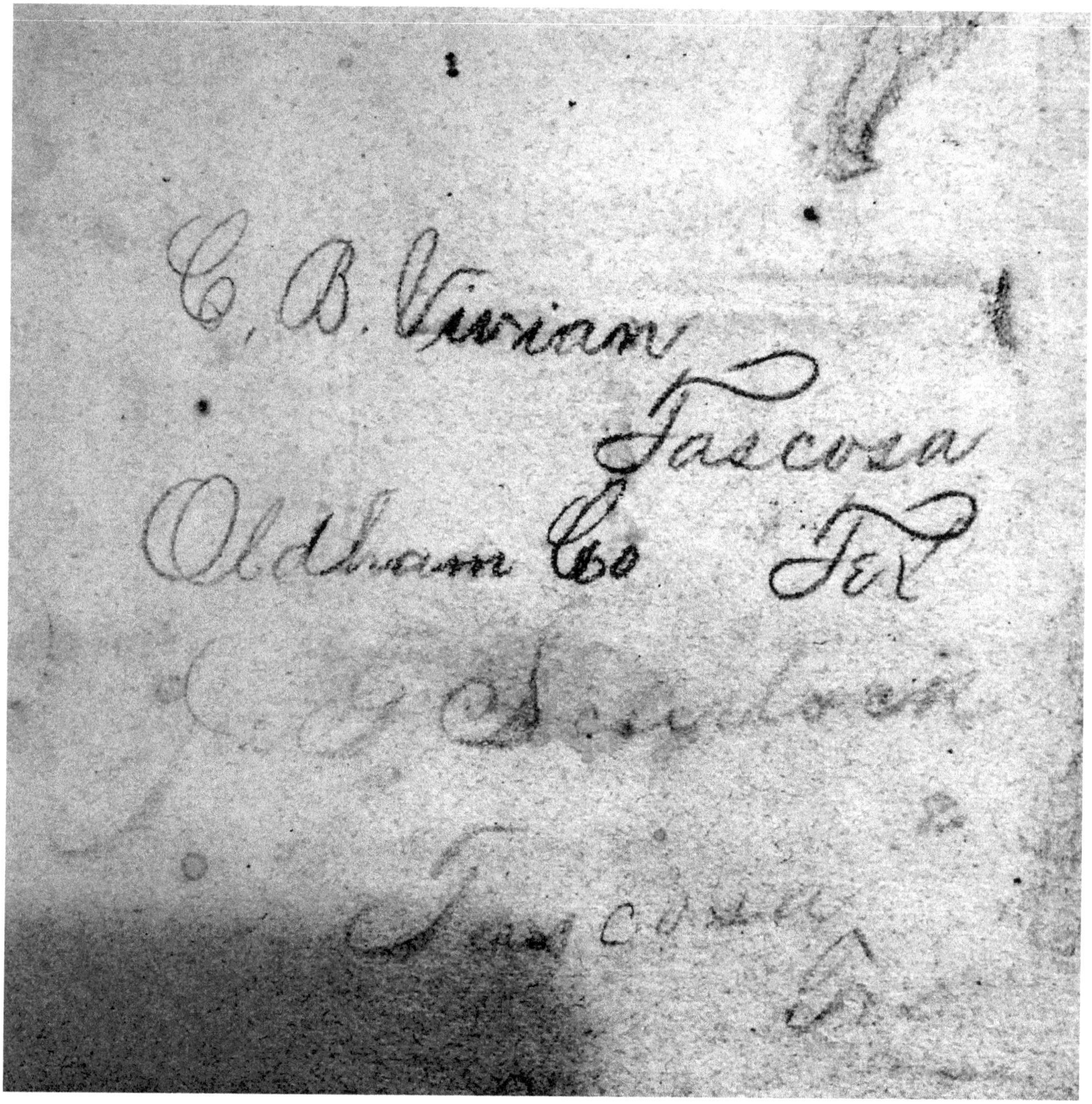

Doc's certificate of membership in the Theosophical Society. See also Rasch's comments at the end of "Man of Many Parts" on the topic.

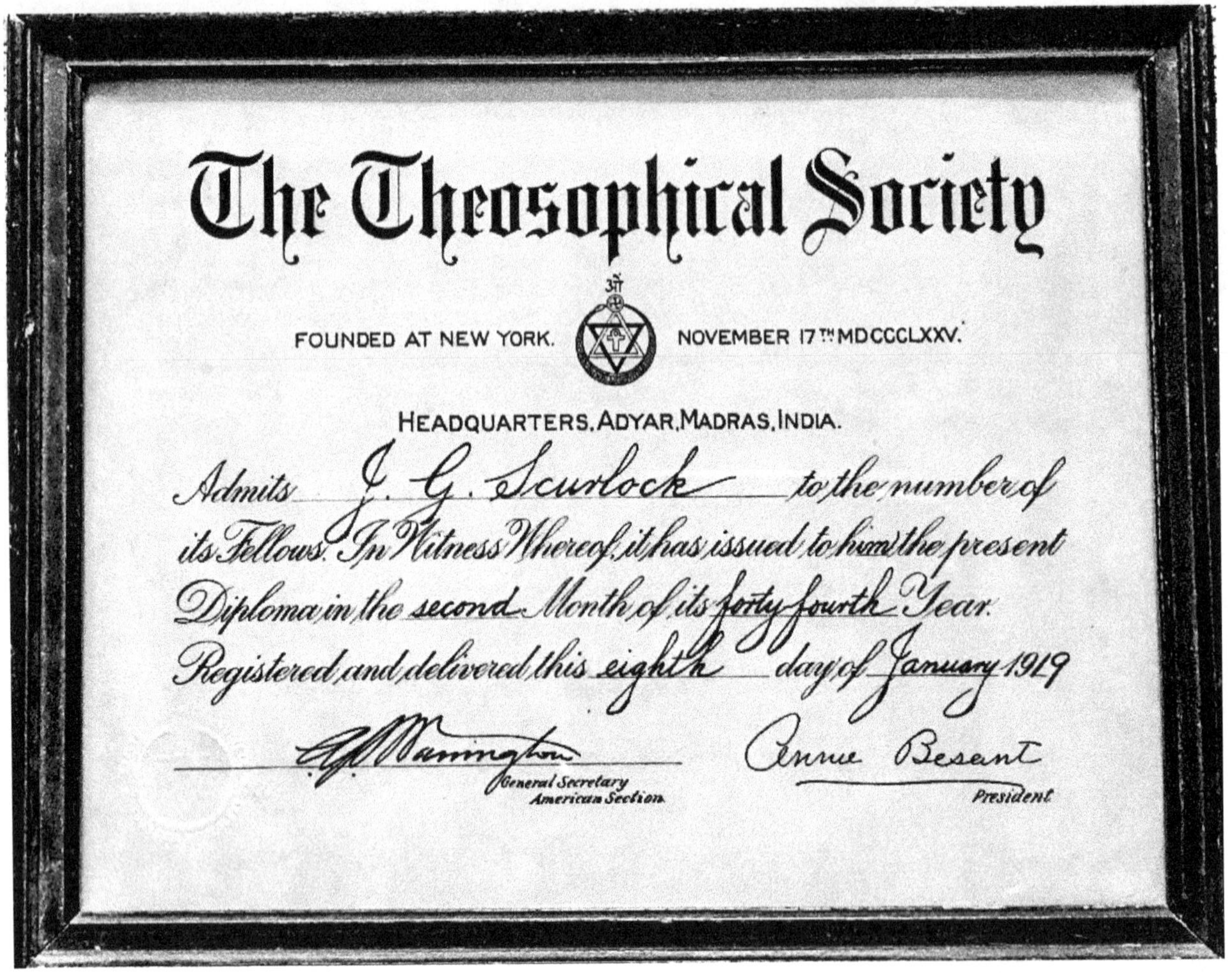

PART VII – DOC'S LEGACY AND THE BUCKBEE LETTERS

THE HISTORY OF THE HISTORY OF DOC SCURLOCK

No one has said it better than Philip Rasch did in a letter dated 23 Apr 1963 to Joe Buckbee:

> "Scurlock was certainly a most interesting personality. It is a great loss that he did not leave an account of his life or a diary, as his views on the Lincoln County troubles would have had major historical importance. I wish I could have known him."

But, alas, Doc didn't leave any such account as far as anyone knows. To the contrary, Doc seemed to want to distance himself from his association with the events of Lincoln and his close association with Billy the Kid and the other Regulators. Doc turned down interviews and even went so far as to avoid looking straight into the camera when getting his picture taken on a few occasions.

This does not mean that Doc didn't share stories with his family, however. Much of the information we have on the life of Josiah Gordon Scurlock comes from both family and researchers. We might call these two sources the family record and the official record.

In this part we will take a much closer look at how Doc's life has been recorded over the years since his death. We will also analyze some of these records and their sources. Finally, the Joe Buckbee letters are presented here.

We must, out of necessity, begin with the Pat Garrett and Ash Upson collaboration *The Authentic Life of Billy the Kid* that was published in 1881. Largely considered by Lincoln County War and Billy the Kid historians to be an unreliable source on many accounts, it's still worth examining. The question that I've long wondered is whether or not Pat Garrett and/or Ash Upson knew Doc Scurlock? Indications seem to point to, no. Doc is mentioned several times in *The Authentic Life*, but usually he's just listed with the usual cast of people that newspapers mention as being present at certain events. The one anecdote that mentions him is worth examining, though. These two quotes from the book come from the time after the Regulators had raided the Mescalero Apache Indian Reservation Agency resulting in the death of Morris Bernstein on August 5th, 1878.

> "Sheriff Peppin together with his posse had retired from active service after the bloody 19th of July, and law was a dead letter in the county. Immediately after the killing of Bernstein, the Kid, accompanied by O'Folliard, Fred Wayt, Middleton, and Brown, went to Fort Sumner, San Miguel County, on the Rio Pecos, eighty-one miles north of Roswell. Here they established a rendezvous to which they clung to the last chapter of this history. Bowdre and Scurlock, who had married Mexican wives who were devoted to them and followed their fortunes faithfully, remained in Lincoln County for some time. But, in the absence of their leader, they were careful to avoid publicity."

I doubt Doc and Charlie would've called Billy their leader, but Doc was certainly careful to avoid any more publicity. It's also interesting that Garrett/Upson remark that Charlie and Doc remained in Lincoln for some time. What is meant by some time?

Using Doc's Spanish Bible is helpful to some degree. Doc recorded the births and deaths of his family in Spanish in this Bible. His young daughter Marie Elena died on August 17th, 1879, but Doc doesn't state where she died or where she was buried.

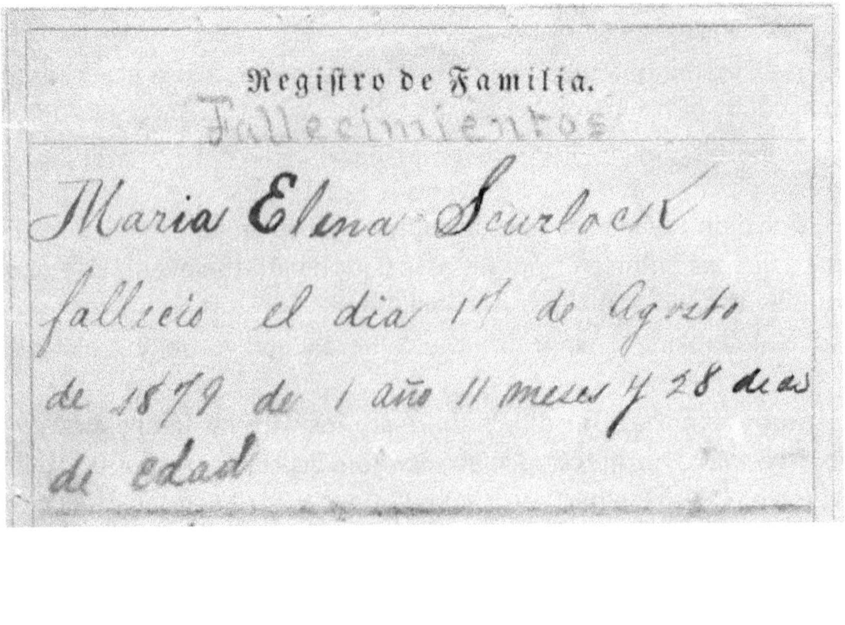
Registro de Familia.
Fallecimientos
Maria Elena Scurlock
fallecio el dia 17 de Agosto
de 1879 de 1 año 11 meses y 28 dias
de edad

He did, however, record the birth locations of his second and third children Viola and Josiah, Jr.

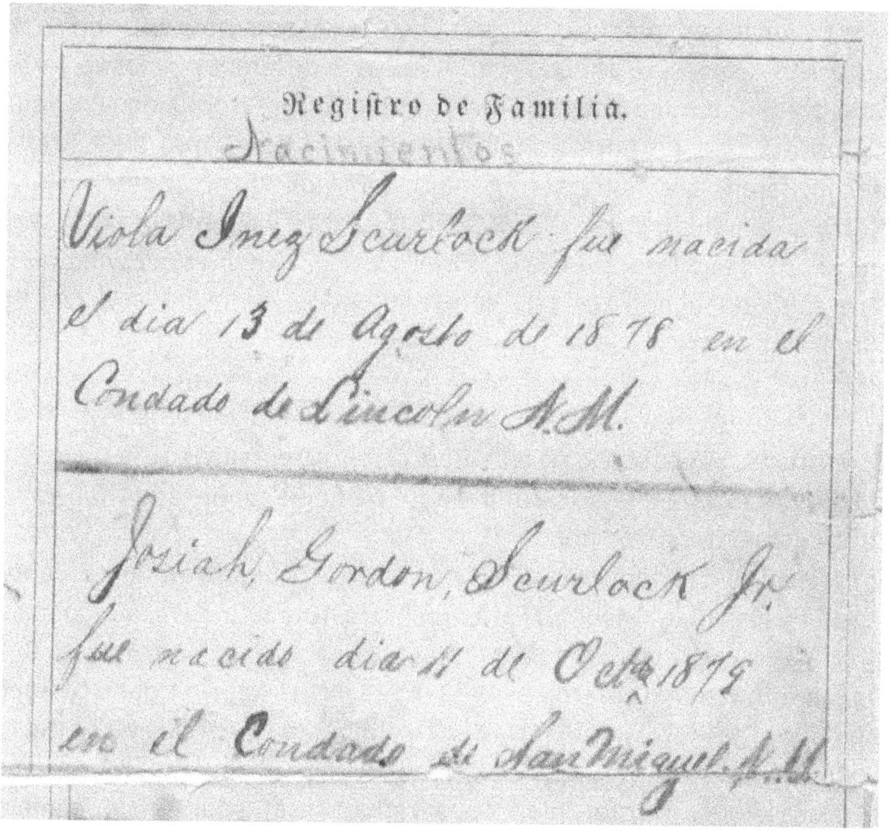

Registro de Familia.

Nacimientos

Viola Inez Scurlock fue nacida el dia 13 de Agosto de 1878 en el Condado de Lincoln N.M.

Josiah, Gordon, Scurlock Jr. fue nacido dia 11 de Oct. 1879 en el Condado de San Miguel N.M.

From these records in Doc's own hand and with the stories passed down through the family, we get the following timeline:

5 Aug 1878 – Bernstein killed.

13 Aug 1878 – Viola born in Lincoln Co.

1 Sep 1878 – Scurlock family relocates to Ft. Sumner according to descendants.

17 Aug 1879 – Marie Elena dies.

11 Oct 1879 – Josiah, Jr. born in San Miguel Co.

It's unknown where the 1 September 1878 date comes from, it was more likely 7 September, but even if it were closer to the end of 1879, this doesn't sound like "some time". The account goes on to tell an anecdote about the cattle stolen from Chisum, rebranded, and sold at Grzelachowski's Ranch at Alamogordo.

> "But the Kid had the money and displayed a rare genius as a financier in its disbursement. Out of about $800 he generously gave Bowdre $30, explaining that he did so because he had a family. O'Folliard, he asserted was a disgrace to the band on account of shabby boots; so he got a new pair as his share. The Mexicans simply got 'the shake'. There was yet Scurlock to dispose of. The Kid got four or five different parties to go to Scurlock and warn him of the intended arrest of the gang by officers from Lincoln County, and this so scared Scurlock that he borrowed fifty pounds of flour from Pete Maxwell, gathered together his family and household goods, and skipped the country. Thus Doc Scurlock henceforth lost to this history. Out of $800, he got fifty pounds of flour, which still stands charged to profit and loss on Pete Maxwell's books. When asked what he would do with his share, the Kid laughed and said he would endow an insane asylum if he could catch Doc Scurlock."

This certainly doesn't sound like an account that would've come from Doc. It also raises several other questions. Supposedly, Charlie had just gotten married, yet, Doc had a wife and children. Why Billy would give Charlie a cut because he had a family and then go to the effort to trick Doc out of a cut seems farfetched.

Out of curiosity, I decided to look in two other accounts from Fulton and Nolan to see how they covered this incident. Maurice Fulton in his *History of the Lincoln County War* states:

> "During the summer and autumn of 1879 the raids of Victorio's band of Apaches occupied the attention of southwestern New Mexico almost to the exclusion of the Lincoln County troubles. Some notice, however, was given Billy the Kid now that he was at large again. In the Las Cruces *Thirty-four* for July 9 appeared a hint of what he was engaged in. 'Kid and Scurlock and others are still in the country. They are reported as getting a crowd together again. No effort is being made to arrest them.' In other words, the Kid and his associates were embarking on a career of cattle and horse stealing. In October a party made up of the Kid, Scurlock, O'Folliard, Bowdre, and two Mexicans stole over a hundred head of Chisum cattle from the Panhandle and then sold them to beef-buyers from Colorado. Chisum, however followed the cattle and recovered them. The story goes that the division of the $800 received for the cattle did not suit Scurlock, and he severed his connection with the gang and left the country for Kansas."

Fulton is a little more unbiased in the telling of this dispute, but where he got that Doc went to Kansas is a mystery. As we'll see later, it appears that most researchers were largely unaware of Doc's life outside of newspaper, court, and military documents until after Philip Rasch contacted the Scurlock family.

Frederick Nolan, in his *The Lincoln County War: A Documentary History* puts it this way:

> "Garrett – or rather Upson – claims the Kid, O'Folliard, Bowdre, Scurlock, and two Mexicans stole 118 head of Chisum cattle from Bosque Grande, drove them up to Yerby's ranch where they rebranded them, and later sold them to some Colorado men at Grzelachowski's ranch at Alamogordo. Around October or November, Scurlock and his wife decided to leave New Mexico for Texas, possibly after a dispute over the division of

the spoils from this transaction. They located in the Panhandle, where Doc settled down and became a highly respected citizen until his death at Eastland nearly fifty years later."

Good 'Ol Nolan, my go-to guy on the Lincoln County War, includes two citations in this account. When you follow these two citations back, you find that numbers twenty-two and twenty-three of Chapter thirty-three point to Garrett's (Upson's) *Authentic Life* and this gem:

22. Garrett, *Authentic Life*, 86.
23. The Garrett-Upson version of Scurlock's departure, albeit written tongue in cheek, is worth noting. Ibid.; Rasch, Buckbee, and Klein, 'Many Parts.'

Is worth noting? What does he mean, here? I can only smile as if Fred has given me a wink because I had just gone down this same rabbit hole of noting the Garrett/Upson version of Scurlock's departure. I just have to smile and say, "You got me hooked, Mr. Nolan. Now, who are these Rasch, Buckbee, and Klein fellows you mention?" Because, as you'll soon see, all roads point back to these three gentlemen. It is the source which *A Documentary History* refers, after all. I think it will do nicely to have Mr. Nolan introduce these men in his own words. This comes from his Introduction to his *The Billy the Kid Reader*:

"There were a few other honorable contributions to the truer story, notable among them William A. Keleher's *The Fabulous Frontier* in 1945 and Irving McKee's biography of Lew Wallace two years later, but it was not until the middle of the century, hard on the heels of the appearance and discrediting of 'Brushy Bill' Roberts – and perhaps even to some degree prompted by it – that a new generation of 'grassroots' researchers ('logical, indefatigable, at horrific dollarage per gram,' as Eugene Cunningham so neatly put it) appeared on the scene and began the long-overdue task of turning legend into history. The watershed came in 1952 with the publication of 'New Light on the Legend of Billy the Kid' by Robert N. Mullin and Philip J. Rasch. From that point forward, dedicated historians such as Maurice Garland Fulton, Keleher, Mullin, and the phenomenal Rasch collectively rewrote the Kid's story, in the process revolutionizing the way the subject was researched and presented."

Philip J. Rasch was born December 3rd, 1909 in Grand Rapids, Michigan. He was a Navy man who was assigned duty on a submarine hunter in WWII. After the war, he transitioned into working with the military specializing in human physiology and fitness. In his spare time, his hobby was researching and writing articles about Billy the Kid, The Lincoln County War, and related material about New Mexican and Texan history. Rasch would go in search of records and family members trying to uncover the lives of numerous players in the events.

For the most part, Doc's life story had not resided in the records and newspapers where he is listed, but with the Scurlock family, who had steadfastly accumulated and collected their own records and artifacts. It seemed that no one really ever attempted to focus on writing a historically accurate biographical sketch of Doc until Joe Buckbee sent a letter to Rasch after reading one of his articles in *Frontier Times* in 1959. Rasch jumped at the opportunity to learn more about Doc from Joe.

Prior to this partnership, Doc had appeared in numerous documents, but it would require the family to fill in the gaps and answer numerous questions that researchers like Rasch, Mullin, Fulton, and Ketring had about Doc.

Joseph E. "Joe" Buckbee was born in Granbury, Texas in 1910. He was the son of Martha Ethlinda "Linda" Scurlock who married Columbus Edward Buckbee. Doc went to live with Linda around 1926, so Joe spent several years with Doc before Doc died. He supplied several family stories that helped Philip Rasch and Karl Klein, a historian who lectured at the University of Texas in Austin, to create the first biographical sketch of Doc called "Man of Many Parts". It was published in January of 1963 in *The English Westerner's Brand Book*. It was reprinted in the following:

- Rasch, P. (1995), *Trailing Billy the Kid*, The National Association for Outlaw and Lawman History, Inc.

If we take a look at Rasch, Buckbee, and Klein's references from *Man of Many Parts*, we'll find the following:

- Nine historical records contemporaneous to events (all contained in this volume).
- Garrett & Upson's *Authentic Life of Billy the Kid,* 1881 (Rasch cites the 1954 edition).
- J. Evetts Haley's piece called "Horse Thieves", 1930.
- George Coe's *Frontier Fighter,* 1934.
- Three of his own previously published works: "The Pecos War", 1956; "Prelude to the Lincoln County War: The Murder of John Henry Tunstall", 1957; and "The Story of Jessie J. Evans", 1960 (Rasch was notorious for citing his own, earlier works).

George Coe's book is largely considered to suffer from "fuzzy memory" syndrome due to the amount of years between the events and his remembering them in his memoires. For example, Coe confuses the timeline of Frank Freeman's exploits in Lincoln. He blends two separate events, but then places them after Tunstall's death, when Frank Freeman was killed in August of 1877 and Tunstall was killed in February 1878.

The piece called "Horse Thieves" was written by James Evetts Haley. Haley was born July 5th, 1901 in Belton, Texas. He was a historian for the Panhandle-Plains Historical Society and the Panhandle-Plains Historical Museum. This article mentions Doc in several places, but they are references to Frank Coe getting the posse together which culminated in the deaths of Chihuahua, Nicas Meras, and Jesus Largo. First, he states:

> "The next morning he was ready to take the trail with a motley array of fighting men. He had the cowboy Charlie Bowdre, one of the men who with unfailing devotion followed upon the heels of Billy the Kid. He had Doc Scurlock, another Texan, who as a cowboy defied the power of John Chisum."

Obviously, Haley didn't know that Doc was really from Alabama. And then the story concludes with this:

"Legend tells how Frank Coe slid off his big bay horse, and how Largo, who knew what to expect, looked at the pinon and looked at the horse. As a cowboy he had eaten jingle-bob beef with Scurlock, and now tried to embrace him crying 'Doc! Doc!' But Scurlock pushed him away, saying he did not know him."

Haley got this story straight from Frank Coe as his source when he interviewed Frank. See also Nolan's *A Documentary History* and his citation for this account.

Rasch's three articles, plus one additional I'll cite called "Rise of the House of Murphy", 1956, can all be found in two books:

- Rasch, P. (1997), *Gunsmoke in Lincoln County*, The National Association for Outlaw and Lawman History, Inc. (contains "The Rise of the House of Murphy", The Pecos War", and "Prelude to War: The Murder of John Henry Tunstall"). It should be noted that Prelude to War in this edition is the 1970 reprint and not the earlier 1957 edition.
- Rash, P. (1998), *Warriors of Lincoln County*, The National Association for Outlaw and Lawman History, Inc. (contains "The Story of Jessie J. Evans").

To begin with, The Rise of the House of Murphy contains this reference to Doc:

"That spring a promising young bad man, Josiah G. 'Doc' Scurlock, succeeded in getting his name in the papers by stealing three horses, two saddles and a gun and making off to Arizona with them. Unfortunately for the peace of the community, he returned the following year and seems to have something of a career of carrying deadly weapons, threatening the citizens, obstructing the laws and generally making a nuisance of himself"

In the footnote for this entry we find:

"See causes 213, 220, 223, 226, 230 Lincoln County. Scurlock was born in Alabama about 1850. He is described as 'being between five feet eight or ten inches high, light hair, light complexion, front teeth out, writes a good hand, quick spoken, and usually makes a good impression on first acquaintance.' *Arizona Citizen*, quoted in Silver City *The Herald*, May 9, 1875."

It's worth noting that Rasch gets Doc's birth year correct here, but lists the errant birth year from his death certificate in "Man of Many Parts". It's unknown how he knew this because he also cites the 1875 article (the first mention of Doc in a paper) that also states he is 22. The math would suggest that Doc was born in 1853 if this were true, yet Rasch knew the 1850 date. As to the causes, three of the five are presented in this volume: 220, 226, and 230.

And also from 1956 in "Pecos War" we find Rasch making this comment:

"Little is known concerning the antecedents of Scurlock and Bowdre, but these two have a rather extensive record in the Lincoln criminal files. Charges of carrying deadly weapons, threatening a citizen, assault, and disguising themselves to obstruct the laws are to be found. Apparently, no serious penalty was incurred in the present instance."

Rasch's citation for this lists, once again, the causes cited above, but also include Charlie's. The Pecos War also includes the story of Doc taking Chisum's stuff in 1875, the Jesus Largo story, and includes the story of Bowdre and Freeman drunkenly whooping up the town and resulting in the killing of Freeman and the capture of Doc and George Coe.

In the 1957 "Prelude to the Lincoln County War" piece, Rasch only mentions Doc when he's included in lists of people. In the 1960 "The Story of Jessie J. Evans", Rasch mentions Doc in the affair where Dick Brewer, Charlie Bowdre, and Doc try to retrieve Brewer's horses from Shedd's ranch and the incident of the Huston Chapman killing.

In light of all this, the Buckbee letters give us insight into the kinds of things that researchers such as Rasch, Mullin, and Fulton knew and didn't know. Even Lewis Ketring's comment that "I was surprised in reading your letter that Scurlock had arrived in New Mexico in 1873, as I had always believed he had arrived sometime in the 1876-77 period" is enlightening about what Ketring knew.

Joe Buckbee also sent a letter to *True West* which was published and caused a little stir in the interest of Doc. It is included in the Buckbee letters as well.

While "Man of Many Parts" might be considered the first true biographical sketch of Doc's life, it certainly isn't the only one. The following lists in chronological order other biographical sketches that have been published over the years.

- Payne, V. (1989), The True Doc Scurlock Story, *Eastland County Newspapers*
- Gomber, D.(1998), Doc Scurlock, Drew Gomber's Western Destinies, *Vision Magazine*, page 9.
- Scurlock, J. D. (1999), From the Lincoln County War to the Eastland Library: Josiah Gordon Scurlock, Cisco Press – Eastland Telegram – Ranger Times, Sunday Mar 14, 1999
- Havelka, H. (1999), Farmer, Rancher, Road Hand . . . Gunslinger?, *Transportation News*, Novemeber 1999.
- Scurlock, D. (2001), Physician, Gunfighter, and Family Man, *Dona Ana County Historical Society, Vol. III, No. 1*
- Payne, V. (2007), Doc Scurlock, Frontier Legend, Buried in Eastland, *The Texas Messenger, Vol. 13, No. 4, Winter*
- Boardman, M. (2019), The Real Doc, *True West*, July, 2019

The two articles by Viola Payne are similar in content, for the most part. Viola worked with Doc's grandson through his son John Joshua Scurlock named Joseph "Jake" Scurlock. Jake's daughter Jodi also assisted her father with his research. Jake was born in 1925 and died in 2001.

Drew Gomber is the resident historian in Lincoln and has long been the go-to man for taking a tour of Lincoln. I had the pleasure of meeting Drew in Lincoln in October of 2018. This trip was also special because of the pleasure of meeting Reagan Scurlock, Doc's grandson through his son Josiah G. Scurlock, Jr. Reagan was 102 years old at this meeting. He knew Doc personally as a boy when Doc began to teach him his letters and numbers. Talking with both Drew and Reagan was truly an amazing opportunity for me in this research.

The article by John Daniel Scurlock comes from Doc's Uncle Daniel Norman Scurlock's line (the number of Daniel Norman Scurlocks becomes confusing). Daniel Norman Scurlock (Priestly's brother) had a son named Daniel Norman Scurlock, Jr. He had a son named Claude Leslie Scurlock. Claude and Claude's son J.D. worked on the family history as well.

In the 1998 book by Rosemary Corley Neal, Claude's granddaughter through his daughter Lois Blanche Scurlock Corley, entitled *Tidewater to Texas: The Scurlocks and Their Wives* she states:

> "This branch of the Scurlocks seems to have taken an early interest in the family history. Much family correspondence and many notes made by Daniel Scurlock, his son Claude Leslie and grandson John Daniel are presently owned by the writer. Priestly's famous letter has been preserved and a photostat of the original, plus a contemporary transcription made by Daniel are also among these private items, cited as 'Scurlock papers' below with full details."

The article by Dan Scurlock also comes from a family member. Dan actually lived at Fort Sumner for many years. Dan is believed to be the grandson of Doc's brother, who was named Daniel Norman Scurlock.

The article by Helen Havelka is an interesting piece. Helen worked with an engineer employed with the Texas Department of Transportation named Larry Smith for this article. When Larry was a Boy Scout, his troop's community project was on Doc's grave and tombstone.

Most recently, Mark Boardman, one of the editors at *True West* magazine did a feature on Doc in their issue about Lincoln subtitled "Billy the Kid Walks the Deadliest Street in America". A great issue packed with fascinating information on Lincoln.

It is to the meticulous researchers such as Rasch, Ketring, Fulton, Mullin, Boardman, and Gomber and the many Scurlock family members who have done such a great job of preserving Josiah Gordon "Doc" Scurlock's history that we owe much of the contents of this volume.

The following 16 pages are the Joe Buckbee letters, 1959-1965.

1839 West Fifth St.
San Pedro, Calif.

July 27, 1959

Mr. Joe Buckbee
3710 Lake Austin Blvd.
Austin, Texas

Dear Mr. Buckbee:

Your letter came today and I am answering immediately, as I leave for New Mexico on another research trip later this week. My note to FRONTIER TIMES was most fortunate, since it brought me a letter and several pictures from one of Dick Brewer's relatives.

As to how I found your grandfather: I was in the Barker Texas History Center at your University above five years ago doing a little reading. I was attending a Navy course at the University at the time and put in all my spare time in the Center. While looking thru the Panhandle-Plains Historical Review, XXIII:71, 1950, I saw a mention of the name Scurlock. The next day I rushed to the Texas Archives, went thru the 1880 Census and lo and behold!

Naturally, I should like to ask you several questions:

1. Can you tell me when and where he was born? According to one of the contemporary papers, he was born in Alabama about 1850, but I have not been able to pin it down any closer than that.

2. Do you know where the nickname "Doc" came from? There is a story in Lincoln that he had studied medicine at one time, but I know of no authority to substantiate this.

3. I note that you say he died in 1929. Can you tell me when and where?

4. Is it possible to obtain a picture of him? I have never seen one. What did the "G" in his name stand for?

5. What can you tell me of his career after he left Lincoln County?

I have quite a bit of material on his life in Lincoln County, most of it taken from the court records and concerned with disturbances of the peace in one way or another. He and Bowdre must have been close friends, since their names are both shown on many of the charges. I have always wondered whether people who led such exciting lives in their youth could settle down to a staid middle age. I have a reprint of an article in which I cited some of this material and will send it to you under separate cover.

I shall certainly look forward to hearing from you. Thanks for writing.

Sincerely,

Philip J. Rasch

Philip J. Rasch

Note on Doc Scurlock:

When it got too hot in New Mexico for Doc Scurlock, he appears to have settled down quietly in the Panhandle of Texas where he was listed by the 1880 census on June 1 with his occupation listed as keeping "mail station".

His place of residence - and work - was at the LX headquarters on the north side of the Canadian River (about a mile and a half downstream from the present bridge on Highway 87.) The listing reads: (from the Potter County census rolls)

Copy of a note from S. R. Archambeau, President, Panhandle-Plains Historical Society

Scurlock, Josiah G.-White - Male - age 30 - married -occupation "keeping mail station"- born in Alabama - father born in Ga - mother in Ala.

- Antonia M.- white -female - age 19 - married - wife "keeping house" - Born in N.M. - father -N.M. mother born in N.M.

- Viola J. - white - female - age 2 - single - daughter- - born in N.M. - father born Ala -mother N.M.

- Josiah G. Jr.-white - Male - age 9 months - son - - born in N.M. - father born Ala - Mother N.M.

The mail station he was keeping was on the Mobeetie to Tascosa to Fort Bascom to Las Vegas mail-hack line. He was not the postmaster, but merely looked after the horses that served as relay teams.

****

It appears that this is the latest word about whatever happened to this member of the Billy-the-Kid gang. Thought you might like to have this for your files.

- Reference: The Federal Census of 1880 in the Panhandle. Panhandle Plains Historical Review - 1950.

1839 West Fifth St.
San Pedro, Calif.

January 18, 1960

Mr. Joe Buckbee
3710 Lake Austin Blvd.
Austin, Texas

Dear Mr. Buckbee:

While working on my Lincoln County material tonight I cam across mention of Doc Scurlock. This reminded me that I had written to you in July of last year and had never received an answer. I am wondering whether you received my letter.

There is quite a bit of material on Scurlock in Lincoln County and if you are interested I believe we could put together a good biographical account of his life. I made a copy of the item I saw tonight for you and it is enclosed.

Sincerely,

Philip J. Rasch

Philip J. Rasch

1839 West Fifth St.
San Pedro, California

February 4, 1960

Mr. Joe Buckbee
The Dam Confectionery
3710 Lake Austin Blvd.
Austin, Texas

Dear Mr. Buckbee:

I have your letter of the 31st and am so excited that I know I cannot sleep unless I answer it. The Kid has been done to death, while Scurlock and Bowdre are all but unknown. This will be new material. By all means let me have copies of the pictures, his handwriting, the sketch of his life, and any other dope. I will have to go thru my material item by item and copy off anything referring to him. I'll just send it on to you from time to time, with or without comment. I'll warn you in advance that some of it may shake you. He was a rough boy in his youth.

I wonder how much of my Lincoln County material you have read. I have tried to be scrupulously fair and to say nothing which I cannot document. However, I can understand your feeling that I am partial to the Murphy cause. In their later years Mrs. McSween and the Coe boys talked freely and at length about their side of the troubles. They managed to build up an impression that the McSween-Tunstall party was very much wronged. Meanwhile the Murphy side kept quiet. Many of them held responsible positions in New Mexico, and they considered that to tell their side of the story would only stir up old troubles. As a result writers like Burns popularized the saintly McSween and the glamourous Kid.

In part also this resulted from the fact that much important material was not available. Angel's reports on his investigations were accessible in part at least, but it was only after Eisenhower became president and appointed Admiral somebody-or-other to go over the records of the War and Navy Departments and removed the "classified" status from all material not affecting national security that the Army files were opened. I was able to obtain then a microfilm of Dudley's court of inquiry. This comprised over 2,000 pages and took me better than two years to transcribe. I also obtained the records of the office of the adjutant general, which contained the weekly reports submitted by the commanding officer at Fort Stanton. Also the reports of the investigations by Colonel Watkins and by Angel of affairs at the Mescalero Agency, etc. etc. Some I still have not seen; evidently I shall have to go to Washington before I can go over the reports of General Hatch and Angel's investigation of Catron has almost entirely disappeared from the National Archives. The story this new material brings out is a bit different from the usual version.

Meanwhile an English correspondent, Fred Nolan, finally persuaded the Tunstall family to permit him to write the story of Tunstall's life. They had previously loaned some of their material to Colonel Fulton, but they turned over to Fred a whole batch of letters etc. that had never been out of their possession. As a result we have a completely new picture of this young man.

With this sort of material in my possession, the Dolan side's descendants have opened up a bit. Of course, what they have to say is mostly family tradition and must be taken with handfulls' of salt. Some of it is as obviously wide of the facts as is Coe's book. However, some documents have been preserved and I have acquired several pictures.

Granting Murphy etc. all of the faults they care to ascribe to them, the fact remains that practically everyone on the opposite side had something to gain by driving them out of the county. I'll copy off and enclose a newspaper item that gives their side of the story to some extent, and there is much truth in what they say.

I have two other reprints around; I'll dig up copies and send them on to you; also one which does not directly concern Scurlock but is part of the Lincoln County War picture.

I note you say that he was born in 1850; however, his death certificate gives the date as January 11, 1849.

By all means let me have any material which would "reveal much of the other side." Even if something should be apparently minor in nature, it might tie in with something I know and clear up another dark corner.

At an off hand guess, I would say that we have probably two to three years work in front of us. I only hope that you will enjoy it as much as I expect to. I should like to suggest you check with the Barker Texas History Center and see whether they have any record of Scurlock. So far as I know, the Center is still in charge of Dr. Llerena Friend. I have met her personally and have had quite a bit of correspondence with her and she is most obliging. I am sure that she would be glad to help a fellow citizen of Austin even more than she would a Californian. The newspaper collection at the Library may also prove helpful as we are able to date things.

So far as pictures are concerned, I can say at once that I have never seen a photo of Scurlock and have no idea of his appearance other than the newspaper quotation.

Did your grandfather ever say anything about Bowdre's background? He is said to have come from Louisiana, but I do not know whether this is so or not.

Sincerely,

Phil Rasch

1839 West Fifth St.
San Pedro, Calif.

May 30, 1960

Mr. Joe Buckbee
The Dam Confectionery
3710 Lake Austin Blvd.
Austin, Texas

Dear Mr. Buckbee:

I received the two pictures of Doc Scurlock and naturally I was delighted to finally see them. I took them to our best photography shop to have copies made. Unfortunately, they are tied up with high school graduation photos at the moment and it will probably be two weeks or so before they can get to them. They say that they have to entirely rearrange their camera room to do copy work and that they do it only once a month or so. So don't think I am stealing them if you don't get them right back.

I'll try to determine whether there is any record of his having gone to school in Tampico, but I have never had much luck with Mexican queries and will be happily surprised if we get an answer of any kind.

According to the 1880 census, he had two children - Viola J. and Josiah G. Jr. Did he ever have any more?

One thing we must have is a copy of the obituary which appeared in the Eastland paper at the time of his death. I have written the TELEGRAM's editor, but received no answer. Do you know anyone there who could go to the newspaper office and make a copy for us?

I am enclosing some more material, and will be eager to see what else your family has. In one of your first letters you said that you could certainly "reveal much of the other side" of the Lincoln County War. I am anxious to have you write about it.

I expect to go to New Mexico in mid-June for a week of research.

Yours very truly

Philip J. Rasch

Philip J. Rasch

1839 West Fifth St.
San Pedro, Calif.

June 16, 1960

Mr. Joe Buckbee
The Dam Confectionery
3710 Lake Austin Blvd.
Austin, Texas

Dear Mr. Buckbee:

I got the pictures back about an hour or so ago and am immediately preparing the originals for return to you. The copying job was fairly expensive, but came out quite well.

I have been in New Mexico all week, but did not turn up anything new on Scurlock. I had a letter from Frank Coe's daughter just before I left and she was greatly interested to learn that I had been in touch with you.

A few more items are also enclosed, but have not had time to do much work lately.

Am looking forward to hearing from you after you have talked with your family.

Sincerely,

Philip J. Rasch

1839 Chandeleur Dr.
San Pedro, Calif.

August 10, 1962

Mr. Joe Buckbee
The Dam Confectionery
3710 Lake Austin Blvd.
Austin, Texas

Dear Joe:

I received your letter of July 17 okay. In the meantime I have been putting a first draft together to see what we had and where there were gaps. On the whole we seem in good shape chronologically. What I would like to do now is to get some "human interest" into it.

In one of your earlier letters you mentioned you could tell a story about how "Doc" lost his front teeth. This sounds like the sort of thing which would be helpful and I would like to have the dope on this.

Did your grandfather ever say anything about individuals in Lincoln as people - particularly did he ever express opinions about McSween, Billy the Kid, or Charles Bowdre?

You mention Fernando Herrera. Do you have any family records showing when and where he was born and when and where he died? At the Five Days Fight at Lincoln he was in the Montano house in the group led by Martin Chavez and distinguished himself by fatally wounding Charles Crawford, alias Lalacooler, or Lally Cooler.

The sort of thing I need now is what he might have told his grandson when reminiscing about his life in those days. Comments on things as he saw them.

I expect to go to Roswell next year and will look for the Coe article. The papers etc. there are in a museum run by people whose principal interest is art. They pay little attention to history and and not very helpful. I was there last year but they were expanding the art gallery and all the papers were stored in a barn out of town and could not be used.

I guess by now Klein is in the northwest, so you won't be seeing him.

Best regards,

Phil Rasch

1839 Chandeleur Dr.
San Pedro, California

April 23, 1963

Mr. Joe Buckbee
Dam Confectionery
3710 Lake Austin Blvd.
Austin, Texas

Dear Joe:

I am glad that your Mother and uncle were satisfied with the Scurlock story. These things are difficult to handle. If you emphasize the outlaw side the family is apt to become irritated; if you emphasize the good citizen side, the readers fall asleep. Scurlock was certainly a most interesting personality. It is a great loss that he did not leave an account of his life or a diary, as his views on the Lincoln County troubles would have had major historical importance. I wish I could have known him.

The paper has been accepted for publication in the English Westerners Brand Book. They were not sure which issue would carry it, as they have to fit various papers to each other so that they come out with the right number of pages. However, there seems to be no doubt in their minds but that we shall see it this summer by the latest. I shall, of course, see to it that copies are sent to you.

It was a pleasure to work with you on this. Wish you had some more famous relatives we could write up!

Sincerely,

Phil Rasch
Phil Rasch

June 23, 1964

Mr. Joe Austell Small
Western Publishing , Inc.
P. O. Box 5008
Edgecliff
Austin, Texas

Dear Joe:

I am sending you the enclosed information that we talked of previously.

Please feel free to edit this if you think it is suitable for publication.

If you have any questions concerning this information, please let me know. I will look forward to seeing you again soon.

With Best Regards,

Joe Buckbee

JB/tl

Dear Joe;

I am the grandson of "Doc" J. G. Scurlock, who in his day consorted with such colorful characters as "Billy the Kid" and many others who came to life in stories he told to me as I sat around at his feet as a boy.

As I was reading in your February issue the story of the Cattle Kings, the words jumped out at me at the period in July 15, 1874 with regard to "Indians killed Jack Holt of the Roswell community in 1873." I find these dates and incidents to be amazingly accurate according to Grandad who was there working with Jack Holt when he was killed. Grandad ("Doc" Scurlock) and Jack Holt were working together as line riders for John Chisum. The two of them were out riding line when suddenly as they approached a canyon they were surprised by approximately five indians (Grandad said there were from five to seven altogether). Almost immediately Holt was killed, as were both the horses. Grandad hid among the rocks and exchanged shots with them most of the evening. As the evening wore on, it became evident that he was getting lower and lower on ammunition. He decided to let up on the shooting. . . not knowing how long he would be able to held out against them. When he did quit shooting and the atmosphere grew quiet, the Indian chief came forward (thinking he was out of ammunition) and Grandad stood up quickly and shot him. At this the rest of the Indians began to yelp like a pack of cyotes and took for cover.

He waited for night and safety before he walked twenty miles for help. When he returned with help they found the dead chief gone. Holt's body was still there however and they were amazed that he had not been scalped but Grandad and his companions were shocked to find that his right arm had been removed at the elbo. They wondered at this and could not imagine why the Indians had done this.

36 SOUTH LA SENDA DRIVE
THREE ARCH BAY
SOUTH LAGUNA, CALIFORNIA

December 16, 1964

Mr. Joe Buckbee,
3710 Lake Austin Blvd.,
Austin, Texas.

Dear Mr. Buckbee:

Your letter in the current issue of TRUE WEST was of more than passing interest to me. Since my boyhood and young manhood in the Southwest at the turn of the century I been gathering pictures and what factual information I could concerning the more notable characters who played prominent roles in the West Texas-Arizona-New Mexico frontier.

Do you have a photograph of your grandfather which you will permit me to have copied, or which you can have copied for me at my expense?

You may be interested in some of the items I have picked over the years concerning the "muy hombre" Doc Scurlock:

1) b. Tallapoosa; Alabama, Jan 11, 1850. d. Eastland 7-25-29
2) Wife, Antonia, b. June 23, 1860 . d. 11-27-1912, Eastland . Father, Anglo; mother, of native Mexican extraction.
3) "Had been well ecucated for the practive of medicine; quiet, well regarded by his neighbors in New Mexico. good farmer and good family man. Prior to Lincoln County War, he devoted part of this time--without any compensation--to teaching school for his own and the neighbors' children."
(Maurice Garland Fulton to R.N.M. Dec., 1947.)
4) Chisum cowboy, 1873-4; later farmer on the Ruidoso.
5) Assets of McSween estate list a note for $275.00, due in six months, dated 6-25-77, at 25% per year interest.

6) Drawn unwillingly into the Lincoln County War. harassed by Dolan contingent due to his frienship with Charley Bowdre and other neighbors .

7) Arrested by Sheriff Brady, "Murphy-Dolan Sheriff" between August 12 and 15th, at his Ruidoso farm, charged with being a member of the Nelson gang of horse thieves.

8) "After the Lincoln County War, Doc Scurlock went to Central America."
(Letter from Herbert Cody Blake, in R. N. M. file.)

Some of which may be true, some not. You doubtless have much more data than that above. And if you will help me in the photograph matter, I shall be most grateful.

R N Mullin

R. N. Mullin

Eastland, Texas
August 31, 1964

Mr. Lewis Ketring, Jr.,
Manitou Springs, Colo.

Dear Sir:

In reply to your letter I have found very little about Mr. Josiah G. Scurlock. I found at the City Hall the Death Certificate which stated that Mr. J. G. Scurlock died July 25, 1929; was a white male, widower; died of heart failure, Dr. L. C. Brown signed death certificate; his fathers' name was Presley Scurlock and his mothers' maiden name was Ester Brown. Burial in Eastland Cemetery.

I found the grave in the Eastland Cemetery and the information on the tombstone is:

Scurlock	Wife
Josiah G.	Antonia
Born Jan. 11, 1850	Born June 13, 1860
Died July 25, 1929	Died Nov. 27, 1912

Nearby were 2 other tombstones of Scurlocks'. Whether or not they are the same family I do not know. One was:

Liddie E. Scurlock
B. Aug. 19, 1882
D. Aug. 15, 1952 } wife

Wm. A. Scurlock
B. April 14, 1893
D. May 6, 1933 } husband

The other grave was of a Civil War vet. with no date of death, just
Co. A. 63 Ala. Inf. Daniel N. Scurlock
CSA

I have asked several old timers about Mr. Scurlock but as yet I haven't found anyone who knew him. They all say, "The name is familiar" but they can't seem to remember the man.

Hoping this information will help you,

Yours truly,

Mrs. W. E. Cushman

Librarian, Eastland Public Library

P. S. I wonder if he were in the oil business? Boyce House doesn't mention him in his books about Eastland County (that we have)

114 Canon Ave
Manitou Springs, Colorado

January 14, 1965

Mr. Joe Buckbee,
3710 Lake Austin Blvd.,
Austin, Texas

Dear Mr. Buckbee:

I was most interested in reading your letter which appeared in the latest issue of True West Magazine, and surprised to see the names of Jack Holt and J.G. Scurlock mentioned. References to Jack Holt's death at the hands of Indians in 1873 are few, and until your letter in TW telling in detail facts surrounding this historical episode, I had located only two others. One is the reference you mentioned in your letter("Cattle Kings" article), and the second is an unpublished referance that the late Lincoln County Historian Maurice G. Fulton made, in which he says,

> "Most vulnerable to Indian attacks were the isolated camps of Chisum's men. More than once, while stealing the stock, did the Indians kill the employees in charge. Probably Newt Huggins came to his death in this way in 1873 in what is now known as Huggins Arroyo. The next year a cowboy named Jack Holt met his death in an Indian attack on a camp at Eighteen Mile Bend on the Rio Pecos."

So according to Fulton, Holt died in 1874, not '73. I have been trying to locate somekind of newspaper account of it, but haven't found any as yet.

I hope you don't mind my writing you, but I have been interested in the early happenings of Lincoln County and southern New Mexico since my high school days in '57, and now being stationed at Fort Carson for a tour in the Army, I find a lot of enjoyment in learning all I can concerning the history of Lincoln county during my leisure hours.

Since those early high school days when I read the first accounts of the happenings of the Lincoln County War period, I have made an effort to learn all I can concerning the histories of the many participants, which in many instances is a difficult operation. Also since those early days when I first became acquainted with the many stories of the pioneers of Lincoln county, the one person I have always admired for his actions during the trying times of the "War" period is Josiah G. Scurlock. I have tried and tried to learn something of his history with small sucess. Finally I learned that he had died in Eastland, Texas and am attaching a copy of the letter I received from the Eastland Public Library.

If it is at all possible, I would appreciate very much if you could tell me a little of your grandfathers history. Was it true that he was actually a doctor? One of the things I would like to find out is what he did after the "War" ceased in 1878? The late historian Fulton used to write that Scurlock was one of the real pioneers of Lincoln County and that his siding with the Tunstall-McSween group did much to show other residents of the county that their cause was an upright one. Fulton even remarked that Scurlock had served as a school teacher while there.

-2-

I was surprised in reading your letter that Scurlock had arrived in New Mexico in 1873, as I had always believed he had arrived sometime in the 1876-77 period.

Did your grandfather even have his picture taken? Collecting photographs of the early Lincoln County people is often times difficult, and I would appreciate help you might be able to give in this direction.

My interest in these early Lincoln County pioneers is nothing more then a hobby with me, and while I have read all of the books relating to this subject, gaining new information is difficult, especially being stationed here in Colorado. When I leave to return to my home state of California I want to make a trip through New Mexico and see the many historical places of interest.

I would appreciate very much hearing from you, and hope my letter hasn't bored or tired you out in any way.

Sincerely,

Lewis Ketring Jr.

Lewis Ketring

Rt. 1, Box 134
River Road
Sneads Ferry, N.C. 28460

28 March 1965

Mr. Joe Buckbee
Dam Confectionery
Lake Austin
Austin, Texas

Dear Joe:

I saw a letter from you in one of the Western magazines a while back so I take it you are still in the land of the living.

There is not much good to be said about North Carolina, so I am doing a lot of writing. I'm trying to collect a paragraph now on each of The Regulators. As I recall, you told me Fernando Herrera was the father of Mrs. Scurlock. Can you give me any dope on him - when and where born and when and where he died, in particular?

Have you seen William Brent's THE COMPLETE AND FACTUAL LIFE OF BILLY THE KID? He is about 40 years behind in the research that has been done on the Kid. The book is worthless. Someone named Koop claims to have found record of the Kid's life in Kansas before he went to New Mexico and is bringing out a booklet on it. Might be worth reading.

Hope everything is going well for you.

Sincerely,

Phil

Philip J. Rasch

PART VIII – AUTHENTICATED PHOTOS OF DOC

Earliest known photo of Josiah Gordon Scurlock

Josiah Gordon Scurlock with wife Antonia Miguela de Herrera Scurlock.

Doc's family circa 1898: L-R – Martha Ethlinda "Linda" Scurlock, Amy Antonia Scurlock (taller girl), Delores "Lola" Scurlock (in front of Amy), Josiah Gordon Scurlock, Jr. (standing in back middle), Antonia (Doc's wife seated holding child), Josephine "Gladys" Scurlock (on Antonia's lap), Prestley Fernando Scurlock, William Andrew Scurlock, Doc, and John Joshua Scurlock.

According to the descendants of William Marcellus Armstrong, Doc's nephew, the below photo was taken in approximately 1919 in Eastland County. "Sellie" had gone bankrupt in Dressy, running the Dressy Mercantile Co. (a general store he owned). After the bankruptcy the family moved to Eastland. In late 1917 or early 1918, they arrived by covered wagon just in time for the oil boom. The McCluskey No. 1 well in Eastland County struck oil on October 28, 1917. All of the available lumber in the area went for building oil derricks, and there was none available for building houses. So for several months, or even a year or two, the family lived in tents.

Front Row (left to right) -- Effie Sawyer, unknown, unknown, unknown, Pauline Scurlock (girl holding left side of covered wagon "hoop"), unknown, unknown, Ward Armstrong, Flois Armstrong, unknown, unknown, unknown, Lois Armstrong.

Back Row (left to right) -- unknown, unknown, unknown, unknown, Amy Scurlock, Daniel Scurlock (directly in center), Thelma Armstrong, Johnny Scurlock, William Marcellus "Sellie" Armstrong, Josiah Doc Scurlock (looking to the side), Will Sawyer, Anna E. (Guy) Armstrong, Lizzie Sawyer.

Doc holding granddaughter Gladys Marie "Rae" Scurlock.

From another reunion, Doc is looking to the side again. L-R: Daniel Norman Scurlock (brother of Doc), John Dargon Scurlock (brother of Doc), Josiah Gordon "Doc" Scurlock, Andrew Jackson "Jack" Smith (brother-in-law of Doc), and William Marcellus Armstrong (nephew of Doc),

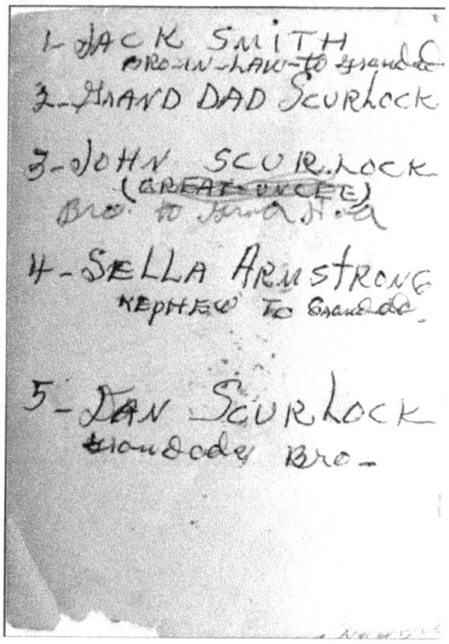

1- JACK SMITH
BRO-IN-LAW-TO Grandad
2- GRAND DAD SCURLOCK
3- JOHN SCURLOCK
(GREAT UNCLE)
Bro. to [illegible]
4- SELLA ARMSTRONG
NEPHEW TO Grandad
5- DAN SCURLOCK
Grandads Bro.

Lola died in October 1916, so this was likely taken in 1915 or 1916.

Josiah G. "Doc" Scurlock is pictured with a daughter, Lola. This photograph was made around 1920, when "Doc" was 70 years old.

This photo was autographed and sent to Mike Stewart, great grandson of Doc, by Keifer Sutherland, who portrayed Doc. Mike was consulted on the life of Doc for the Young Guns movies by various historians. Yes, The Scurlock family is well aware of the historical discrepancies, that's why we dedicated a whole chapter to it.

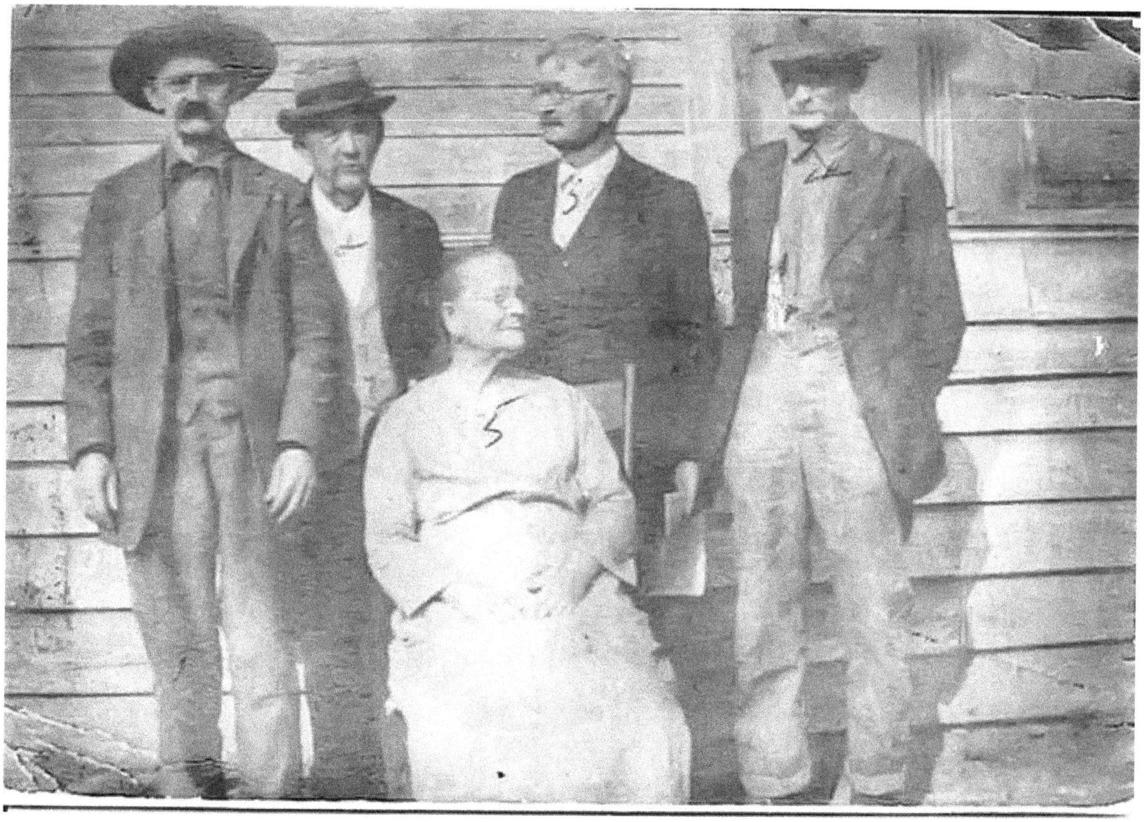

L-R: Andrew Jackson "Jack" Smith (Doc's brother-in-law), Daniel Norman "Dan" Scurlock (Doc's brother), Mary Ann Scurlock-Smith (Doc's sister), Josiah Gordon "Doc" Scurlock (looking to the side), and John Dargon Scurlock (Doc's brother)

A one-of-a-kind picture of Doc showing his missing teeth as he clowns with his siblings Daniel, Mary, and John.

Provenance of the below photo hasn't been proven to be Doc! Even though numerous sources use this image as one of Doc, this is likely Doc's sister Mary and her husband Jack Smith. Jack's also standing beside Doc in a later picture where Doc is looking to the side.

This photo fell out of one of Doc's books and was assumed to be him and Antonia, however, it's more likely that Doc was keeping a picture of his sister Mary and brother-in-law Jack Smith in the book. It was often commented by the family that Jack and Doc favored each other. Below are further comparisons.

The man in the upper right is confirmed to be Jack Smith. The two bottom photos are known photos of Doc.

This is another photo of Jack Smith compared to the photo in question.

The photo on the right is a known photo of Mary Ann Scurlock, Doc's sister.

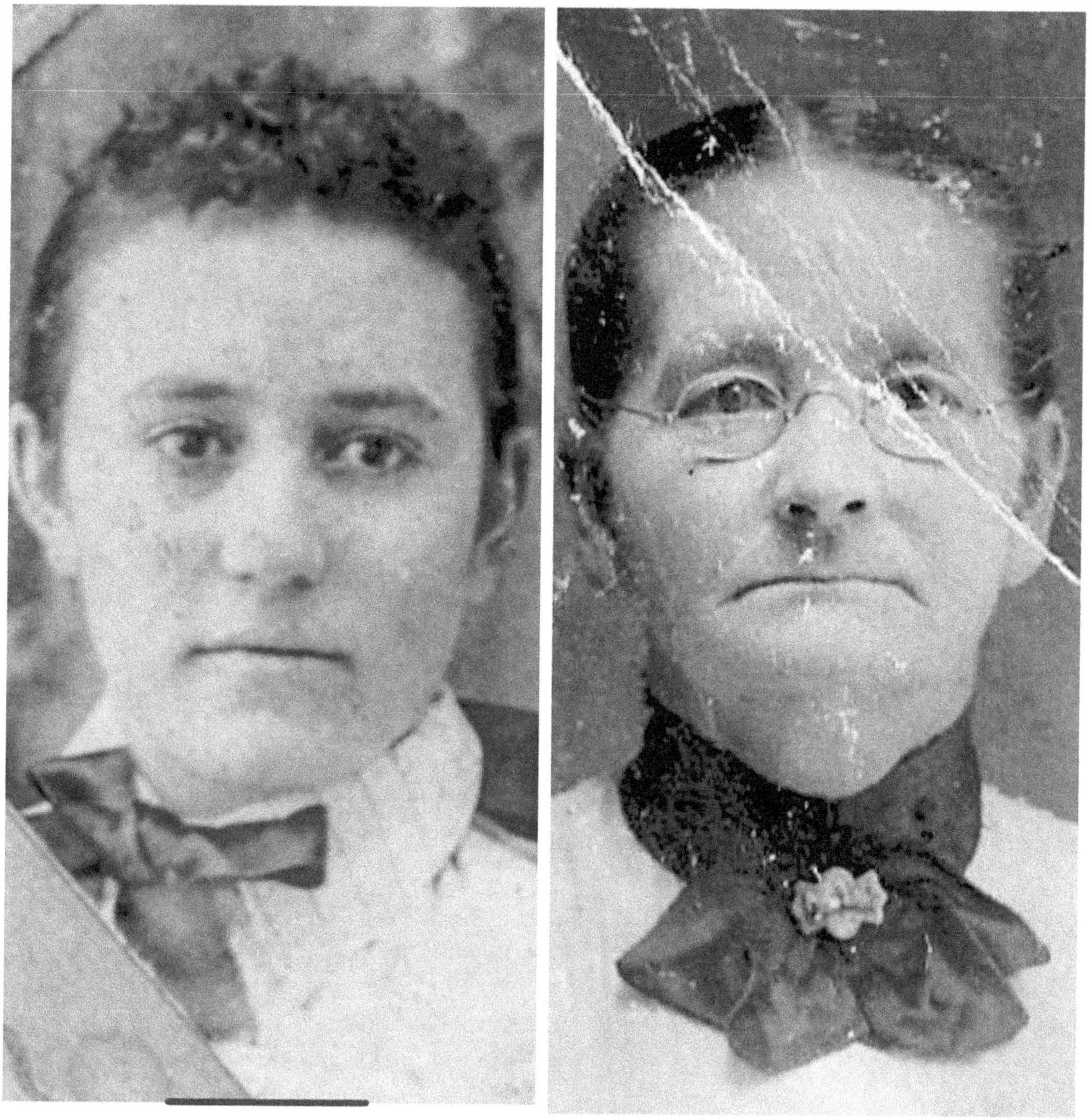

This is another look at Mary Scurlock Smith compared to the photo in question.

Antonia had a longer face than Mary's round face. This photo compares a known photo of Antonia Herrera Scurlock with the photo in question.

The man on the left is known to be Jack Smith. Notice how much he resembles later pictures of Doc.

Below right is another picture with unconfirmed provenance. A descendant of Doc's sister Mary Scurlock Smith possesses this photo, but it hasn't been conclusively identified as being Doc. The photo on the left is a confirmed picture of Doc for comparison.

Antonia Herrera Scurlock.

The following pictures are of Doc's children.

Josiah Gordon Scurlock, Jr. (Reagan Scurlock's Father).

Josiah Gordon Scurlock, Jr. and John Joshua Scurlock.

Prestley Fernando Scurlock.

Amy Antonia Scurlock.

Martha Ethlinda Scurlock.

William Andrew Scurlock on left, unknown on right.

Delores "Lola" Scurlock.

Prestley Fernando and William Andrew Scurlock.

Josephine "Gladys" Scurlock with husband William Franklin Pearson.

Joe Buckbee, Sr., Doc's grandson.

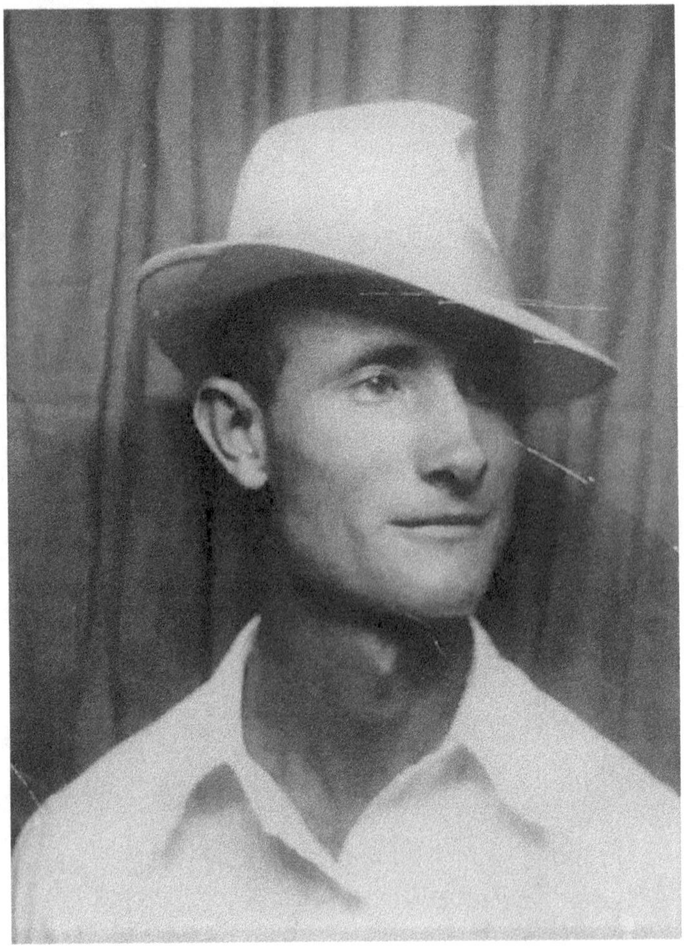

PART IX – CENSUS RECORDS FOR JOSIAH GORDON SCURLOCK

Doc appears on the censuses of 1850, 1860, 1880, 1890, 1900, 1910, and 1920. He hasn't been found on the 1870 and 1890 censuses. He likely didn't get enumerated in 1870 because he was in Mexico at that time. The 1890 census was mostly lost due to fire and water damage.

YEAR	COUNTY/STATE	OCCUP.	FAMILY
1850	Tallapoosa, Alabama	Teacher (Priestly)	Presley (Priestly) 44 Easther 29 Rhodia (Rhoda) Ann 13 William 11 Sampson 9 Daniel 4 Josiah 1
1860	Tallapoosa, Alabama	Farmer (Priestly)	Presley Sherlock (Scurlock)54 Esta A. (Easter) 40 Sampson V. 19 Daniel 14 Josiah 10 Nancy 8 Joshua 6 Mary 3 Martha L. 1
1870 – No census record found			
1880	Potter, Texas	Keeping Mail	Joseah (Josiah) 29 Antonia 19 Viola J. 2 Josiah 8 mo.
1890 – No census record found			
1900	Hood, Texas	Farmer	Jacob G. (Josiah) 50 Antonia M. 39 Josiah G. 20 John J. 19 Amy A. 15 Marta E. 14 Prestley F. 11 Dolores 9 William A. 7 Josephine G. 4

1910	Hood, Texas	Farmer	Jonah G. (Josiah) 60 Ammie N. (Antonia) 49 Prestley F. 21 Lola 19 William A. 17 Josephine J. 14
1920	Hood, Texas	Clerk Retail Grocery	Jos. G. (Josiah) 70

138

SCHEDULE I.—Free Inhabitants in Township 19 in the County of Tallapoosa State of Alabama enumerated by me, on the 28 day of Nov 1850. Eli T. Pruney Ass't Marshal.

Dwelling-houses numbered in the order of visitation.	Families numbered in the order of visitation.	The Name of every Person whose usual place of abode on the first day of June, 1850, was in this family.	Age.	Sex.	Color, {White, black, or mulatto.	Profession, Occupation, or Trade of each Male Person over 15 years of age.	Value of Real Estate owned.	Place of Birth. Naming the State, Territory, or Country.	Married within the year.	Attended School within the year.	Persons over 20 y'rs of age who cannot read & write.	Whether deaf and dumb, blind, insane, idiotic, pauper, or convict.
1	2	3	4	5	6	7	8	9	10	11	12	13
[illegible]	[illegible]	Martha Bonham	25	F				Geo				
		Elizabeth	6	"				Ala		1		
		James	4	M				"				
		Henry	2	"				"				
999	999	William Flemmington	35	M		Farm	500	S C				
		Mary	19	F				"				
		Caroline	15	"				Geo		1		
		Joseph	12	M				"		1		
		William	10	"				"				
		Samuel	8	"				"				
		Martha	5	F				"				
		Elizabeth	2	"				Ala				
		Elizabeth Hancock	23	F		Farm		Geo				
		John Millman	19	M		"		"				
1000	1000	Presley N. Scurlock	44	"		Teacher	125	"				
		Esther	29	F				"				
		William	11	M				Ala		1		
		Simpson	9	"				"		1		
		Daniel	4	"				"				
		Josiah	1	"				"				
		Rodia Ann Sharlock	13	F				Geo		1		
1001	1001	Henry Jackson	62	M		Mechanic	435	"				
		Delila	53	F				"			1	
		Permelia	18	"				Ala				
		Isaac Jackson	25	M		Farm		"				
		Monsenia	18	F				Geo				
1002	1002	Manuel Pliler	50	M		Farm		S C				
		Polly	45	F				"			1	
		Barbary	23	"				"			1	
		Manuel	20	M		Farm		"				
		Malinda	17	F				"		1		
		Patrick	17	M		none		"		1		
		Nancy	15	F				"		1		
		Buck	13	M				"		1		
		Peter	11	"				"		1		
		Mary	10	F				"				
		Lize	8	"				Ala				
		Toddy	6	"				"				
1003	1003	Conrad Pliler	30	M		Farm	300	Geo			1	
		Mary	22	F				"			1	
		Joseph	½	M				Ala				
		Martha Kilgore	22	F				Geo				

Page No. 107

301

SCHEDULE 1.—Free Inhabitants in Western Division (Beat 2) **in the County of** Tallapoosa **State of** Alabama **enumerated by me, on the** 8th **day of** Aug **1860.** [illegible] **Ass't Marshal.**

Post Office [illegible]

	Dwelling-houses—numbered in the order of visitation.	Families numbered in the order of visitation.	The name of every person whose usual place of abode on the first day of June, 1860, was in this family	Description: Age	Sex	Color, White, black, or mulatto.	Profession, Occupation, or Trade of each person, male and female, over 15 years of age.	Value of Estate Owned: Value of Real Estate.	Value of Personal Estate.	Place of Birth, Naming the State, Territory, or Country	Married within the year.	Attended School within the year.	Persons over 20 y'rs of age who cannot read & write.	Whether deaf and dumb, blind, insane, idiotic, pauper, or convict.	
	1	2	3	4	5	6	7	8	9	10	11	12	13	14	
1			Sarah	26	F					Georgia			1		1
2	130	130	[illegible] Burlock	41	M		Farmer	1000	400	Do					2
3			[illegible]	11	F					Do					3
4			Sampson W	17	M					Alabama					4
5			Daniel	14	M					Do					5
6			Josiah	10	M					Do		1			6
7			Nancy	8	F					Do		1			7
8			William	6	M					Do					8
9			Mary	3	F					Do					9
10			Martha L	1	F					Do					10
11	131	131	Elizabeth Miller	40	F			1000	500	Georgia					11
12			William B	17	M					Alabama		1			12
13			Martha	1[illegible]	F					Do		1			13
14			Mary E	12	F					Do		1			14
15			Benjamin Barton	11	M					Do		1			15
16	132	132	[illegible] Betty	2[illegible]	M		Farmer	250	200	Georgia					16
17			[illegible]	21	F					Do			1		17
18			George M	1	M					Alabama					18
19			Frances Whaley	18	F					Do		1			19
20	133	133	Allen J. Wood	3[illegible]	M		Farmer	500	1600	Georgia					20
21			Louisa	2[illegible]	F					Do			1		21
22			[illegible]	7	F					Alabama					22
23			Rachel	4	F					Do					23
24			Wiley [illegible]	4	M					Do					24
25			[illegible]	2	M					Do					25
26	134	134	James Barrow	23	M		Farmer		100	Georgia			1		26
27			[illegible]	23	F					Alabama					27
28	135	135	[illegible] Jones	3[illegible]	M		Blacksmith	500	250	Georgia					28
29			[illegible]	23	F					Do					29
30			[illegible]	8	M					Alabama		1			30
31			[illegible]	7	F					Do		1			31
32			[illegible]	2	M					Do					32
33			John Hancock	2[illegible]	M					Georgia					33
34	136	136	[illegible]	[illegible]	M		Farmer	250	75	Do			1		34
35			[illegible]	30	F					Do			1		35
36			Robert F	10	M					Alabama		1			36
37			Mary E	[illegible]	F					Do					37
38			James	7	M					Do		1			38
39			Martha	5	F					Do					39
40			Sarah	4	F					Do					40

No. white males, 20 No. colored males, No. foreign born, No. blind, 3,750 7,605 No. idiotic,

No. white females, 20 No. colored females, No. deaf and dumb, No. insane, No. paupers, No. convicts,

10

[7-296.]

Received Sept 1880

A.

Page No.

Supervisor's Dist. No. 3

Enumeration Dist. No. 197

Note A.—The Census Year begins June 1, 1879, and ends May 31, 1880.

Note B.—All persons will be included in the Enumeration who were living on the 1st day of June, 1880. No others will. Children BORN SINCE June 1, 1880, will be OMITTED. Members of Families who have DIED SINCE June 1, 1880, will be INCLUDED.

Note C.—Questions Nos. 13, 14, 22 and 23 are not to be asked in respect to persons under 10 years of age.

82

SCHEDULE 1.—Inhabitants in ______________, in the County of Potter, State of Texas enumerated by me on the 15th 16th & 17 day of June, 1880.

Travis Leach
Enumerator.

Dwelling No. (1)	Family No. (2)	Name (3)	Color (4)	Sex (5)	Age (6)	Relationship (8)	Single (9)	Married (10)	Occupation (13)	Months unemployed (14)	Birthplace (24)	Father's birthplace (25)	Mother's birthplace (26)
22	27	Moore Wm	W	M	30		/		Raising Cattle		Mo	Ken	Penn
		True Ebin E	W	M	32	Servant	/		Herding Horses		Me	Me	Me
		Erskine Clement	W	M	22	Servant	/		Keeping Books		Mass	Mass	Me
		Lawrence George O C	W	M	20	Servant	/		Herding Cows		Con	N H	Mass
		Carter Frederick	W	M	26	Servant	/		Cooking		Mass	N H	Me
		Bates Frank C	W	M	22	Servant	/		Herding Cows	4	Mass	Mass	Mass
		Brown Stephen J	W	M	25	Servant	/		Herding Cows		Iowa	Penn	Penn
		Barnes Jay	W	M	30	Servant	/		Herding Cows		Kansas		
		Bell John	W	M	28	Servant	/		Herding Cows		Kan	Iowa	Mo
		Bell Wm	W	M	20	Servant	/		Herding Cows		Kan	Iowa	Mo
		Betts John	W	M	25	Servant	/		Herding Cows		Tex	Tex	Tex
		Chambers Alonzo	W	M	31	Servant	/		Herding Cows		Tex	Mo	Mo
		Coffee Thomas	W	M	26	Servant	/		Herding Cows		Tex	Mo	Kan
		Green Wm	W	M	24	Servant	/		Herding Cows		Tex	Tex	Tex
		Gates Loren	W	M	21	Servant	/		Herding Cows		N Y	N Y	N Y
		Houghton Edward	W	M	25	Servant	/		Herding Cows		Tex	Tex	Tex
		Munroe Thomas	W	M	25	Servant	/		Herding Cows		Mo	Mo	Mo
		McClaugherty James	W	M	30	Servant	/		Herding Cows		Va	Va	Va
		Peacock John	W	M	22	Servant	/		Herding Cows		Mo	Mo	Mo
		Williams Henry	W	M	25	Servant	/		Herding Cows				
		Wills Amstead	B	M	19	Servant	/		Herding Cows		Tex	Tex	Tex
22	28	Prewo Alexander B	W	M	20		/		Keeping Mail Sta		Mo	Ken	Ken
		Johnson Osburn	W	M	32	Boarder	/		Carrying Mail		Va	Eng	Eng
		Montgomery Samuel	Mu	M	28	Boarder	/		Hunting Horses		Miss	Eng	Penn
		Scurlock Josiah G	W	M	30			/	Keeping Mail Sta		Ala	Geo	Ala
		Antonia M	W	F	19	Wife		/	Keeping House		New Mexico	N M	N M
		Viola J	W	F	2	Daughter	/				N M	Ala	N M
		Josiah J	W	M	1/12	Son	/				N M	Ala	N M

I hereby Certify that I have this day (finished) Completed the Enumeration of Enumeration District No 197 of Supervisor District No 3 Tex as required by Law and according to my oath of office to the best of my ability Said District Comprising the counties of Gray Carson Potter Moore Hutchinson and Roberts

Dated Mobeetie this 21st day of June A D 1880

7—224.

TWELFTH CENSUS OF THE UNITED STATES.

1624 281 A

SCHEDULE No. 1.—POPULATION.

State Texas
County Hood
Township or other division of county Justice's Precinct 3
Name of incorporated city, town, or village, within the above-named division, X
Supervisor's District No. 4
Enumeration District No. 94
Sheet No. 10
Name of Institution, X
Ward of city, X

Enumerated by me on the 11 day of June, 1900, John T. Browning, Enumerator.

37

Street	House Number	Dwelling No. (1)	Family No. (2)	Name (3)	Relation (4)	Color (5)	Sex (6)	Month (7)	Year (7)	Age (8)	Marital (9)	Years married (10)	Mother of how many children (11)	Children living (12)	Birthplace of person (13)	Birthplace of father (14)	Birthplace of mother (15)	Year of immigration (16)	Years in U.S. (17)	Naturalization (18)	Occupation (19)	Months not employed (20)	Attended school (21)	Can read (22)	Can write (23)	Can speak English (24)	Owned or rented (25)	Free or mortgaged (26)	Farm or house (27)	No. of farm schedule (28)
				Lambert James E	Son	W	M	July	1886	13	S				Texas	Texas	Texas				Farm Laborer	0		yes	no	yes				
				— Burl W	Son	W	M	June	1889	11	S				Texas	Texas	Texas				Farm Laborer	0		yes	yes	yes				
				— Earl A	Son	W	M	June	1889	11	S				Texas	Texas	Texas				Farm Laborer	0		yes	yes	yes				
				— David	Son	W	M	Dec	1894	5	S				Texas	Texas	Texas													
		158	168	Barton Joshua	Head	W	M	Dec	1827	72	M	51			S Carolina	Virginia	S Carolina				Farmer	0		yes	yes	yes	R		F	174
				— Cordelia	Wife	W	F	Aug	1840	59	M	51	8	7	Georgia	Georgia	S Carolina							no	no	yes				
			169	Barton Jessie	Head	W	M	May	1873	27	M	5			Georgia	S Carolina	Georgia				Farmer	0		yes	yes	yes	O	F	F	175
				— Lee	Wife	W	F	May	1877	23	M	5	2	2	Texas	Virginia	Georgia							yes	yes	yes				
				— Early	Son	W	M	Aug	1895	4	S				Texas	Georgia	Texas													
				— Mary	Daughter	W	F	Dec	1899	6/12	S				Texas	Georgia	Texas													
		159	170	Carney William	Head	W	M	Sept	1872	27	M	3			Georgia	Georgia	Georgia				Farmer	0		yes	yes	yes	O	M	F	176
				— Lithie	Wife	W	F	May		19	M		1	1	Georgia	Georgia	Georgia							yes	yes	yes				
				— Mattie	Daughter	W	F	Aug	1898	1	S				Texas	Georgia	Georgia													
		160	171	Adkisson James	Head	W	M	Dec	1870	29	M	6			Texas	Texas	Texas				Farmer	0		yes	yes	yes	R		F	177
				— Mary E	Wife	W	F	Aug	1871	28	M	6	1	1	Texas	Texas	Texas							yes	yes	yes				
				— Mary L	Daughter	W	F	Jan	1894	5	S				Texas	Texas	Texas													
		161	172	Saul Charley	Head	W	M	Jan	1852	48	M	22			Texas	Texas	Texas				Farmer	0		yes	[illegible]	[illegible]	R		F	178
				— Mary A	Wife	W	F	Nov	1860	39	M	22	6	6	Illinois	Illinois	Illinois							yes	yes	yes				
				— [illegible] B	Daughter	W	F	Feb	1879	21	S				Texas	Texas	Illinois				Farm Laborer	3		yes	yes	yes				
				— Bessie M	Daughter	W	F	Nov	1880	19	S				Texas	Texas	Illinois				Farm Laborer	3		yes	[illegible]	[illegible]				
				— Lizzie L	Daughter	W	F	Jan	1883	17	S				Texas	Texas	Illinois				At School		3	yes	yes	yes				
				— Marsella	Son	W	M	July	1885	14	S				Texas	Texas	Illinois				At School		3	yes	yes	yes				
				— Earl N	Daughter	W	F	Oct	1887	12	S				Texas	Texas	Illinois				At School		3	yes	yes	yes				
				— Jessie E	Son	W	M	Feb	1890	10	S				Texas	Texas	Illinois				At School		3	yes	yes	yes				
				Robertson Bert	Boarder	W	M	Jan	1881	19	S				Texas	Georgia	Georgia				Farm Laborer	0		yes	yes	yes				
		162	173	Smith Mack D	Head	W	M	Aug	1867	32	M	5			Texas	Georgia	Texas				Farmer	0		yes	yes	yes	R		F	179
				— Dola	Wife	W	F	July	1874	26	M	5	3	2	Texas	Alabama	Alabama							yes	yes	yes				
				— Addie	Daughter	W	F	May	1897	3	S				Texas	Texas	Texas													
				— Aubrey	Son	W	M	May	1900	1/12	S				Texas	Texas	Texas													
				Means [illegible]	Brother	W	M	July	1866	33	M	11			Texas	Indian Ter	Georgia				Farmer	0		yes	yes	yes	R		F	180
		163	174	Scurlock Joseph	Head	W	M	Jan	1850	50	M	24			Alabama	Georgia	Alabama				Farmer	0		yes	yes	yes	O	M	F	181
				— Antonia M	Wife	W	F	June	1860	39	M	24	11	8	New Mexico	New Mexico	New Mexico							no	no	yes				
				— Josiah G	Son	W	M	Oct	1879	20	S				New Mexico	Alabama	New Mexico				Farm Laborer	4		yes	yes	yes				
				— John J	Son	W	M	May	1881	19	S				Texas	Alabama	New Mexico				Farm Laborer	3		yes	yes	yes				
				— Amy A	Daughter	W	F	July	1884	15	S				Texas	Alabama	New Mexico				Farm Laborer	3		yes	yes	yes				
				— Maria E	Daughter	W	F	May	1886	14	S				Texas	Alabama	New Mexico				Farm Laborer	3		yes	yes	yes				
				— Prestley F	Son	W	M	Aug	1888	11	S				Texas	Alabama	New Mexico				Farm Laborer	3		yes	yes	yes				
				— Dolores	Daughter	W	F	Mar	1891	9	S				Texas	Alabama	New Mexico							yes	yes	yes				
				— William A	Son	W	M	Apr	1893	7	S				Texas	Alabama	New Mexico													
				— Josephine G	Daughter	W	F	Aug	1895	4	S				Texas	Alabama	New Mexico													
		164	175	Hays Elisha	Head	W	M	Mar	1821	79	Wd				S Carolina	S Carolina	S Carolina				Farmer	0		yes	no	yes	O	F	F	182
				— Sampson J	Son	W	M	Mar	1852	48	S				Georgia	S Carolina	S Carolina				Farmer	0		no	no	yes	R		F	183

DEPARTMENT OF COMMERCE AND LABOR—BUREAU OF THE CENSUS

THIRTEENTH CENSUS OF THE UNITED STATES: 1910—POPULATION

State: Texas
County: Wood
Township or other division of county: Justice Precinct 4
Name of incorporated place:
Name of institution:
Enumerated by me on the ___ day of ___, 1910. Mrs. Henry J. Kerr, Enumerator.

Supervisor's District No. 12
Enumeration District No. 40
Sheet No. 7 B
Ward of city:
9426

Street: Acton-Weatherford Road (lines 51–85); "Wilderness" Road (lines 86–100)

Line	Dwelling	Family	Name	Relation	Sex	Race	Age	Marital	Yrs. married	Children born	Children living	Birthplace	Father's birthplace	Mother's birthplace	Language	Occupation	Industry	Employer/worker	Out of work	Weeks out	Read	Write	School	Ownership
51			Mayfield, Clark J.	Son	M	W	11	S				Texas	Texas	Kentucky	English	None					yes	yes	yes	
52			—— Alvin J.	Son	M	W	7	S				Texas	Texas	Kentucky	English	None							yes	
53			—— John	Father	M	W	63	Wd				Mississippi	Mississippi	Mississippi	English	None					yes	yes		
54	128	128	Tidwell, William F.	Head	M	W	45	M1	23			Alabama	Alabama	Alabama	English	Farmer	General farm	OA			yes	yes		R 7/22
55			—— Mary F.	Wife	F	W	44	M1	23	7	5	Alabama	Georgia	Alabama	English	None					yes	yes		
56			—— John J.	Son	M	W	20	S				Alabama	Alabama	Alabama	English	Laborer	Farm work	W	no	8	yes	yes		
57			—— James D.	Son	M	W	18	S				Texas	Alabama	Alabama	English	None					yes	yes	No	
58			—— William P.	Son	M	W	15	S				Texas	Alabama	Alabama	English	None					yes	no	yes	
59			—— Margie L.	Daughter	F	W	9	S				Texas	Alabama	Alabama	English	None					yes	no	yes	
60	129	129	Tidwell, Thomas F.	Head	M	W	23	M1	5			Alabama	Alabama	Alabama	English	Laborer	Odd jobs	W	yes	24	yes	yes		1 H 2-1-0-0
61			—— Effie C.	Wife	F	W	24	M1	5	1	1	Texas	Iowa	Iowa	English	None					yes	yes		
62			—— Venita C.	Daughter	F	W	3	S				Texas	Alabama	Texas		None								
63	130	130	Scurlock, Josiah G.	Head	M	W	60	M1	33			Alabama	Georgia	Alabama	English	Farmer	General farm	OA			yes	yes		R 7/23
64			—— Antonia M.	Wife	F	W	49	M1	33	11	8	New Mexico	New Mexico	New Mexico	English	None					yes	yes		
65			—— Presley F.	Son	M	W	21	S				Texas	Alabama	New Mexico	English	Farmer	General farm	OA			yes	yes		R 7/24
66			—— Lola	Daughter	F	W	19	S				Texas	Alabama	New Mexico	English	None					yes	yes		
67			—— William A.	Son	M	W	17	S				Texas	Alabama	New Mexico	English	None					yes	yes		
68			—— Josephine G.	Daughter	F	W	14	S				Texas	Alabama	New Mexico	English	None					yes	yes	yes	
69	131	131	Smith, William M.	Head	M	W	65	M1	27			Alabama	Virginia	Alabama	English	Farmer	General farm	OA			yes	yes		O F F 125
70			—— Hester G.	Wife	F	W	54	M1	27	9	8	Kansas	Kentucky	Kentucky	English	None					yes	yes		
71			—— Bruce G.	Son	M	W	33	S				Texas	Alabama	Texas	English	Farmer	General farm	OA			yes	yes		R 7/26
72			—— Maggie L.	Daughter	F	W	14	S				Texas	Alabama	Kansas	English	None					yes	yes	yes	
73			—— Williana C.	Daughter	F	W	11	S				Texas	Alabama	Kansas	English	None					yes	yes	yes	
74	132	132	Wilkerson, Eugene R.	Head	M	W	34	M1	9			Texas	Texas	Texas	English	Farmer	General farm	OA			yes	yes		O M F 127
75			—— Martha J.	Wife	F	W	21	M1	9	3	3	Texas	Georgia	Georgia	English	None					yes	yes		
76			—— Frederick C.	Son	M	W	8	S				Texas	Texas	Texas	English	None					yes	yes	yes	
77			—— Richard H.	Son	M	W	6	S				Texas	Texas	Texas		None								
78			—— Henry E.	Son	M	W	[illegible]	S				Texas	Texas	Texas		None								
79	133	133	Riley, Jackson W.	Head	M	W	60	M2	20			Tennessee	Tennessee	Tennessee	English	Farmer	General farm	OA			No	No		O F F 128
80			—— Nancy E.	Wife	F	W	44	M2	20	5	5	Alabama	Alabama	Alabama	English	None					yes	yes		
81			—— William A.	Son	M	W	17	S				Texas	Tennessee	Alabama	English	None					yes	yes		
82			—— Cora B.	Daughter	F	W	16	S				Texas	Tennessee	Alabama	English	None					yes	yes	yes	
83			—— Emma C.	Daughter	F	W	14	S				Texas	Tennessee	Alabama	English	None					yes	yes	yes	
84			—— Alice A.	Daughter	F	W	10	S				Texas	Tennessee	Alabama	English	None					yes	yes	yes	
85			—— Annie May	Daughter	F	W	8	S				Texas	Tennessee	Alabama	English	None							yes	
86	134	134	Duckworth, Hugh	Head	M	W	37	M1	2			Texas	Arkansas	Arkansas	English	Farmer	General farm	OA			yes	yes		O F F 129
87			—— Ida E.	Wife	F	W	25	M1	2	1	1	Texas	Georgia	Texas	English	None					yes	yes		
88			—— Hugh Jr.	Son	M	W	[illegible]	S				Texas	Texas	Texas		None								
89	135	135	Grammer, Oscar R.	Head	M	W	33	M1	7			Alabama	Alabama	Alabama	English	Farmer	General farm	OA			yes	yes		O F F 130
90			—— Bessie L.	Wife	F	W	30	M1	7	3	3	Texas	S. Carolina	S. Carolina	English	None					yes	yes		
91			—— Ida L.	Daughter	F	W	7	S				Texas	Alabama	Texas	English	None							yes	
92			—— Gena M.	Daughter	F	W	5	S				Texas	Alabama	Texas		None								
93			—— Walter T.	Son	M	W	1	S				Texas	Alabama	Texas		None								
94			Stribling, Myrtle	Sister-in-law	F	W	20	S				Texas	S. Carolina	S. Carolina	English	None					yes	yes		
95	136	136	Ratliff, James N.	Head	M	W	37	M1	16			Texas	Mississippi	Texas	English	Farmer	General farm	OA			yes	yes		O F F 131
96			—— Ada O.	Wife	F	W	34	M1	16	5	5	W. Virginia	W. Virginia	W. Virginia	English	None					yes	yes		
97			—— Mary E. J.	Daughter	F	W	14	S				Texas	Texas	W. Virginia	English	None					yes	yes	yes	
98			—— Dollie J.	Daughter	F	W	12	S				Texas	Texas	W. Virginia	English	None					yes	yes	yes	
99			—— Olive	Daughter	F	W	9	S				Texas	Texas	W. Virginia	English	None					yes	yes	yes	
100			—— Katie	Daughter	F	W	5	S				Texas	Texas	W. Virginia		None								

STATE Texas — COUNTY Eastland — TOWNSHIP OR OTHER DIVISION OF COUNTY Justice Precinct No 1 — NAME OF INSTITUTION X

DEPARTMENT OF COMMERCE—BUREAU OF THE CENSUS 38

FOURTEENTH CENSUS OF THE UNITED STATES: 1920—POPULATION

NAME OF INCORPORATED PLACE X — WARD OF CITY X

ENUMERATED BY ME ON THE 16th DAY OF February, 1920. Mary Williams, ENUMERATOR 8757

SUPERVISOR'S DISTRICT NO. 17 — ENUMERATION DISTRICT NO. 92 — SHEET NO. 24 A

Line	Mark	Dwelling	Family	Name	Relation	Home owned or rented	Sex	Color or race	Age	Marital	Attended school	Read	Write	Birthplace	Father's birthplace	Father's mother tongue	Mother's birthplace	Speaks English	Occupation	Industry	Employer/wage/own	Code
1	+	564	576	Livingstone, Lula	Servant		F	B	38	M		yes	yes	Texas	Texas		South Carolina	yes	Cook	Boarding House	W	952
2	+	565	577	Scurlock, Jos. B.	Head	1 R	M	W	70	Wd		yes	yes	Alabama	Georgia		Alabama	yes	Clerk	Retail Grocery	W	707
3	+	566	578	Blaine, Ben S.	Head	1 R	M	W	24	M		yes	yes	Oklahoma	United States		United States	yes	Tool Dresser	Oil well	W	136
4				—— Mamie	wife		F	W	24	M		yes	yes	Texas	Tennessee		[illegible]	yes	None			
5	+	567	579	Roney, William H.	Head	1 R	M	W	40	M		yes	yes	West Virginia	United States		West Virginia	yes	Driller	Oil well	W	096
6				—— Nora	wife		F	W	34	M		yes	yes	West Virginia	West Virginia		West Virginia	yes	None			
7				—— Virginia	Daughter		F	W	9	S	yes			Ohio	West Virginia		West Virginia		None			
8				—— James	Son		M	W	7	S	yes			Ohio	West Virginia		West Virginia		None			
9	+	568	580	Lusk, Chas L.	Head	1 R	M	W	24	M		yes	yes	Texas	Texas		Texas	yes	Hauling	Team	W	612
10				—— Della	wife		F	W	22	M		yes	yes	Texas	Texas		Texas	yes	None			
11				—— George	Son		M	W	5	S	yes			Texas	Texas		Texas		None			
12	+	569	581	Graves, Alford L.	Head	1 R	M	W	44	M		no	yes	Texas	Alabama		Texas	yes	Hauling	Team	W	612
13				—— Selma	wife		F	W	33	M		yes	yes	Texas	Arkansas		Arkansas	yes	None			
14				—— Herman	Son		M	W	16	S	yes	yes	yes	Texas	Texas		Texas	yes	Hauling	Team	W	612
15				—— Virgil	Son		M	W	15	S	yes	yes	yes	Texas	Texas		Texas	yes	None			
16				—— Carrel	Son		M	W	12	S	yes	yes	yes	Texas	Texas		Texas	yes	None			
17				—— G. W.	Son		M	W	8	S	yes			Texas	Texas		Texas		None			
18				—— Josiah	Son		M	W	5	S	yes			Texas	Texas		Texas		None			
19				—— J. M.	Son		M	W	2	S				Texas	Texas		Texas		None			
20				—— Robert	Son		M	W	[illegible]	S				Texas	Texas		Texas		None			
21				—— John	Father		M	W	70	Wd		yes	yes	Alabama	Alabama		Georgia	yes	None			1
22	+	570	582	Cox, Fred M.	Head	1 R	M	W	26	M		yes	yes	Texas	Texas		Texas	yes	Tool Dresser	Oil well	W	136
23				—— Ella	wife		F	W	18	M	yes	yes	yes	Texas	Texas		Mississippi	yes	Keeper	Boarding house	W	906
24	+	571	583	Ratliff, W. H.	Head	1 R	M	W	75	M		yes	yes	Mississippi	Tennessee		Alabama	yes	Servant	Lodging house	W	966
25				York, Fred A.	Lodger		M	W	45	M		yes	yes	Kansas	California		California	yes	Laborer	Oil field	W	096
26	+	572	584	Hood, Albert L.	Head	1 R	M	W	34	M		yes	yes	Texas	United States		United States	yes	Foreman	Oil Lease	W	070
27				—— Ruth	wife		F	W	26	M		yes	yes	Texas	Arkansas		Texas	yes	None			
28				—— Bess	Daughter		F	W	1 1/2	S				Texas	Texas		Texas		None			
29	+	573	585	Justice, James A.	Head	1 R	M	W	29	M		yes	yes	Texas	Missouri		Missouri	yes	Laborer	Oil field	W	096
30				—— Iris	wife		F	W	30	M		yes	yes	Texas	Texas		Texas	yes	None			
31				—— Nancy	Daughter		F	W	7	M	no			Texas	Texas		Texas		None			
32	+	574	586	Morrell, Robt. A.	Head	1 R	M	W	42	M		yes	yes	Texas	Texas		Texas	yes	Hauling	Team	W	612
33				—— Hilda	wife		F	W	42	M		yes	yes	Texas	Tennessee		Tennessee	yes	None			
34				—— William	Son		M	W	18	S	yes	yes	yes	Texas	Texas		Texas	yes	Hauling	Team	W	612
35				—— Cordia	Daughter		F	W	16	S	yes	yes	yes	Texas	Texas		Texas	yes	None			
36				—— Mary	Daughter		F	W	12	S	yes	yes	yes	Texas	Texas		Texas	yes	None			
37				—— Viva	Daughter		F	W	11	S	yes	yes	yes	Texas	Texas		Texas	yes	None			
38				—— Louis	Son		M	W	8	S	yes			Texas	Texas		Texas		None			
39				—— Dora	Daughter		F	W	5	S	no			Texas	Texas		Texas		None			
40				—— Laura	Daughter		F	W	3 1/2	S				Texas	Texas		Texas		None			
41	+	575	587	Coley, Benj.	Head	1 R	M	W	60	M		yes	yes	Ohio	Ohio		Ohio	yes	Water Tender	Oil well	W	096
42				—— Lina	wife		F	W	60	M		yes	yes	Ohio	Germany	German	Ohio	yes	None			
43	+	576	588	Coley, William	Head	1 R	M	W	27	M		yes	yes	Ohio	Ohio		Ohio	yes	Driller	Oil well	W	096
44				—— Beulah	wife		F	W	24	M		yes	yes	Ohio	Ohio		Ohio	yes	None			
45				—— Dorothy	Daughter		F	W	6	S				Ohio	Ohio		Ohio		None			
46	+	576	589	Johs, Jacob C.	Head	1 R	M	W	50	M		yes	yes	Ohio	Ohio		Ohio	yes	Driller	Oil well	W	096
47				—— Leta	wife		F	W	46	M		yes	yes	Ohio	Ohio		Ohio	yes	None			
48				—— Chas.	Son		M	W	7	S	yes			Ohio	Ohio		Ohio		None			
49	+	577	590	Walker, Leon G.	Head	1 R	M	W	21	S	yes	yes	yes	Alabama	Alabama		Alabama	yes	Laborer	Pipe line	W	686
50				Nelson, William A.	Partner		M	W	18	S	yes	yes	yes	Texas	Texas		Texas	yes	Laborer	Pipe line	W	686

www.ingramcontent.com/pod-product-compliance
Lightning Source LLC
Chambersburg PA
CBHW081118030125
19857CB00031B/340

9 798606 91491